The Psychological Birth of the Human Infant

Titles of Related Interest

TUSTIN, F.: Autistic Barriers in Neurotic Patients
DAWS, D. & BOSTON, M. (eds): The Child Psychotherapist
SIDOLI, M. & DAVIES, M. (eds): Jungian Child Psychotherapy
NEUMANN, E.: The Child
MANNONI, M.: The Child, his 'Illness' & the Others
WEININGER, O.: Children's Phantasies
FREUD, A.: Normality & Pathology in Childhood

THE PSYCHOLOGICAL BIRTH OF THE HUMAN INFANT

Symbiosis and Individuation

BY

MARGARET S. MAHLER
FRED PINE
ANNI BERGMAN

Routledge
Taylor & Francis Group
LONDON AND NEW YORK

First published 1975 by Hutchinson & Co (Publishers) Ltd

Published 1985 by Karnac Books Ltd

2 Park Square, Milton Park, Abingdon, Oxfordshire OX14 4RN
52 Vanderbilt Avenue, New York, NY 10017

Routledge is an imprint of the Taylor & Francis Group, an informa business

First issued in hardback 2019

British Library Cataloguing in Publication Data
Mahler, Margaret S.
The psychological birth of the human infant:
symbiosis and individuation
1. Children to 3 years. Development
I. Title. II. Pine, Fred. III. Bergman, Anni
155.4'22

ISBN: 978-0-946439-12-6 (pbk)
ISBN: 978-0-367-32858-0 (hbk)

CONTENTS

Part IV

Summary and Reflections

Appendices

The Data Analysis and Its Rationale: A Case Study in Systematic Clinical Research

ACKNOWLEDGMENTS

MANY colleagues and friends have contributed their help and encouragement during the years of the study which this volume describes. Among those who have worked with us directly on this research we particularly wish to express our appreciation and gratitude for their invaluable help to John B. McDevitt, M.D.; Ernest Abelin, M.D.; Edith Atkin; Iris Cohen-Wiley; Manuel Furer, M.D.; William Greenspon, M.D.; Ann Haeberle-Reiss, Ph.D.; Margaret Hawkins; Robert Holter, M.D.; Emmagene Kamaiko; Kitty La Perriere, Ph.D.; Kerstin Kupferman; David L. Mayer, M.D.; Herman Roiphe, M.D.; Laura Malkenson Salchow; and many others. Our thanks are due also to Mary E. McGarry, M.D.; Sally Provence, M.D. of the Child Study Center of Yale University, New Haven; and Miriam Siegel, Ph.D., New York, for their consultative work.

For the most part our research was carried out at the Masters Children's Center in New York, whose Board of Managers continued to sponsor the Mahler–McDevitt follow-up study under the direction of Dr. John B. McDevitt and Anni Bergman. While we certainly are grateful to all members of the Board, our particular gratitude goes to Jessie Stanton, Kay Eppler, G. Kenneth Crowther, and Adelaide de Menil.

We are also grateful to the following agencies and foundations whose financial help made it possible to bring our research to fruition over a period of fifteen years: The Field Foundation (New York); The Foundation's Fund for Research in Psychiatry (New Haven); The Foundation for Research in Psychoanalysis (Los Angeles); The Grant Foundation (New York); The Robert P. Knight Foundation (New Haven); The Menil Foundation (Margaret S. Mahler Research Fund, Houston, Philadelphia, and New York); The National Association for Mental Health (New York); The Psychoanalytic Research and Development Fund (New York); The Strick Foundation (Philadelphia); The Taconic Foundation (New York). The lion's share of financial support was supplied by Grant No. MH08238, The National Institute of Mental Health, USPHS (Washington, D. C.).

We are particularly grateful to Dr. Ernest Abelin for his careful editing and revising of this volume. The continuity of Parts I, II, III, and IV, is due to a great extent to his valuable suggestions.

For editorial assistance, we wish to thank Caryl Snapperman, Kitty Ball Ross, and Keri Christenfeld. For her aid in typing early stages of several chapters of the manuscript, we would like to thank Lillian Rothenberg. We are also indebted to Mary M. Sweeney, who, among many other assistants, stood by with patient help in typing many drafts of the material and rushing the manuscript to meet deadlines.

Finally, the senior author wishes to express her sincere appreciation and gratitude to the Menil Foundation which, through its generosity in creating the Margaret S. Mahler Research Fund, made it possible for the senior author to devote her time and efforts to studying the material and refining her thoughts that went into the writing of this book. Dr. Selma Kramer, Dr. Robert Prall, and the Philadelphia Child Psychoanalytic Group, as well as other members of the Philadelphia Psychoanalytic Institute, gave their invaluable help by cooperating with The Menil Foundation in setting up and carrying out the aims of the research fund.

MARGARET S. MAHLER
FRED PINE
ANNI BERGMAN

INTRODUCTION AND HISTORICAL REVIEW

As EARLY AS 1949, Mahler first adumbrated her theory that schizophrenia-like infantile psychosis syndromes were either autistic or symbiotic in origin, or both.[1] In 1955, with Gosliner, she introduced her hypothesis of the universality of the symbiotic origin of the human condition, as well as the hypothesis of an obligatory separation-individuation process in normal development.[2]

These hypotheses led to a research project on "The Natural History of Symbiotic Child Psychosis," carried out at the Masters Children's Center in New York, under the direction of Mahler and Dr. Manuel Furer (co-principal investigators). The project was sponsored by the National Institute of Mental Health, USPHS. It was designed to study the gravest deviations of the assumed normal symbiotic phase and the complete failure of the obligatory intrapsychic separation-individuation process. The yield of this research is described in *On Human Symbiosis and the Vicissitudes of Individuation: Volume I, Infantile Psychosis.*[3]

In its earliest stages, the research was limited to the study of symbiotic psychotic children and their mothers. However, the necessity of further validation of the above hypotheses in normal human development became more and more apparent to the two principal investigators of the project. A comparative parallel study was needed with normal babies and their mothers to substantiate the universality of the hypotheses. Hence in 1959, investigation of a control group of "average mothers and their normal babies" was begun at the Masters Children's Center. A pilot study, "The Development of Self-Identity and Its Disturbances," was made possible by grants from the Field Foundation and the Taconic

[1] See "Clinical Studies in Benign and Malignant Cases of Childhood Psychosis —Schizophrenia-Like," *Am. J. Orthopsychiatry*, 19:297, footnote.

[2] See "On Symbiotic Child Psychosis: Genetic, Dynamic and Restitutive Aspects," in *The Psychoanalytic Study of the Child*, Vol. 10. New York: International Universities Press, pp. 195–212.

[3] M. S. Mahler. New York: International Universities Press, 1968.

Foundation. Its aim was to learn how healthy children attain their sense of "individual entity" and identity. Ann Haeberle-Reiss (research psychologist), Anni Bergman, and later Edith Atkin worked with Mahler and Furer on this pilot study.

When in the very beginning of the 1960s, the National Association of Mental Health expressed its interest in a comparative investigation within our framework of "The Development of Intelligence in Schizophrenic Children and a Control Group of Normal Toddlers," the complementariness of the two research projects became more apparent. Dr. David L. Mayer was added to our research staff, and many of the workers who hitherto had been exclusively engaged in the symbiotic psychosis study now joined the work of the normative study as research psychiatrists or participant observers.

The complementariness of the two research projects called for a sophisticated innovative methodology, which was initiated in 1961 by Dr. Fred Pine. (The 1963 paper by Pine and Furer, "Studies of the Separation-Individuation Phase: A Methodological Overview," is relevant for the understanding of that stage of our overall work.)[4]

As the methodology evolved and led to more systematic, psychoanalytically oriented observations, the joint efforts of Mahler, Furer, Pine, Bergman, and many co-workers resulted in further constructions; the additional hypothesis of four subphases of the normal or near-normal separation-individuation process was formulated.[5] After the formulation of this additional hypothesis, it became apparent that its validity had to be checked by repeating and extending the study to another group of average mothers and their normal babies.

In February 1963, Mahler applied to the National Institute of Mental Health for a research grant. In her application she stated that on the basis of her previous work, she and her co-workers found that the roots of infantile psychosis are to be sought in the second half of the first year and in the second year of life. This time span came to be recognized as the "separation-individuation phase" of development. Mahler stated that the purpose of the proposed study was to verify the occurrence of the four subphases of the separation-individuation process by longitudinal

[4] In *The Psychoanalytic Study of the Child,* Vol. 18. New York: International Universities Press, pp. 325–342.

[5] See Mahler and Furer, "Description of the Subphases. History of the Separation-Individuation Study." Presented at Workshop IV: "Research in Progress." American Psychoanalytic Association, St. Louis, May 4, 1963; and Mahler, "Studies of the Process of Normal Separation-Individuation: the Subphases." Presented to the Philadelphia Psychoanalytic Society, November 15, 1963.

study of another group of mother-child pairs—and to delineate both the patterns of mother-child interaction typical of each subphase and the developmental patterns of the child occurring at each subphase. It was felt that added systematic knowledge about this little-known period of development could be applicable in the prevention of severe emotional disturbance. Funds for such a study were granted (MH08238) by the National Institute of Mental Health for 5 years (later extended). The results of this research are described in the present volume.

Dr. John B. McDevitt became our associate in 1965 and since that time has invaluably enhanced the systematization, as well as the scope and precision, of our work. However, rather than participating in the writing of this volume, he preferred to devote his time to important aspects of the study that are of special interest to him and to the ongoing follow-up study.

The Psychological Birth of the Human Infant: Symbiosis and Individuation is divided into four parts. The authors thought it would be salutary first to present a background against which the formulations explicated in Parts II and III could be viewed. In Part I, Chapter 1 (written by Pine and Mahler), we therefore integrate the ideas contained in 20 or more widely scattered relevant papers by Mahler and her co-workers, past and present. This opening chapter was greatly influenced by our joint discussions. (The minutes of our staff conferences are utilized in this as well as in other chapters.)

Part I, Chapter 2, as well as the Appendices (written by Pine), describes the evolution and the functioning of the research setting from a methodological point of view. We believe the correlation of Pine's work with that of Mahler and Bergman becomes evident in Parts II and III.

In Part II, Chapters 3 through 6, Bergman and Mahler describe their clinical study of the first three subphases of the separation-individuation process and provide illustrative vignettes. Chapter 7 deals with the fourth subphase and with object constancy in its psychoanalytic (emotional) sense.

In Part III, contributed by Mahler and Bergman, the "subphase histories" of five representative children in interaction with their mothers are presented. Thus, in this section we attempt to document the implications of the broad middle range of "variations of normalcy" contained in Part II. From our observational study, as well as our clinical work, the subphase developmental histories of the representative cases seem to prove quite dramatically the conceptualizations of McDevitt and Pine, on which the seventh chapter of the book essentially is based.

In the concluding Part IV, Mahler summarizes the results of the observational study and offers some amplifications and changes in the focusing of hitherto accepted metapsychological concepts. She also points to a few (by no means all) specific areas that she and her co-workers found to be in particular need of further psychoanalytic research.

MARGARET S. MAHLER
FRED PINE
ANNI BERGMAN

Part I

Separation-Individuation in Perspective

CHAPTER 1

Overview

THE biological birth of the human infant and the psychological birth of the individual are not coincident in time. The former is a dramatic, observable, and well-circumscribed event; the latter a slowly unfolding intrapsychic process.

For the more or less normal adult, the experience of himself as both fully "in," and fully separate from, the "world out there" is taken for granted as a given of life. Consciousness of self and absorption without awareness of self are two polarities between which he moves with varying ease and with varying degrees of alternation or simultaneity. But this, too, is the result of a slowly unfolding process.

We refer to the psychological birth of the individual as the *separation-individuation process*: the establishment of a sense of separateness from, and relation to, a world of reality, particularly with regard to the experiences of *one's own body* and to the principal representative of the world as the infant experiences it, the *primary love object*. Like any intrapsychic process, this one reverberates throughout the life cycle. It is never finished; it remains always active; new phases of the life cycle see new derivatives of the earliest processes still at work. But the principal psychological achievements of this process take place in the period from about the fourth or fifth month to the thirtieth or thirty-sixth month, a period we refer to as the *separation-individuation phase*.

The normal separation-individuation process, following upon a developmentally normal symbiotic period, involves the child's achievement of separate functioning in the presence of, and with the emotional availability of the mother (Mahler, 1963); the child is continually confronted with minimal threats of object loss (which every step of the maturational process seems to entail). In contrast to situations of traumatic separation, however, this normal separation-individuation process takes place in the setting of a developmental readiness for, and pleasure in, independent functioning.

Separation and individuation are conceived of as two complementary developments: separation consists of the child's emergence from a symbiotic fusion with the mother (Mahler, 1952), and individuation consists of those achievements marking the child's assumption of his own individual characteristics. These are intertwined, but not identical, developmental processes; they may proceed divergently, with a developmental lag or precocity in one or the other. Thus, premature locomotor development, enabling a child to separate physically from the mother, may lead to premature awareness of separateness before internal regulatory mechanisms (cf. Schur, 1966), a component of individuation, provide the means to cope with this awareness. Contrariwise, an omnipresent infantilizing mother who interferes with the child's innate striving for individuation, usually with the autonomous locomotor function of his ego, may retard the development of the child's full awareness of self-other differentiation, despite the progressive or even precocious development of his cognitive, perceptual, and affective functions.

From the observable and inferred beginnings of the infant's primitive cognitive-affective state, with unawareness of self-other differentiation, a major organization of intrapsychic and behavioral life develops around issues of separation and individuation, an organization that we recognize by terming the subsequent period the separation-individuation phase. In Part II we will describe the steps in this process (the subphases), beginning with the earliest signs of differentiation, proceeding through the period of the infant's absorption in his own autonomous functioning to the near exclusion of mother, then through the all-important period of rapprochement in which the child, precisely because of his more clearly perceived state of separateness from mother, is prompted to redirect his main attention back to mother, and finally to a feeling of a primitive sense of self, of entity and individual identity, and to steps toward constancy of the libidinal object and of the self.

We wish to emphasize our focus on *early* childhood. We do not mean to imply, as is sometimes loosely done, that every new separation or step toward a revised or expanded feeling of self at any age is part of the separation-individuation process. That would seem to us to dilute the concept and erroneously to direct it away from that *early intrapsychic achievement of a sense of separateness that we see as its core*. An old, partially unresolved sense of self-identity and of body boundaries, or old conflicts over separation and separateness, can be reactivated (or can remain peripherally or even centrally active) at any and all stages of life; but it is the original infantile process, not the new eliciting events or situations, to which we shall address ourselves.

In terms of its place in the larger body of psychoanalytic theory, we consider our work to bear especially on two main issues: adaptation and object relationship.

Adaptation

It was rather late in the developmental history of psychoanalysis that Hartmann (1939) began to bring a perspective on adaptation into psychoanalytic theory. Perhaps that is because, in the clinical psychoanalysis of adults, so much seems to stem from within the patient—from his long-standing character traits and dominating fantasies. But in work with infants and children, adaptation impresses itself forcibly on the observer. From the beginning the child molds and unfolds in the matrix of the mother-infant dual unit. Whatever adaptations the mother may make to the child, and whether she is sensitive and empathic or not, it is our strong conviction that the child's fresh and pliable adaptive capacity, and his need for adaptation (in order to gain satisfaction), is far greater than that of the mother, whose personality, with all its patterns of character and defense, is firmly and often rigidly set (Mahler, 1963). The infant takes shape in harmony and counterpoint to the mother's ways and style —whether she herself provides a healthy or a pathological object for such adaptation. Metapsychologically, the focus of the *dynamic* point of view —the conflict between impulse and defense—is far less important in the earliest months of life than it will come to be later on, when structuralization of the personality will render intra- and intersystemic conflicts of paramount importance. Tension, traumatic anxiety, biological hunger, ego apparatus, and homeostasis are near-biological concepts that are relevant in the earliest months and are the precursors, *respectively*, of anxiety with psychic content, signal anxiety, oral or other drives, ego functions, and internal regulatory mechanisms (defense and character traits). The *adaptive* point of view is most relevant in early infancy—the infant being born into the very crest of the adaptational demands upon him. Fortunately, these demands are met by the infant's ability, in the pliability and unformedness of his personality, to be shaped by, and to shape himself to, his environment. The child's facility for conforming to the shape of his environment is already present in early infancy.

Object Relationship

We feel that our contribution has a special place in the psychoanalytic study of the history of object relationship. Early psychoanalytic writings showed that the development of object relationship was dependent upon the drives (Freud, 1905; Abraham, 1921, 1924; Fenichel, 1945). Concepts such as narcissism (primary and secondary), ambivalence, sadomasochism, oral or anal character, and the oedipal triangle relate simultaneously to problems of drive and of object relationship (cf. also Mahler, 1960). Our contribution should be seen as supplemental to this in showing the growth of object relationship from narcissism in parallel with the early life history of the ego, set in the context of concurrent libidinal development. The cognitive-affective achievement of an awareness of separateness as a precondition of true object relationship, the role of the ego apparatuses (for example, motility, memory, perception) and of more complex ego functions (such as reality testing) in fostering such awareness are at the center of our work. We try to show how object relationship develops from infantile symbiotic or primary narcissism and alters parallel with the achievement of separation and individuation, and how, in turn, ego functioning and secondary narcissism grow in the matrix of the narcissistic and, later, the object relationship to mother.

In terms of its relationship to clinical psychopathological phenomena, we consider our work to bear on what Anna Freud (1965*b*) has called developmental disturbances, which the developmental flux of energy (E. Kris, 1955) may even out during later development, or which, in certain instances, may be precursors of infantile neurosis or middle range pathology. In rare cases, in which the subphase development was severely disordered or unsuccessful, we found, as did others such as Frijling-Schreuder (1969), Kernberg (1967), and G. and R. Blanck (1974), that borderline phenomena or borderline states, and even psychosis, may result.

This volume, in contradistinction to the volume on infantile psychosis (Mahler 1968*b*), deals predominantly with average development and makes contributions to the understanding of, at most, middle-range pathology.

In the study of infantile psychoses, both in the predominantly autistic (Kanner, 1949) and in the predominantly symbiotic syndromes (Mahler, 1952; cf. also Mahler, Furer, and Settlage, 1959), children were observed who seemed either unable to enter or ever to leave the delusional twilight state of a mother-infant symbiotic common orbit (Mahler and

Furer, 1960; cf. Mahler, 1968*b*). These are children who may never show responsivity to, or the capacity of adapting to, stimuli emanating from the mothering person, that is to say, children who cannot utilize a "mothering principle" (Mahler and Furer, 1966). Or, on the other hand, they may show panic at any perception of actual separateness. Even the exercise of autonomous functions (for example, motility or speech) may be renounced or distorted to preserve the delusion of the unconditionally omnipotent symbiotic unity (cf. Ferenczi, 1913).

In either event, these children are deficient in the capacity to use the mother as a beacon of orientation in the world of reality (Mahler, 1968*b*). The result is that the infant personality fails to organize itself around the relationship to the mother as an external love object. The ego apparatuses, which usually grow in the matrix of the "ordinary devoted" mothering relationship (see Winnicott, 1962) fail to thrive; or, in Glover's terms (1956), the ego nuclei do not integrate, but secondarily fall apart. The child with predominantly autistic defenses seems to treat the "mother in the flesh" (Bowlby, Robertson, and Rosenbluth, 1952) as nonexistent; only if his autistic shell is threatened by penetration from human intrusion does he react with rage and/or panic. On the other hand, the child with a predominantly symbiotic organization seems to treat the mother as if she were part of the self, that is, as not separate from the self but rather fused with it (Mahler, 1968*b*). These latter children are unable to integrate an image of mother as a distinct and whole external object; instead, they maintain the split between the good and the bad part-objects and alternate between wanting to incorporate the good or expel the bad. In consequence of one or the other of these solutions, adaptation to the outside world (most specifically represented in a developing object relationship to mother [or father]) and individuation leading to the child's unique personality do not unfold evenly from an early stage onward. Thus, essential human characteristics get blunted and distorted in their rudimentary stage or fall apart later on.

The study of the normal symbiotic period, and of normal separation and individuation, helps make the developmental failures of psychotic children more comprehensible.

Some Definitions

We have found, in discussions and presentations over the years, that three of our basic concepts are misunderstood often enough to warrant clarification. First, we use the term *separation* or *separateness* to refer to the *intrapsychic* achievement of a sense of separateness from mother and, through that, from the world at large. (This very sense of separateness is what the psychotic child is unable to achieve.) This sense of separateness gradually leads to clear intrapsychic representations of the self as distinguished from the representations of the object world (Jacobson, 1964). Naturally, in the normal course of developmental events, real physical separations (routine or otherwise) from mother are important contributors to the child's sense of being a separate person—but it is the sense of being a separate individual, and not the fact of being physically separated from someone, that we will be discussing. (Indeed, in certain aberrant conditions, the physical fact of separation can lead to ever more panic-stricken disavowal of the fact of separateness and to the delusion of symbiotic union.)

Second, we use the term *symbiosis* (Mahler and Furer, 1966), similarly, to refer to an intrapsychic rather than a behavioral condition; it is thus an inferred state. We do not refer, for example, to clinging behavior, but rather to a feature of primitive cognitive-affective life wherein the differentiation between self and mother has not taken place, or where regression to that self-object undifferentiated state (which characterized the symbiotic phase) has occurred. Indeed this does not necessarily require the physical presence of the mother, but it may be based on primitive images of oneness and/or scotomatization or disavowal of contradictory perceptions (see also Mahler, 1960).

Third, Mahler (1958*a* and *b*) has earlier referred to infantile autism and symbiotic psychosis as two extreme disturbances of identity. We use the term *identity* to refer to the earliest awareness of a sense of being, of entity—a feeling that includes in part, we believe, a cathexis of the body with libidinal energy. It is not a sense of *who* I am but *that* I am; as such, this is the earliest step in the process of the unfolding of individuality.

Symbiotic Psychosis and Normal Separation-Individuation: A Review

Historically, the senior author's observations of normal development and of the mother-infant dyad gradually led to the study of pathological phenomena, including child psychosis. Of course, the turn from problems of normal development was never complete. Although the immediate predecessor of the current work was the study of symbiotic psychosis of early childhood, we would, at this time, like to show the ways in which that study led naturally to our reconsideration of normal development.

On the Hypothesis of a Normal Separation-Individuation Phase

In our previous research on the natural history of symbiotic child psychosis (with Furer), we reached rock bottom when we tried to understand why those child patients were unable to develop beyond a (distorted) symbiotic phase, why they even had to reach back into bizarre life-maintaining mechanisms of a secondary autistic nature (Mahler and Furer, 1960; Mahler, 1968*b*). To understand this, we felt we had to know more about the steps that lead to normal individuation and, in particular, more about coenesthetic, preverbal, and early boundary-forming experiences which prevail in the first two years of life.

We began to ask various questions. What was "the ordinary way" of becoming a separate individual that these psychotic children could not achieve? What was the "hatching process" like in the normal infant? How could we understand in detail the ways in which the mother—as catalyst, activator, or organizer—contributed to these processes? How did the vast majority of infants manage to achieve the second, seemingly very gradual, psychic birth experience which, beginning during the symbiotic phase, gives way to the events of the separation-individuation process? And what, by contrast, were the genetic and structural features that prevented the prepsychotic child from achieving this second birth experience, this hatching from the symbiotic mother-infant "common boundary"?

By 1955 (Mahler and Gosliner), we began to be able to articulate a conception of a normal separation-individuation phase.

> Let us, for the sake of brevity, call [this] period . . . the *separation-individuation phase* of personality development. It is our contention that this separation-individuation phase is a crucial one in regard to the ego and the development of object relationships. It is also our contention that the characteristic fear of this period is separation anxiety. This separation anxiety is not synonymous with the fear of annihilation through abandonment. It is an anxiety which is less abruptly overwhelming than the anxiety of the previous phase. It is, however, more complex, and later we hope to elaborate on this complexity. For we need to study the strong impetus which drives toward separation,[1] coupled with the fear of separation, if we hope to understand the severe psychopathology of childhood which ever so often

[1] We know now that the drive is not toward separation per se, but the innate given is the drive toward individuation, which cannot be achieved without autonomous separation.

begins or reveals itself insidiously or acutely from the second part of the second year onward.

> This separation-individuation phase is a kind of second birth experience which one of us described as "a hatching from the symbiotic mother-child common membrane." This hatching is just as inevitable as is biological birth (Mahler and Gosliner, 1955, p. 196).

Furthermore:

> For purposes of understanding our points, we propose focusing on the position of defense of the eighteen- to thirty-six-month infant, to defend his own evolving, enjoyable, and jealously guarded self-image from infringement by mother and other important figures. This is a clinically important and conspicuous phenomenon during the separation-individuation phase. As Anna Freud [1951*b*] has pointed out, at the age of two and three a quasi-normal negativistic phase of the toddler can be observed. It is the accompanying behavioral reaction marking the process of disengagement from the mother-child symbiosis. The less satisfactory or the more parasitic the symbiotic phase has been, the more prominent and exaggerated will be this negativistic reaction. The fear of reengulfment threatens a recently and barely started individual differentiation which must be defended. Beyond the fifteen- to eighteen-month mark, the primary stage of unity and identity with mother ceases to be constructive for the evolution of an ego and an object world (Mahler and Gosliner, 1955, p. 200).

Today, we would date the onset of separation-individuation much earlier, and we can add considerably to those early formulations.

On the Hypothesis of Anxiety Attendant upon the Awareness of Separateness

It was hypothesized (Mahler, 1952) that in certain toddlers the maturational spurt of locomotor and other autonomous ego functions takes place concomitantly with a lag in emotional readiness to function separately from the mother and produces organismic panic, the mental content of which is not readily discernible because the child (still in the preverbal stage) cannot communicate (cf. also Harrison, 1971). This panic never consolidates into an appropriate signal anxiety, but retains the character of acute or insidious organismic distress, with the child's concomitant inability to utilize the "other" as external organizer or auxiliary ego. This further arrests structuralization of the ego. The very fact that the more or less built-in maturation proceeds while psychological development does not[2] renders the rudimentary ego extremely brittle. Dedifferentiation and fragmentation may result, and the well-known clinical picture of infantile psychosis then ensues (Mahler, 1960).

[2] See Hartmann, Kris, and Loewenstein (1946) for a discussion of maturation and development.

Overview

This view of intrapsychic events remains, of course, a hypothesis—especially in light of the preverbal nature of the phenomena which it is meant to explain. However, it seems to fit very well the observable clinical data—which are not hypothetical but descriptive—regarding loss of already achieved autonomous functions and a halt to subsequent development. This fragmentation may occur any time from the end of the first and in the course of the second year of life. It may follow a painful and unexpected trauma but often follows upon a seemingly minor event, such as a brief separation or a minor loss. Those observations ultimately led us to study the toned-down "panics" in the normal infant and toddler during separation-individuation and the way in which the mother and child, as a unit and as individuals, coped with them. Our increasing knowledge of the developmental tasks that confront the normal infant and later the normal toddler during the separation-individuation phase, and the trials and difficulties and momentary regressions seen in the behavior of these children, provide the basis for formulating our theoretical framework for understanding benign and transient disturbances, and neurotic ones, as well as the rare occurrences of more severe and lasting reactions shown by symbiotic psychotic children at an early or later age.

On the Hypothesis of the Development of a Sense of Identity

A third hypothesis (Mahler, 1958*a* and *b*) states that normal separation-individuation is the first crucial prerequisite for the development and maintenance of the "sense of identity." Concern with the problem of identity arose from observing a puzzling clinical phenomenon, namely, that the psychotic child never attains a feeling of wholeness, of individual entity, let alone "a sense of human identity." Autistic and symbiotic infantile psychoses were seen as two extreme disturbances of the sense of "identity" (Mahler, 1958*a*): it was clear that in those rare conditions something had gone basically astray at the very root, that is, in the very earliest interactions within the mother-infant unit. Briefly, one could summarize the central hypothesis as follows: whereas in primary autism there is a deanimated, frozen wall between the subject and the human object, in symbiotic psychosis there is fusion, melting, and lack of differentiation between the self and the nonself—a complete blurring of boundaries. This hypothesis ultimately led us to the study of the normal formation of separate entity and identity (cf. Mahler, 1960).

On the Catalyzing Function of Normal Mothering

A fourth hypothesis grew from an impressive and characteristic observation that the symbiotic psychotic children were unable to use the mother as a real external object as a basis for developing a stable sense of separateness from, and relatedness to, the world of reality. Work with normal mother-child pairs developed our interest in the modalities of contact between mother and infant at differing stages of the separation-individuation process: in the modalities by which contact was maintained even while symbiosis waned; and in the specific role of the mother in facilitating not only the separateness of the child but also the specific patterning of his individuating personality by complementarity, contrast, identification, or disidentification (Greenson, 1968).

Thus, the central ideas of the work with symbiotic psychotic children grew and transformed smoothly and with continuity into the organizing ideas of the work with normal mother-infant pairs. So too did our more formal efforts at research, as we shall now describe.

In the late 1950s at the Masters Children's Center in New York City, Furer and Mahler had started a systematic study of "The Natural History of Symbiotic Child Psychosis."[3] It was a therapeutic action research in which we used the so-called tripartite design (child, mother, and therapist) first applied by Dr. Paula Elkisch (1953). We attempted to establish what the late Augusta Alpert (1959) would have called a *corrective symbiotic relationship* between mother and child, with the therapist acting as a bridge between them. Concurrently with the above project, the pilot phase of an observational study of *normal* mother-child pairs was begun. The latter was a bifocal observational study (that is, with focus on mother and child) of more or less randomly selected mother-infant pairs, in which the mother-child units were compared with one another and with themselves over time. These studies of symbiotic infantile psychosis and of normal mother-infant pairs ran parallel for about 4 years and have continued separately for another 7 years.

The studies of average mother-infant pairs continued on a larger scale and more systematically from 1963 on.[4] The questions to which we

[3] Grant M-3353 of the National Institute of Mental Health, USPHS 1959/1960–1962/1963, "The Natural History of Symbiotic Child Psychosis," M. S. Mahler and M. Furer, co-principal investigators.

[4] It continued as a follow-up study by Dr. J. B. McDevitt, Anni Bergman, and associates under the auspices of the board of the Masters Children's Center until December 31, 1974. It is now sponsored by the Margaret S. Mahler Research

originally addressed ourselves were oriented to two main hypotheses: (1) that there exists a *normal* and *universal* intrapsychic separation-individuation process which is preceded by a normal symbiotic phase; and (2) that in certain predisposed but *extremely rare* cases the maturational spurt of locomotion and other autonomous ego functions, when coupled with a concomitant lag in emotional readiness for functioning separately from mother, gives rise to organismic panic. It is this panic that causes ego fragmentation and thus results in the clinical picture of symbiotic infantile psychosis (Mahler, 1960). We have since learned that there are innumerable degrees and forms of partial failure of the separation-individuation process.

The method of study of the normal separation-individuation process approximated the method used in the study of "The Natural History of Symbiotic Child Psychosis" (the tripartite design) and was characterized by the continual presence of the mother, by a physical setup specifically designed for, and uniquely suited to, observation of the infant's readiness for active experimentation at separation and return, and by the opportunity to observe the infant's reaction to passive separation experiences.

The work on the normal separation-individuation phase has had in turn considerable feedback to the earlier work on symbiotic child psychosis. Not only has our description of the subphases in the development of separation-individuation made it possible for us to anticipate and conceptualize some of the progressive changes seen in the symbiotic psychotic child during the course of his intensive therapy (cf. Bergman, 1971; Furer, 1971; Kupferman, 1971), but our very formulations (given in part above) about the symbiotic psychotic child bear the mark of our later understanding of the separation-individuation process (Mahler and Furer, 1972; Mahler, 1969*b*, 1971).

A Preliminary Note on Observation and Inference

The question of the kind of inferences that can be drawn from direct observation of the preverbal period is a most controversial one. The problem is complicated by the fact that not only is the infant preverbal, but that the verbal means of the observer-conceptualizer lend themselves

---

Fund of The Menil Foundation through a gift given anonymously to the Medical College of Pennsylvania.

only very poorly to the translation of such material. The problems of psychoanalytic *re*construction here find their parallel in the problem of psychoanalytic construction—the construction of a picture of the inner life of the preverbal child, a task in which coenesthetic empathy, we believe, plays a central role. Although we cannot ultimately prove the correctness of such constructions, we nonetheless believe that they can be useful, and we are committed to attempting their formulation.

Analysts have taken positions that vary along a broad spectrum regarding efforts to understand the preverbal period. At one extreme stand those who believe in innate complex oedipal fantasies—those who, like Melanie Klein and her followers, impute to earliest extrauterine human mental life a quasi-phylogenetic memory, an inborn symbolic process (Mahler, 1969; Furer, quoted by Glenn, 1966). At the other end of the spectrum stand those Freudian analysts who look with favor on stringent verbal and reconstructive evidence—organized on the basis of Freud's metapsychological constructs—yet who seem to accord preverbal material little right to serve as the basis for even the most cautious and tentative extension of our main body of hypotheses. They demand that these hypotheses also be supported by reconstruction—that is to say, by clinical and, of course, predominantly verbal material. We believe that there is a broad middle ground among analysts who, with caution, are ready to explore the contributions to theory that can come from inferences regarding the preverbal period (Mahler, 1971).

Generally, in making inferences regarding the preverbal period from clinical psychoanalytic data, analytic theorists are asserting their right always to ask "Why?" "How did it come about?" and to answer by tracing earlier and earlier verbalizable memories, and ultimately to connect these memories to preverbal (but manifestly observable) phenomena of infancy that are isomorphic with the verbalizable clinical phenomena; for example, Freud's (1900, p. 271) comments on dreams of flying and the infant's experience of being swooped up by adults (cf. also Anthony, 1961). That is, we study phenomena of the preverbal period that appear (from the outside) to be the kinds of experience that match up with what patients are only later able to report during analysis, in their verbalizable recollections, that is, free associations, without at that point being aware of their origins.

As in clinical psychoanalysis, our method of working was from beginning to end characterized by "free-floating attention" in order to take in the usual and the expectable, but more particularly the unexpected, surprising, and unusual behaviors and transactional sequences. As the psychoanalytic instrument, especially the ear (see Isakower, 1939), functions during analysis, so, in psychoanalytic infant observation, the psychoanalytic eye lets itself be led wherever the actual phenomenological sequences lead (cf. A. Freud, 1951*b*).

But beyond these general modes of psychoanalytically derived observations, the observer of the child in the preverbal period has a special observational opportunity: the opportunity to observe the body in movement. To explain one of our major bases for making inferences from nonverbal behavior, let us briefly refer to the significance of the kinesthetic function and the function of motility in the growing child. As set forth in a number of papers in the 1940s (Mahler, 1944; Mahler, Luke, and Daltroff, 1945; Mahler and Gross, 1945; Mahler, 1949*a*), the observation of motor, kinesthetic, and gestural (affectomotor) phenomena of the entire body can have great value. It permits one to infer what is going on inside the child; that is to say, the motor phenomena are correlated with intrapsychic events. *This is particularly true in the first years of life.*

Why is this so? Because the motor and kinesthetic pathways are the principal expressive, defensive, and discharge pathways available to the infant (long before verbal communication takes their place). We can make inferences from them to inner states because they are the end products of inner states. One cannot be certain of the inner state, but, in the effort to infer it, multiple, repeated, and consensually validated observations and inferences offer some safeguard against total error.[5] Furthermore, in the preverbal period, by definition, speech has not yet assumed the major expressive function it will later serve, thus leaving the task of communication predominantly to the mimetic, the motor, and the gestural spheres. And finally, in the very young child, changes like modulation, inhibition, stylization, and defensive distortion of bodily expression have not yet been learned.

The young child's rich and expressive affectomotor (gestural) behavior of his entire body, as well as the back-and-forth movement of approach and appeal behaviors and distancing behaviors between infant and mother—their frequency, amplitude, timing, and intensity—served as important guidelines, furnishing many clues to phenomena we encounter through verbal communication at later ages. We watched the infant's expressive motility as it progressed beyond immediate discharge of instinctual drive, by way of the detour functions provided by the primitive ego's abilities

[5] Kestenberg's important work bears witness to how much we may learn from movement patterns of mother and infant (1965*a*, 1965*b*, 1967*a*, and 1971). Unfortunately, it was beyond the scope of our research methodology to create a general guideline by which the motor, especially the expressional or affectomotor, phenomena could be more specifically and teachably used as referents to intrapsychic processes. Hopefully, future researchers will undertake such a project.

to delay, to learn, and to anticipate. We observed and assessed the infant's autonomous and conflict-free motor functioning, with special regard to progressive steps in his separation-individuation process. In short, the observation of motor-gestural behaviors gave us important clues to intrapsychic events, and the substantive formulations to which we shall soon turn have been influenced by such observations (see Homburger, 1923; Mahler, 1944; Mahler, Luke, and Daltroff, 1945).

Instead of entering further into the general controversy regarding observation of preverbal infants and the legitimacy of inferences about the evolution of intrapsychic phenomena, we would like to present the history, methods, and tentative results of one such effort.

CHAPTER 2

Evolution and Functioning of the Research Setting

IN this chapter we describe the slow evolution of a way of working. It is a way of working that was at first highly clinical, fairly unsystematic, and yet extraordinarily stimulating. Later, we became more systematic—too systematic at times, in the sense that our systems of data collection lost touch with the natural flow of the material—but we were able, we feel, to redress the balance and to develop reasonably flexible modes of organizing the data. These shifts coincided to some extent with a change in the physical location of the work and with a progressive step in our formulations (we shall describe these later). Overall, however, our continuing aim was to find a way of working that seemed to us to strike an appropriate balance between free-floating psychoanalytic observation and pre-fixed experimental design.

We know that our procedures are subject to serious criticism from both quarters, and indeed we are quite capable of leveling those criticisms at ourselves. In particular we are well aware of our problems of evidence, of establishing, if not proof, at least approximations to it. From the standpoint of psychoanalysis, our infant-toddler observations do not give us the opportunity for confirmation through self-report, through the emergence of confirming memories, through symptom changes—those indicators of confirmation of interpretation that are usually relied upon in clinical psychoanalysis. But, though we lack subjective reports (at the earlier ages—though not with the older toddlers or mothers) and certainly do not maintain a blank-screen transference relationship to the subjects of our study, we nonetheless observe with a "psychoanalytic eye"—informed by all of our past encounters with intrapsychic life, letting our attention follow the paths suggested by the phenomena before us. Turning to the other pole: from the standpoint of rigorous experimentation, we certainly have not achieved freedom from bias, from halo, from evaluative considerations, in our assessment of evidence. But though our approach is frankly highly clinical and open-ended, we arranged the work so that we could have *repeated encounter* with phenomena in a *somewhat standardized* situation, and subject to a fair degree of *consensual validation.*

The initial, less systematic phase of the work was, as we said, extraordinarily productive and led us to the formulations regarding the subphases of the separation-individuation process we have already alluded to and which we will describe more fully in the next section. This productivity was no doubt an outcome of the very newness of the work at that time; multitudes of observations and ideas unfolded before and within us, many, many of which seemed new and fresh. But the productivity was probably also due to our (it now seems) wise decision to let the mothers and their babies show us the paths the research should follow—the way and the degree to which each mother wished to use the Center and the participant observers, the pace and the degree to which they were ready to reveal themselves to us, the extent to which each mother would choose to take active responsibility for the care of her child at the Center, and the like. This left our procedures less systematic, but attuned to the needs of our subjects of study. Aspects of the physical setting also helped. In our initial location, for example, the babies' bathroom was close to the nursery room, in fact in the midst of the nursery (see Diagrams 1 and 2), divided only by a low accordion gate from the babies' area of the room. Later, when we moved upstairs in the same building and had more elaborate, "better" toddler bathrooms at the end of the long hall, we found ourselves deprived of that most important opportunity to observe with ease the children's toileting behavior, that is, the toddlers' curiosity and fascinated play with water and other contents of the toilet bowl, their curiosity about their own and each others' bodies and functionings in that fascinating room. We were also deprived later on of the chance to see the mothers' behavior while diapering and their reaction to the infants' and toddlers' sneaking under the gate into the bathroom, and so on.

When, about half way through the study, we did move (upstairs in the same building), our quarters were much less cramped (see Diagram 3). But, beyond that, our attempt for a while to do (what seems to us now) a too inflexible study of certain of the data brought us again into a period

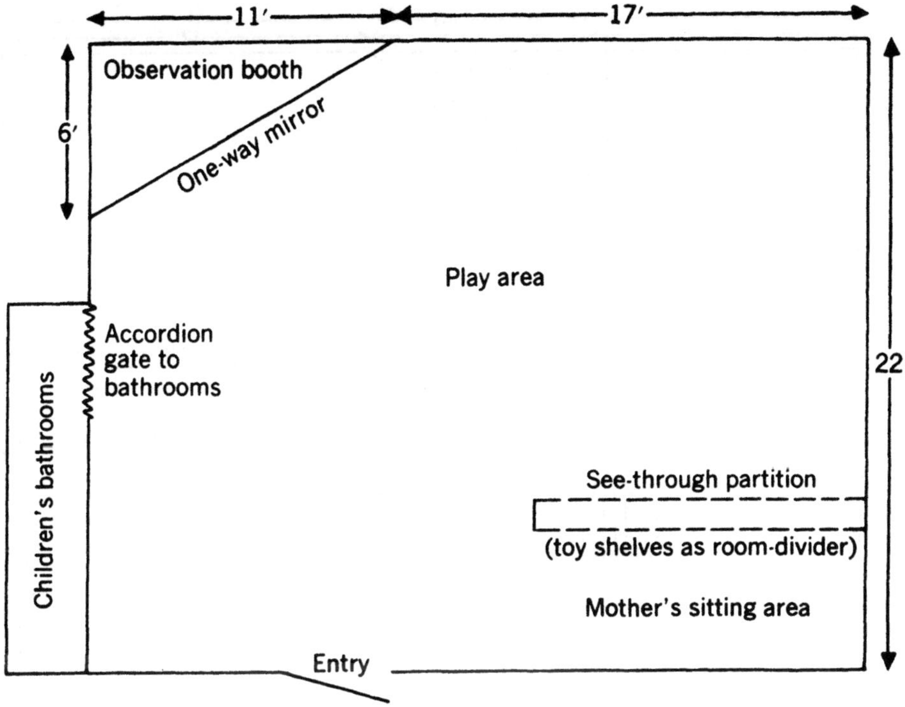

DIAGRAM 1

MOTHER-INFANT ROOM. INITIAL SETTING.

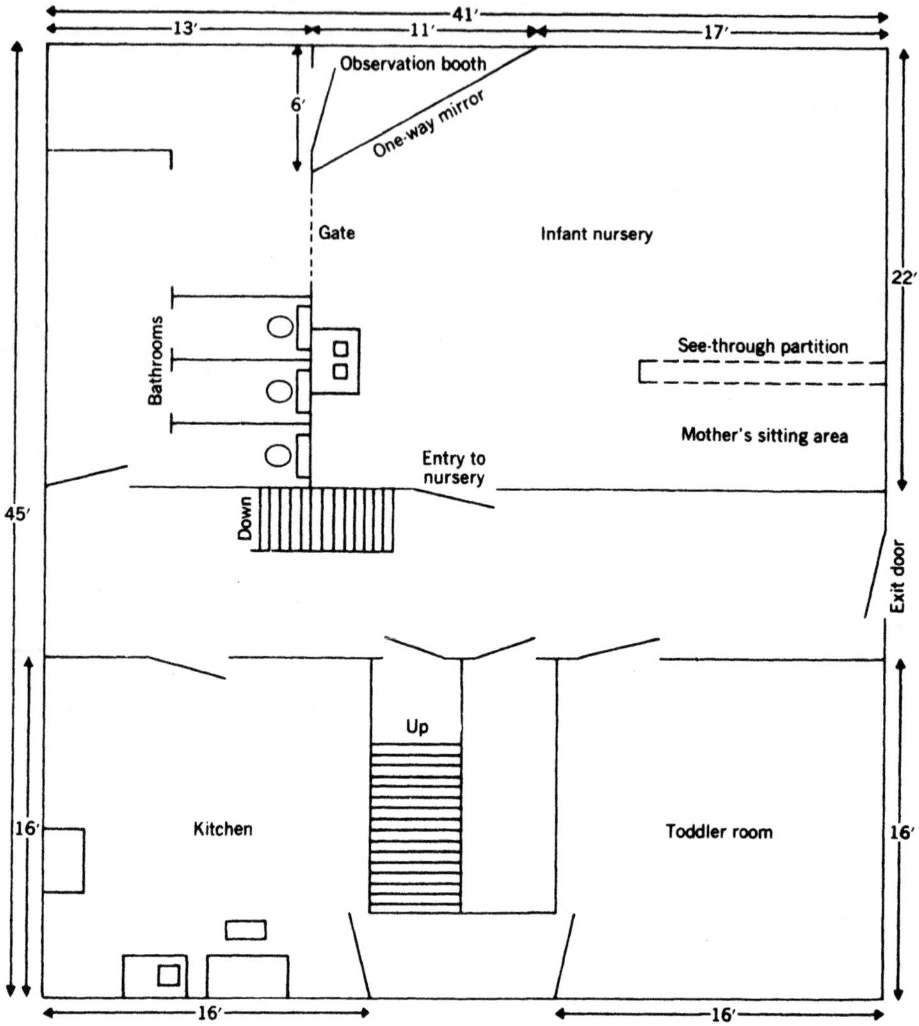

DIAGRAM 2

FLOOR PLAN. INITIAL SETTING.

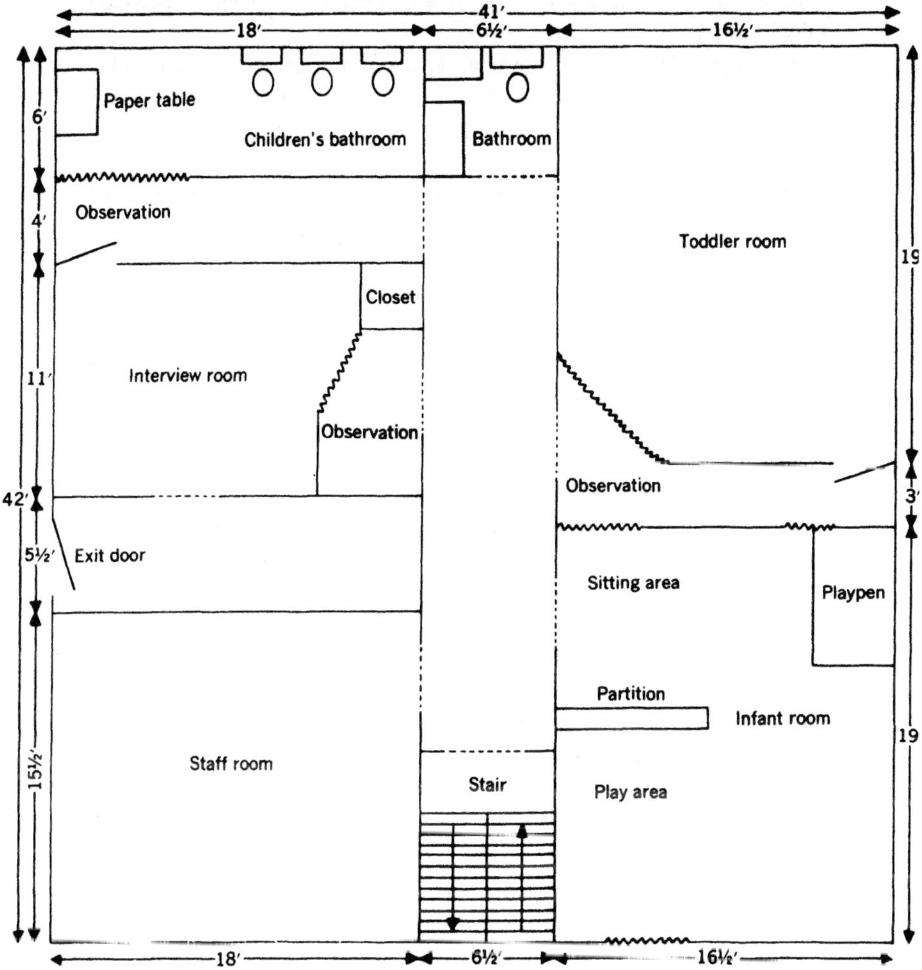
41′
18′
6½′
16½′
Paper table
Children's bathroom
Bathroom
6′
Observation
4′
Toddler room
19
Closet
Interview room
11′
Observation
Observation
42′
3′
5½′
Exit door
Sitting area
Playpen
Partition
Infant room
19
Staff room
15½′
Stair
Play area
18′
6½′
16½′

where we had to refind our way to an appropriate balance between clinical and systematic study.

This chapter describes the physical setting of our research, in particular in relation to the opportunities it presents for observation of phenomena relevant to the separation-individuation process, but also including some historical perspectives on the evolution of various aspects of the design. A summary of the varieties of data available to us, with discussion of issues surrounding these data, appears in Appendix A. The appendices also include: (1) a discussion of the "method of the method"—that is, of the rationale of our approaches to data analyses; (2) a look at some of our midway attempts at formal data collection and quantitative analysis which, while contributing to the development of a more precise language for us, floundered because they were either too focused, unable to keep up with the growth processes in the children, prematurely codified, or all of these; and (3) a review of each of our three later approaches to the data (orienting questions, area observations derived from our psychoanalytically oriented frame of reference, and formulations regarding early character formation as the outcome of the separation-individuation process).

In describing here the physical setting of the work and its history, we hope that our later ways of dealing with the available data will emerge for what they are: attempted solutions to the task of grappling with immense quantities of data without getting lost in detail and while keeping an eye on our goal—the study of the separation-individuation process.

The Setting and Its Rationale

The method of procedure has, for the most part, relied upon a descriptive, clinical approach with observations of mother-child pairs occurring in an essentially naturalistic setting. The original (downstairs) setting was chosen so as to permit the occurrence and study of those behaviors which were assumed to be of particular relevance to an understanding of the separation-individuation process.

Let us repeat a general description of the original setting of the mother-infant room that we gave some years ago (see Pine and Furer, 1963) and complete it with more details. The work with the normal babies took place in a playroom setting where a group of babies played, busied themselves in a large playpen, or played on a mattress or on the floor. They seemed to experiment actively in the playpen; for example, with their body's growing integration, they sat up and toppled down, they stretched to reach and handle a toy, they strained to turn toward mother, whose voice they may have heard but who may not have been in their visual field. They looked at her from inside the playpen and with smiles and cooing would invite her to come and play. They played with toys themselves, especially with those suited to make "interesting spectacles last" (Piaget, 1937). The mothers were free to talk with one another and to interact with their babies as they pleased.

We wanted, and apparently succeeded in creating, a situation where the spontaneous day-to-day relationship of mother to child could be observed in a natural setting. The playroom had a small area reserved as a sitting room for the mothers, in which they would chat, sip coffee, or read—and from which they had a full view of, and free access to, the children. There was another much larger area that had many attractive and colorful toys, and the children tended, as soon as they could, to move back and forth freely between the toy area, the section where the mothers generally sat, and all other parts of the room. The mother-child separation was by no means complete in the physical arrangements of the room; it was quite unlike a day-care center or a school situation where, for example, the mother relinquishes charge of her child to the nurse or the teacher for a period. It was more like an outdoor playground setting where the children play where they please while the mothers sit on benches and talk—with their children in full view and with the opportunity to attend to whatever mothering is required of them. Diagram 1 shows our initial mother-infant room.[1]

Opportunities to Observe Separation

It was clear from the outset that the central phenomenon under study, the intrapsychic process of separation and individuation, was not susceptible to direct observation; but cues to the intrapsychic process could come from observation of mother-child interaction, and so the intrapsychic process could be inferred from behaviors that were indeed observable. At the beginning of our study when our observations were concentrated mostly on children in the second year of life, we felt that most of our cues to the intrapsychic process would come from the observation of those routine separation experiences, both active and passive, that presented

[1] This setting, as it turned out, was much more successfully arranged originally than it was later on, when there was (because of the location of the entrance door and the general architectural layout of the room) more confusion through intermingling of mothers, infants, and occasionally even toddlers.

themselves daily, initiated by the child, by the mother, or by the observer. From the start, when we observed children not earlier than from 9 to 10 months on, certain kinds of separations were available to our observations. These were the ones that took place in the presence of the mother: an infant crawling or walking across the room momentarily cannot find his mother's face among the many present; the mother is inattentive, perhaps simply talking to others, and so on. From very early on, separations of a passive sort, being left instead of leaving, also occurred. The mother left the room for a moment or two, or she left for half an hour or more for an interview with one of the staff (when on occasion and as needed, the child might come with her). Or, when the child was a bit older and had been at the Center for a while, mother might be gone for an entire morning. After some time we introduced a "toddler room" into which the children would graduate when they were able to spend larger amounts of time away from mother with a "teacher" in a nursery-school-like setting. Thus, we had an observational situation that provided many opportunities for the observation of mother-infant separations and reunions.

During the later phase of our research (after March 1962), when we had come to realize that the intrapsychic separation experiences begin much earlier, we extended our observations to babies, beginning at around 4 months of age. We observed the holding behavior of mothers with their infants and the molding behavior of infants with their mothers. We observed infants alternately melting into, versus stiffening and stemming against, the mother's body. These and other observations gave us insights into the lap baby's earliest boundary formation within symbiosis much before the baby's earliest approach and distancing behaviors in space would occur. Then we were most carefully observing the earliest signs of differentiation (see Part II, Chapter 4). The infant stiffens and distances in the mother's arms (cf. Mahler, 1963). He cannot crawl yet, but still he alternately distances and fuses with, that is, seems to melt into the mother's body—then the outside world beckons and competes with the hitherto exclusive attention to the mother (cathexis is drawn from the symbiotic orbit) (see Spock, 1963). As soon as the infant's apparatuses mature sufficiently, he may slide down from the mother's lap, thence he crawls, paddles, and still later walks away from the mother.

To give a fuller picture of some of the details of separation to which both settings have permitted us to address ourselves, let us mention some of the questions which have stimulated, and been stimulated by, our observations at various times in the study. How does a mother carry her child when she arrives: Like a part of herself? Like another human being? Like an inanimate object? How does the young infant react to the mother's taking off his wraps? Once in the room, does the mother separate herself from the child physically and/or emotionally, or is there an "invisible bond" between baby and mother even across some physical distance? Does the mother know what is happening to her infant even though he is at some distance from her? How quickly, how readily, and how appropriately does she respond to his needs? Does the mother keep her infant in her arms a great deal? Does she make a gradual transition by taking him slowly to the playpen, for example, and staying with him until he is comfortable, perhaps offering him a toy? Or can't she wait to be rid of him, dumping him into the playpen immediately upon arrival and turning her attention to other things, perhaps her newspaper or conversation, turning to the child to overstimulate him only as her own needs demand it? In sum, we found that the observations in the infant room showed us the individual characteristics, as well as the development, of the mother in her mothering. We were able to formulate the characteristics of the interchange between mother and her babe-in-arms, of mother's interchange with her rapidly crawling or paddling older infant, with the child who begins to show interest in "other-than-mother" persons, with the vigorously exploring toddler, and with the child who begins to talk and can make his needs known in new ways. We were able to study the mother's ways of separating herself from the young infant and her responses to separation initiated by the child later on.

On the other side of the dyad, we also observed at what time of the infant's life he became aware of his mother, or rather we attempted to study and formulate the many, many, very gradual waxing and waning steps of development that lead to a recognition of the mother as a separate being. We observed how the infant reacts to the "holding behavior" of his particular mother, later on his straining a bit away from her, as if to have a better look at her and investigating mother (and "other"). From around 5 months we had cues to infer boundary formation, thence active separations from his mother. Does he try, when at some distance, to bridge the gap visually, vocally, or somewhat later in a locomotor fashion by actively seeking out his mother and demanding her attention by the more differentiated means now at his disposal? Beyond this, still in the infant room we observed the child's reaction to his peers, to adults other than mother (of varying degrees of familiarity to him), and the conditions under which he related to, or more or less vigorously rejected, substitutes for his mother. The mother's actual absences from the mother-infant room, especially those that we planned in connection with her weekly interviews, afforded a quasi-experimental separation experience.

We studied the child's reaction to the mother's departure, his behavior while she was out of the room, his response to her return—the phenomena of the reunion—each of these in relation to the progressions and regressions during the separation-individuation process.

The Rationale for the Establishment of a Toddler Room

Already in the downstairs setting we took a small office space and converted it into a senior toddler playroom, partly because the senior toddlers' expansive and vigorous activity endangered the safety of the infant on the floor, and partly because they showed us that they needed a separate room to engage in age-appropriate play activities with the playroom teacher and increasingly with one another. We took a small adjoining room—the only available one—into which one of the participant observers (*qua* nursery teacher) moved with the older toddlers (approximately age 2 and up). This allowed us to follow maturing reactions to leave-takings from and by the mother, and we especially learned a great deal from toddlers who were eminently verbal. The separations were different in that phase of our study in which, because of the smallness of the toddler room and the intimacy among the play-teacher, the mother, and the toddler, the mothers would leave the building much more often to go shopping, to the laundromat, or home.

We noted in particular that, perhaps because of the smallness of the room downstairs, one or the other of the toddlers became very possessive of the room (the space) and would roughly close out any intruder, for example, another mother who had no child there, or other participant observers, including the principal investigator. This somehow was reminiscent of the territorial claims or possessiveness of the animal world. In the upstairs setting, we planned the toddler facilities carefully from the very beginning. It was a large room in its own right on the same side of the corridor as the infant room and was connected with the infant room by that corridor. The participant observer who moved into the toddler room in both settings was a seasoned nursery school teacher. Among other things, she had the task of observing to an increasing extent the by-then verbal and other behavioral sequences during play, and the toddlers' interaction with her and with each other.

The participant observer was as passive as the situation permitted, yet assisted the toddlers in their play, attended to their needs, and functioned as go-between for the toddler and his mother. (Diagrams 2 and 3 show the relationship between the infant nursery and the toddler room in our initial and later settings, respectively.)

Whereas we learned precious leave-taking and reunion reactions even in our improvised primitive setting downstairs, the final setting of the toddler room was carefully planned from the very start and the new layout gave us richer data in these respects. As we mentioned before and as Diagram 3 shows, it was as large or larger than the mother-infant room and offered the opportunity for the infant in the early practicing-crawling phase to discover its novel world and atmosphere and show us his reaction when he discovered it.

The toddler room was discovered by most infants already in their expansive early practicing subphase, their crawling period. Most crawling or paddling infants have the urge to get beyond thresholds anyway, to venture beyond the nursery in homes as well. In our upstairs setting they learned to crawl into the corridor that connected the two nurseries; they would paddle into the dressing room across the hall, and by chance they might crawl further toward the often open door (on the same side of the corridor where their nursery was) and peek into the toddler room. They would stop at the threshold and at first would rapidly crawl back to "home base" where mother was. They might peek into the toddler nursery, being very much interested in expanding their horizon. Sometimes they had older siblings in that room. But only some months later, when the "junior toddler" felt for the first time secure on his feet, did he occasionally drift or warily venture beyond the threshold of the interesting other playroom. Some weeks later he would actively seek out that room which had so much more diversification; there was more exciting action going on there between senior toddlers and their nursery teacher; there was the opportunity to play with water or with fingerpaints; there were large action toys, such as a seesaw, a tricycle, a hobby horse, as well as a doll corner, large trains, many picture books and puzzles, and story times with the teacher.

In the beginning the mothers followed their toddlers into this room; but one day the senior author decided, after careful thought, that this situation was too uneven, permitted too much intermingling, too much variation on the parts of the different mothers and the different toddlers to be useful to study separation-individuation optimally. On October 4, 1966, she asked the mothers to remain settled in their sitting area in the infant room. Following this, the back-and-forth movement of individual children between two rooms, their becoming aware of being separated (inadvertently and/or through their own doing), and their reactions to this provided us with invaluable data. The way they (through actions, or words, or in emotional expressions) sought to establish their mother's whereabouts gave us important clues about many facets of the child's personality at that time with regard to the development of object constancy, self-awareness, general mood and temperament, frustration tolerance, and many other traits. We were able to see, after a while, the older toddler's increasing ability to maintain longer separations from mother, in many cases functioning better away from mother, which (as we shall fully discuss in Part II, Chapters 5–7) we felt was due to the absence of the conflict between being close to mother and distancing from her. In the more ideal cases, there was adequate acceptance of the teacher as a substitute and ease of reuniting with the mother after short separations. We saw above all, even in normal toddlers, quite unexpectedly rapid alternations from week to week, indeed often from day to day, between progressive and regressive tendencies (from the separation-individuation process point of view).

Other Observational Opportunities

The requirements for an infant nursery of this sort gave us opportunities for observation beyond those related to separation per se. Thus, the mothers were present to care for their infants (as young as 2–3 months at times), and we were able to examine closely affective aspects of the interaction of the mother-child pairs. One major focus was on the quality of the mother's *emotional availability* to the child, and the child's ability to make use of her in the course of the separation-individuation process, to draw from her the necessary "contact supplies" (Mahler, 1963). The conversation between the mothers while their children were in the nursery rooms offered additional insights into the meaning of their maternal behavior; they came to speak comfortably and freely after a while, since the Center became homelike for them (more so in the original cramped natural setup than in the spacious carefully planned upstairs setup).

The child's use of the physical equipment in the room offered additional observational opportunities. Thus, for example, large action toys such as tricycles turned out to be interesting not simply in terms of motor development, but for the opportunity they gave for exuberant expression, well beyond the practicing subphase, an exuberance suggestive at times of fantasies of omnipotence (one of the reasons we had to protect the lap and floor babies from their exuberance). On the other hand, responses to the child's use of these toys sometimes gave us clues to hovering and symbiotic tendencies on the part of a mother and toddler. The rocking horse and large teddy bear at times gave us clear-cut glimpses of autoerotic or contact stimulation. We found that windup, mechanical toys and talking dolls were frightening at times, but that toys where the child controlled the movement could be used with pleasure. In the infant room, and in the toddler room, we had a floor-level mirror which lent itself very well to the study of various mirror reactions of infants from a very early age on. We felt that mirror reactions might offer an avenue into the investigation of the child's developing awareness of his body as distinct from his environment. (During the last two or three years of data collection, Dr. John McDevitt developed an accessory research specifically on the development of mirror reactions.)

Some of the routine equipment and paraphernalia in the infant's room also provided opportunities for observation of phenomena not so clearly related to the separation-individuation process. We could observe mothers who did or did not change diapers when needed, who did or did not feed the children with cookies when appropriate, or who did so at random. There was a playpen which was used for naps as well as for play. We always thought of sleeping as, in part, a separation from mother, this being commonly related to the sleep difficulties of early childhood; but of course we had no opportunity to observe directly the night sleep disturbances so characteristic of the second year. We did not have too clear a view of the relevance of toileting, eating, and other aspects of infant behavior to the separation-individuation process. The facilities of our setting, giving the mothers and children the opportunity to spend part of their lives with us in quite natural interaction, gave us a wide range of observational opportunities, but there were, of course, many things we did not see: a child's falling asleep in his own crib, his reaction to father's coming home from work. In particular, in the upstairs setting we did miss, to a great extent, the opportunities we had had downstairs of watching the daily anal, urinary, and phallic bathroom behavior of the children and their mothers' reaction to those. We tried to make up for some of this through home visits.

The History of the Development of the Setting

The group and the setting did not spring forth full-grown in our planning. At the inception of the project our two major practical concerns were to contact mothers with children at the end of the first and in the second year of life (because we were thinking of the separation-individuation phase as beginning in the second year of life at that point) and to develop and maintain their interest in participating.

The first mothers contacted had older children in the normal nursery group of the Masters Children's Center. As an inducement for participation, a reduction in nursery fee for the older child was given, with a promise of a similar reduction for the younger child when he was old enough. We followed this format with the first three mothers to enter the project. Subsequent to them, however, all others came by word of mouth—actually contacted us—so that our original expectation that we would need a special plan to induce participation appeared superfluous. Each woman who entered the project subsequently over the years had heard about it from one of the participating mothers, became interested, and, after initial screening, joined the group. To some extent, then, these mothers were self-selected, and we did not actively seek a representative sample of any particular group. We did do a cursory screening, however, in our effort to work with more or less normal mothers. We screened out mothers who seemed to show gross pathology on initial contact; we selected only intact families (with mother, father, and child members); and we tried to avoid accepting mothers when we felt that their attendance would be unreliable (for example, if they lived too far away, beyond walking distance).

Because we were initially quite worried whether we would be able to recruit mothers to the project, the fact that this did not present much of a problem is of interest. How did this come about? First, the Center was well known in the neighborhood (as a nursery school, even prior to our work in it). Furthermore, many young, socially mobile, and quite well educated couples live in the area, and it is from this group that our families came. These mothers did not work, because it was not absolutely necessary financially that they do so and because, by and large, they were sufficiently interested in, and aware of, the rewards and problems of child rearing to want to remain with their young children. Thus, they had the time to participate; we, of course, required that the mothers be present and available. It is possible that with less sophisticated and less well educated women we would have had more of a problem. However, all of these women understood the concept of research and had a favorable view of its value, especially because research on infants and mothers touched the central issues of their present lives. Many of the mothers expressed active intellectual interests in child development; others expressed more personal motivations concerning their hope of learning more about their own children. Underlying all of this is the fact that the life of the mother of a very young child can at times be quite a lonely one. Social contacts are necessarily limited, particularly during the day and during the long cold season. From the very start we provided a convenient place—attractive, clean, and safe—for the mothers to let their young, prenursery children engage in active play. We were an indoor playground for mothers otherwise cooped up in small apartments (small because of high rents in the area) with their young children. The Center, and more particularly the atmosphere created by the staff, also provided the women with the comfort of company of their own age and interests. Mothers could also have the feeling of having authorities in child rearing around without having to accept or acknowledge any authoritative suggestion, let alone demand, on their part. The staff inadvertently looked upon the assembled mothers as the "mother's club."

Thus, somewhat contrary to our original expectations, we had little problem in establishing an initial motivation for entering the project. Once we had the group of mothers committed to participation the question of how best to direct the functioning of the group had to be settled. Two considerations were pertinent: (1) the necessity of keeping the mothers interested and maintaining their participation, and (2) the needs of the research. As in any new undertaking, we had only limited knowledge on which to draw. Our general aim was to establish a situation in which the mother-child interaction could be observed in a reasonably *natural setting*. But many questions arose, such as whether to see the mothers individually, in groups of two, three, or more; what problems would arise in handling transference relationships to the participant observers; and how much these observers should have to do with the child or with the mother-child interaction.

Since it was essential that the mothers feel at ease in the situation, we proceeded very slowly at first, seeing them individually and talking with them. From these initial contacts, which took only a couple of weeks, it became evident that some of the women were apprehensive about too close and too concentrated a scrutiny of themselves and their children. We decided quite early, therefore, to have the mothers and children come in groups, rather than alone—at least until we became better acquainted with them. From this decision evolved the group setting which continued in more or less constant form over the years. Some of the mothers also expressed doubts about the amount of time they would have to spend at the Center. Hence, in the beginning of our research we gave them four mornings a week from which to choose at least two for visiting the Center. In this way, we allowed the mothers to show us indirectly the situation and relationship to us with which they were most comfortable; we allowed them to show us their optimally preferred distance or closeness to us and to our setting. One year we even accommodated some mothers who had to attend to older siblings by arranging to see them afternoons in order to have continuity in our work. In allowing this amount of latitude, we were attempting to maintain an easy atmosphere where the mothers felt at liberty to use the Center; thereby we avoided the creation of a more structured situation where we would be requiring certain things from them. This approach seemed particularly necessary, since these were normal, healthy families, which were presumably not motivated to stay with us primarily for therapeutic reasons.

Once the group was meeting regularly, more specific questions arose. Two were particularly pertinent. First, the question arose as to how active each of the participant observers (originally only two) should be with the children. That is, how often should they help a child, stop a quarrel, offer a toy? Because the main requirement of the research was that we be able to observe the mothers and children in as natural a setting as possible, we at first decided on no interference at all. All aspects of child care were to be left to the mothers. We had told the mothers from the start that *they*, not the participant observers, were in charge of the children; the observers were not defined as nursery teachers. However, in spite of this, the mothers had questions in their minds regarding what was expected of them. The problem was enhanced by the fact that the mothers' room was originally separated from the playroom by a ceiling-high partition, with only a rather large doorway between. This meant that the women often could not see their children, and once a child was out of sight there was a tendency to leave caretaking responsibility to the participant observers. The senior author decided within a couple of months that this partition should come down and a waist-high one was substituted in its place. The new partition was not a solid unit, but composed of brass rods with spaces between them. Even a crawling infant could then be seen by its mother and vice versa. There were quite a few mothers who, for their own inner reasons, protested, saying in effect, "but what a waste, you just put the old partitions up!" When the waist-high partition consisting of railings was installed, the reason was given to the mothers, and our desire for them to care for their children was clearly reemphasized. They accepted this willingly and increased their caretaking behavior. (Some, of course, did not; but we could then see this noncaretaking as a relevant characteristic of the particular mother, itself an aspect of her unique mothering behavior.) Once the pattern of maternal caretaking was established, the workers could relax the "no interference" role somewhat in order to play with the children to get a better idea of responsiveness, tolerance of outsiders, attention span, and the like.

The second question, though in a different way, also concerned the degree to which the participant observers would become involved with the mother-child interaction. Very soon after the group started, several of the mothers began asking questions and advice in child rearing. We again decided in favor of less interference. Each question was to be handled as generally and impersonally as possible without causing annoyance or withdrawal on the part of the mothers. In a few cases, it was mutually decided that the particular problem raised was sufficiently important (for example, how to handle the birth of a new sibling) to warrant more attention. In these cases, one of the workers suggested to the mother that she discuss the problem with one of the principal investigators or with her interviewer, and frequently the mothers took advantage of this. This was, indeed, one of the roots of our decision to make more systematic assignments of each mother-child pair to one of the principal investigators or senior staff.

Our decision to limit intervention had several bases, apart from our wish to observe the mother-child interaction in as natural a setting as possible. Our early experiences with the group strongly indicated that these mothers would be most at ease in a permissive and unauthoritative atmosphere. Furthermore, we felt that the development of strong transference feelings to either of the workers would be disruptive both to the natural functioning of the mother and child and perhaps to the group as a whole. Some of this changed over time. We came to recognize that there was, inevitably, a transference on the part of the mother to the interviewer—and to the Center as a symbol—perhaps in part because of our attempts at relative neutrality. Judiciously handled and respected, this could provide an additional strength to the mother's motivation to participate and also provide the basis for giving some helpful comments to mother where necessary.

We said above that the mothers gave us clues regarding how close they wished to be. By and large the mothers did not ask for direct advice, and this fit with the staff's wishes. They accepted the Center's atmosphere with enjoyment and gratitude, but they drew the line at "therapy" and pushed aside direct advice, pompousness, or even professionalism if it appeared in the staff. By and large they kept it so that their relationships to the staff did not extend beyond the Center and its activities.

One final very important piece of history should be recorded. From our third research year onward, we selected only young infants for the study. In the pilot study we took a group of toddlers aged 9 to 20 months. As the study progressed, we came to believe more and more strongly that by the last quarter of the first and during the second year these children were, from the point of view of separation-individuation, in *an advanced stage of that process*, already far removed from the hypothesized prior phase of development, namely, the normal symbiotic phase (Mahler and Furer, 1963*b*). This meant that we could not directly observe the beginnings of the separation-individuation process as the infant evolved from this previous symbiotic phase. We had revised the postulation concerning the age span at which the normal separation-individuation process occurs, so that we now understood it to range from about the fifth month through the second and third years of life. This revision in our theory was made during the third year of the study; from March 1962 on, we began to select for admission only infants considerably younger in age than had been the case during the first 2 years of the study. (See Table 1, pp. 233–234.)

Some Comments on "Clinical" Standardization and Reliability of Observation

The slow evolution of our way of working, which was responsive both to the needs of the research and to the needs of the mother-child pairs, led us to a general format for the work. In retrospect, our feeling is that our established procedure and the uniform spatial and physical arrangements afforded by the Center provided us with an observational situation that was far better standardized than we had dared hope for at the outset.

Our method of working provided us with an abundant observational record of our subject pairs that had considerable continuity. From the fifth month to the completion of the third year of life, we approximated twice-weekly observations, weekly interviews, and bimonthly home visits. This resulted in a richness of data and a frequency and continuity of observations over time which greatly exceed that of most reported studies of similar subject matter. We feel in retrospect that we managed to avoid many of the problems of infrequent, highly selective ratings and write-ups of mother-child pairs in certain specific, selected situations where situational variables are relatively salient in influencing the obtained results. We also avoided problems of rich but hard-to-compare and hard-to-standardize observations through fully naturalistic observation (for example, by relying totally on home visits, playground observations, and the like). While we have not gone so far as to build a home for families to move into, we have nevertheless made our Center almost into an extension of the homes of our subjects. We have been impressed by the great relaxation and ease with which our subjects used our facilities and behaved within them, especially when comparing the behavior of our own mother-child pairs with the behavior of mothers in other, one-time, observational-experimental situations.

We also have not lost the advantage of a situation which is standardized in many respects: the facilities were the same for all mother-child pairs, including the arrangements, the equipment, and to a certain extent, the participant observers. Thus, while we did not have a rigidly structured test situation, neither did we have to contend with a wide range of differences in home layouts, time arrangements, and such. What we contributed was, within limits, identical for each mother and child; they made use of it as they would. It is certainly true that we found variations in the attention the mother paid to the infant with particular observers present, or with many versus few other mothers present; however, in most instances these changes were relatively easily recognizable and became part of the data for study. Some mothers decreased their attention to their children because they somehow felt that there was someone else to help them look after their offspring (despite instructions to the mother that she was responsible for the care of her child while at the Center) or because they were simply more relaxed and less anxious in a protective environment. On the other hand, some mothers, intent on showing off themselves or their infant and/or aided by their freedom from other obligations while at the Center, gave more attention and stimulation to their children than they normally might have, or engaged in such stimulation more at those times when somebody was paying particular attention to them. Occasionally, a mother could be seen to act for, or conversely to inhibit action in front of, the camera; but we have been able to compare these moments with many unphotographed ones and have found that, on the whole, the mothers' behavior was quite consistent.

Another fact to be considered is that, even without our intention or explicit action (quite to the contrary, our general avoidance of guidance and influence), the mere fact of attendance undoubtedly had some influence on the mothers' attitudes and feelings. They probably received a good deal of support from the very fact of being part of a research situation, the prestige of which some of them keenly recognized, and from the interest shown them and their children by the workers. This active participation might have helped them avoid or might have attenuated some of the main hazards of young motherhood, for example, feelings of helplessness, social isolation, and being overwhelmed by the dependence of, and responsibility for, a small being. (In contrast, on rare occasions the reverse was true; thus, a mother could get involved in a competitive quest to be a better mother than others or to show off how well her offspring could do in spite of—or even because of—her demanding, nonindulgent, overambitious, and competitive attitude.) We unhesitatingly would state, however, that even though attendance at the Center may have attenuated or exaggerated or masked these and other stressful areas, it did not obliterate or basically alter them. We found our mothers reacting differentially, in individually characteristic ways, to all of those stresses common to the average mother during the separation-individuation phase.

In summary, then, while our situation was markedly freer and less structured than many, it did have a very definite methodological consistency. Since our mothers were free to come when they wished, their attendance did vary in frequency and in length of each stay. However, it was uniform in the fact that whatever the length and frequency of visits, they were determined by the mother's wish to attend and by her feeling of comfort in staying in the situation. Although the workers' presence was experienced and reacted to by each mother according to her own needs —for some this may have meant the necessity for increased mothering of their child (or of *being mothered themselves*), to some it may have given license to mother less—in either instance the basic characteristics of mothering attitudes did not seem to change. Although there is no doubt that these mothers, who were aware that they were part of a research project, must to some extent have been influenced in their behavior by such awareness, nonetheless we were continually impressed by the great variety of seemingly quite natural individually characteristic behaviors that we were able to observe. Indeed, with the mothers and children seen for two to four mornings a week over a period of years, and often with second (and even third) children, it would be hard to maintain that they showed only a pose and an unrepresentative sample of their behavior with their children in the periods during which we observed them.

Part II

On Human Symbiosis and the Subphases of the Separation-Individuation Process

INTRODUCTION

IN this Part we will present a sequential description of the separation-individuation process and of its forerunners, the normal autistic and the normal symbiotic phases.

Chapter 3 is devoted to the first two phases of mental development. We are aware that it does not contain nearly as much in the way of behavioral characterizations as the subsequent chapters. While we did study the early patterning of the symbiotic phase, we concentrated our efforts on the mother-child interaction and the infant's development from about 4-5 months. As early as 1954-1955 (in cooperation with Dr. Bertram Gosliner, and at the suggestion of Dr. Annemarie Weil[1]), the senior author named that period the *separation-individuation phase.* The principal aim of this book is to relate what we have learned about separation-individuation. We left the extensive, in-depth study of the newborn, of the normal autistic phase, and of the symbiotic first few months of life to other authors, who have carried out this study with much care, ingenuity, and technical and methodological ability.

In fact, the very concepts of the first two phases are situated on a higher level of metapsychological abstraction than the subsequent subphases. They were derived at first through psychoanalytic reconstruction from our study of psychotic and borderline children and adults, as well as from the observational work of other psychoanalytic authors.

By contrast, Chapters 4, 5, and 6 represent a condensation and discussion of an enormous wealth of original behavioral data. In the course of our rather unsystematic naturalistic pilot study (in the late 1950s), we could not help but note certain clusters of variables at specific crossroads of the individuation process. This strongly suggested to us that it would be advantageous to subdivide the data we were collecting on the intrapsychic separation-individuation process in accordance with the repeatedly observable behavioral referents of that process. We divided the process into *four subphases*: differentiation, practicing, rapprochement,

[1] Personal communication.

and "on the way to libidinal object constancy." Chapters 4-7 each deal with one of the subphases.

Chapter 7, however, which deals with the fourth subphase, stands somewhat apart from the first three. It is certainly not by chance that we were unable to give this subphase a simple, one-word label. No doubt, the establishment of both individuality and object constancy are the central issues during this subphase of the separation-individuation process; however, by their nature, one cannot tell clearly when they begin, and even less, when they are achieved. They are part of an ongoing developmental process. Therefore, we prefer to talk of the "beginning of consolidation" of individuality (self-identity or self-constancy, cf. G. and R. Blanck, 1974) and we prefer to talk of the attainment of a degree of object constancy (that is, being on the way to object constancy).

In addition, the beginnings and achievements of intrapsychic representations are much more difficult to ascertain from this subphase on, and they vary considerably from one child to another. Intrapsychic processes are now mediated by verbal and other forms of symbolic expression and have to be inferred from them—very much like in clinical child psychoanalysis. Although we did try to tap these processes by "play sessions," this was not the main focus of our research effort. For all these reasons, Chapter 7 should be understood to be more tentative and speculative than Chapters 4, 5, and 6.

CHAPTER 3

The Forerunners of the Separation-Individuation Process

The Normal Autistic Phase

IN the weeks preceding the evolution to symbiosis, the sleeplike states of the newborn and very young infant far outweigh the states of arousal. They are reminiscent of that primal state of libido distribution which prevailed in intrauterine life and which resembles the model of a closed monadic system, self-sufficient in its hallucinatory wish fulfillment.

Freud's (1911) use of the bird egg as a model of a closed psychological system comes to mind: "A neat example of a psychical system shut off from the stimuli of the external world, and able to satisfy even its nutritional requirements *autistically* . . . is afforded by a bird's egg with its food supply enclosed in its shell; for it, the care provided by its mother is limited to the provision of warmth" (p. 220n.; italics added).

In the normal autistic phase there is a relative absence of cathexis of external (especially distance-perceptual) stimuli. This is the period when the stimulus barrier (Freud, 1895, 1920), the infant's inborn unresponsiveness to outside stimuli, is clearest. The infant spends most of his day in a half-sleeping, half-waking state: he wakes principally when hunger or other need tensions (perhaps what David M. Levy [1937] meant by the concept of affect-hunger) cause him to cry, and sinks or falls into sleep again when he is satisfied, that is, relieved of surplus tensions. Physiological rather than psychological processes are dominant, and the function of this period is best seen in physiological terms. The infant is protected against extremes of stimulation, in a situation approximating the prenatal state, in order to facilitate physiological growth.

Conceptualizing the state of the sensorium metaphorically, we have applied to the first weeks of life the term *normal autism*; for in this stage the infant seems to be in a state of primitive hallucinatory disorientation in which need satisfaction seems to belong to his own "unconditional," omnipotent, *autistic* orbit (cf. Ferenczi, 1913).

As Ribble (1943) has pointed out, it is by way of mothering that the young infant is gradually brought out of an inborn tendency toward vegetative, splanchnic regression and into increased sensory awareness of, and contact with, the environment. In terms of energy or libidinal cathexis, this means that a progressive displacement of libido has to take place from the inside of the body (particularly from the abdominal organs) toward its periphery (Greenacre, 1945; Mahler, 1952).

In this sense, we would propose to distinguish two stages within the phase of primary narcissism (a Freudian concept to which we find it most useful to adhere). During the first few weeks of extrauterine life, a stage of absolute primary narcissism, marked by the infant's lack of awareness of a mothering agent, prevails. This is the stage we have termed *normal autism*. It is followed by a stage of dim awareness that need satisfaction cannot be provided by oneself, but comes from somewhere outside the self (primary narcissism in the beginning symbiotic phase)—Ferenczi's stage of absolute or unconditional hallucinatory omnipotence (1913). Paraphrasing Ferenczi, we might term this stage of primary narcissism the *conditional* hallucinatory omnipotence.

The normal neonate is born with reflex equipment such as the sucking, rooting, grasping, and the *Anklammerung* (clinging) (see Hermann, 1936) probably related to, and complementing, the Moro reflex. However, the reaction which Freud (1895) singled out as most remarkable—the baby's turning his head toward the breast in order to achieve the wished-for pleasure he had experienced in previous encounters with the breast (a derivative of the rooting reflex)—is of a different sort. It is a quasi-coenesthetically acquired pattern of reception in the service of an important "pleasure motivation."

Thus, according to Freud (1895), perception (reception in Spitz's sense) in the service of motivation to gain pleasure was capable of bringing about a "perceptual identity" of an external stimulus with a corresponding pleasurable memory.[1] Turning the head toward the breast (or

[1] Only much later in his writing on *Negation* (1925) did Freud spell out in greater detail the developmental achievement of reality testing that comes about when the image of the lost object can *or cannot* be refound through perception.

nipple) is of the same order of primitive coenesthetic transaction with the "mothering one" as visual pursuit. Visual following, as well as turning toward the breast, shows progression in development, while the primordial sucking, rooting, grasping, and Moro reflexes steadily decline and finally disappear.

The task of the autistic phase is the achievement of homeostatic equilibrium of the organism within the new extramural environment, by predominantly somatopsychic (Spitz), physiological mechanisms.

The newborn brings with him into the outside world the equipment of primary autonomy (Hartmann, 1939). In the normal autistic phase these apparatuses of primary autonomy obey the rules of the coenesthetic organization of the central nervous system: the reaction to any stimulus that surpasses the threshold of reception in the weeks of normal autism is global, diffuse, syncretic—reminiscent of fetal life. (This means that there is only a minimal degree of differentiation, and that various organismic functions are interchangeable.)

Although the autistic phase is characterized by relative absence of cathexis of external stimuli, this does not mean that there can be no responsiveness to external stimuli. Wolff (1959) and Fantz (1961), among others, have clearly demonstrated such responsivity in the newborn, and Wolff additionally describes the fleeting states of "alert inactivity" in which it is most likely to occur. It is this fleeting responsivity to external stimuli that makes for the continuity between the normal autistic phase and later phases.

The Beginning of the Symbiotic Phase

The newborn's waking life centers around his continuous attempts to achieve homeostasis. The effect of his mother's ministrations in reducing the pangs of need-hunger cannot be isolated, nor can the young infant differentiate them from tension-reducing attempts of his own, such as urinating, defecating, coughing, sneezing, spitting, regurgitating, vomiting —all the ways by which the infant tries to rid himself of unpleasurable tension. The effect of these expulsive phenomena, as well as the gratification gained from his mother's ministrations, helps the infant in time to differentiate between a "pleasurable"/"good" quality and a "painful"/ "bad" quality of experience (Mahler and Gosliner, 1955). (This seems to be the first quasi-ontogenetic basis of the later splitting mechanism.)

Through the inborn, autonomous perceptive faculty of the primitive ego, memory traces of the two primordial qualities of stimuli occur within the primal undifferentiated matrix, which Jacobson calls the primal psychophysiological self (in the same sense used by Fenichel and by Hartmann, Kris, and Loewenstein). We may further hypothesize that these are cathected with primordial undifferentiated drive energy (Mahler and Gosliner, 1955).

From the second month on, dim awareness of the need-satisfying object marks the beginning of the phase of normal symbiosis, in which the infant behaves and functions as though he and his mother were an omnipotent system—a dual unity within one common boundary. This is perhaps what Freud and Romain Rolland discussed in their dialogue as the sense of boundlessness of the oceanic feeling (Freud, 1930.)

At this time, the quasi-solid stimulus barrier (negative because it is uncathected)—this autistic shell which kept external stimuli out—begins to crack.[2] Through the aforementioned cathectic shift toward the sensoriperceptive periphery, a protective, but also receptive and selective, positively cathected stimulus shield now begins to form and to envelop the symbiotic orbit of the mother-child dual unity (Mahler, 1967*a*, 1968*b*).

It is obvious that whereas the infant is *absolutely* dependent on the symbiotic partner during the symbiotic phase, symbiosis has quite a different meaning for the adult partner of the dual unity. The infant's need for the mother is absolute; the mother's need for the infant is relative.

The term *symbiosis* in this context is a metaphor. Unlike the biological concept of symbiosis, it does not describe what actually happens in a mutually beneficial relationship between two *separate* individuals of different species. It describes that state of undifferentiation, of fusion with mother, in which the "I" is not yet differentiated from the "not-I" and in which inside and outside are only gradually coming to be sensed as different. Any unpleasurable perception, external or internal, is projected beyond the common boundary of the symbiotic *milieu interieur* (cf. Freud's concept of the "purified pleasure ego," 1915*b*), which includes the mothering partner's gestalt during ministrations. Only transiently—in the state of the sensorium that is termed alert inactivity (cf. Wolff, 1959)—does the young infant seem to take in stimuli from beyond the symbiotic milieu. The primordial energy reservoir that is vested in the

[2] Benjamin and his co-workers (1961) noted an interesting physiological crisis at around 3 to 4 weeks. At that age a maturational crisis occurs. This is borne out in electroencephalographic studies and by the observation that there is a marked increase in overall sensitivity to external stimulation. "Without intervention of a mother figure for help in tension reduction, the infant at that time tends to become overwhelmed by stimuli, with increased crying and other motor manifestations of undifferentiated negative affect."

undifferentiated "ego-id" seems to contain an undifferentiated mixture of libido and aggression. The libidinal cathexis vested in the symbiotic orbit replaces the inborn instinctual stimulus barrier and protects the rudimentary ego from premature phase-unspecific strain, from stress traumata (cf. Kris, 1955; Khan, 1963, 1964).

The essential feature of symbiosis is hallucinatory or delusional somatopsychic *omnipotent* fusion with the representation of the mother and, in particular, the delusion of a common boundary between two physically separate individuals. This is the mechanism to which the ego regresses in cases of the most severe disturbance of individuation and psychotic disorganization, which Mahler (1952; Mahler and Gosliner, 1955) has described as "symbiotic child psychosis."

In the human species, the function of and the equipment for self-preservation are atrophied. The rudimentary (not yet functional) ego in the newborn baby and the young infant has to be complemented by the emotional rapport of the mother's nursing care, a kind of social symbiosis. It is within this matrix of physiological and sociobiological dependency on the mother that the structural differentiation takes place which leads to the individual's organization for adaptation: the functioning ego.

We owe to Spitz's ingenious lucidity much knowledge about how, during the second and third months of life, sensory reception of a contact perceptual nature facilitates the infant's entrance into the symbiotic stage proper. We would only add to Spitz's emphasis that we believe that contact perceptual experiences *of the total body*, especially deep sensitivity of the total body surface (the pressure that the holding mother exercises) in addition to the kinesthetic sense, play an important role in symbiosis as well. Let us not forget what an important longing many fairly normal adults preserve for holding and for being held, for hugging and for being hugged (Hollander, 1970). Beyond Spitz's (1955) primal cavity experiences, these latter modalities play a decisive role in the process of the very young infant's familiarization with his symbiotic partner, the molding behaviors and their variations. All this is still within the realm of coenesthetic global experiences.

Spitz (1965) described how the mouth-hand-labyrinth-skin "unified situational experience" is merged with the first visual image, the mother's face. We found that all other conditions being equal, symbiosis was optimal when the mother naturally permitted the young infant to face her—that is, permitted and promoted eye contact, especially while nursing (or bottle-feeding) the infant, or talking or singing to him.

This brings to mind that Freud (1895) thought "masses in motion" to be the first percept; we now know that *the human face ("en face") in motion* is the first meaningful percept and is the memory engram that elicits the unspecific, so-called social smile. We only have to substitute for Freud's "masses in movement" the vertically moving human face, even disguised with a mask or a symbol of it (Spitz, 1946), and we have our most up-to-date concept of the beginning of perceptual emotional "social" activity of the human being.

The eye-to-eye encounter with even a masked face moving in a vertical direction is the trigger, the organizer or perhaps the "releaser," of the unspecific, so-called social smiling response. This unspecific smiling response marks the entrance into the stage of the need-satisfying object relationship. There is temporary cathexis of the mother and/or her ministrations through the pressure of "need." This corresponds to the entry into that period which we have named *the symbiotic phase.* While primary narcissism still prevails, in the symbiotic phase it is not so absolute as it was in the autistic phase (the first few weeks of life); the infant begins dimly to perceive need satisfaction as coming from some need-satisfying part-object—*albeit still from within the orbit of the omnipotent symbiotic dual unity*—and he turns libidinally toward that mothering source or agency (Spitz, 1955; Mahler, 1969). The need gradually becomes a wish (cf. Schur, 1966) and later the specific "object-bound" affect of longing (Mahler, 1961, 1963, 1971).

Pari passu, and in accordance with the pleasure-pain sequences, demarcation of representations of the body ego within the symbiotic matrix takes place. These representations are deposited as the "body image" (Schilder, 1923; Mahler and Furer, 1966). From now on, representations of the body that are contained in the rudimentary ego mediate between inner and outer perceptions. This corresponds with Freud's (1923) concept that the ego is molded under the impact of reality, on the one hand, and of the instinctual drives, on the other. The body ego contains two kinds of self-representations: an inner core of the body image, with a boundary that is turned toward the inside of the body and divides it from ego, and an outer layer of sensoriperceptive engrams that contributes to the boundaries of the "body self" (cf. Bergmann, 1963, discussing Federn's concepts).

From the standpoint of the body image, *the shift of predominantly proprioceptive-enteroceptive cathexis toward sensoriperceptive cathexis of the periphery* is a major step in development.[3] We did not realize the importance of this shift prior to psychoanalytic studies of early infantile

[3] The well-known peripheral pain-insensitivity, as well as the panic creating hypersensitivity to enteroceptive ("gut") sensations equated with bad introjects *in the psychotic,* bears witness to this.

psychosis. We know now that this major shift of cathexis is an essential prerequisite of body-ego formation. Another parallel step is the deflection —by defense formations such as projection—of destructive, unneutralized aggressive energy, beyond the body-self boundaries (cf. Hoffer, 1950*b*).

The infant's inner sensations form the *core* of the self. They seem to remain the central crystallization point of the "feeling of self," around which a "sense of identity" will become established (Greenacre, 1958; Mahler, 1958*b*; Rose, 1964, 1966). The sensoriperceptive organ —the "peripheral rind of the ego," as Freud called it—contributes mainly to the self's demarcation from the object world. The two kinds of intrapsychic structures *together* form the framework for self-orientation (Spiegel, 1959).

Within the symbiotic common orbit, the two partners or poles of the dyad may be regarded as polarizing the organizational and structuring processes. The structures that derive from this double frame of reference represent a framework to which all experiences have to be related before there are clear and whole representations in the ego of the self and the object world (Jacobson, 1964). Spitz (1965) calls the mother the auxiliary ego of the infant. Similarly, we believe the mothering partner's "holding behavior," her "primary maternal preoccupation" in Winnicott's sense (1958), is the symbiotic organizer—the midwife of individuation, of psychological birth.

Toward the latter part of the symbiotic stage, we generally assume, primary narcissism declines and gradually gives way to secondary narcissism. The infant takes his own body, as well as the mother, as the object of his secondary narcissism. The concept of narcissism, however, remains rather obscure in both psychoanalytic theory and usage unless we place sufficient emphasis on the vicissitudes of the aggressive drive.

During the course of normal development, protective systems safeguard the infant's body from the oral-sadistic pressures which begin to constitute a potential threat to his body integrity from the fourth month on (Hoffer, 1950a). The pain barrier is one such device. In addition, Hoffer (1950b) particularly emphasized that adequate libidinization of the body, within the mother-infant relationship, is important for the development of the body image.

Only when the body becomes the object of the infant's secondary narcissism, via the mother's loving care, does the external object become eligible for identification. To quote Hoffer (1950a, p. 159), from the age of 3 or 4 months on, "primary narcissism has already been modified, but the world of objects has not necessarily yet taken on definite shape."

Normal autism and normal symbiosis are prerequisite to the onset of the normal separation-individuation process (Mahler, 1967*a*; Mahler and

Furer, 1963*a*). Neither the normal autistic, the normal symbiotic, nor any subphase of separation-individuation is completely replaced by the subsequent phase. From a descriptive point of view, it is possible to see similarities among them: they can be conceptually differentiated on the basis of clusters of behavioral phenomena, but they overlap considerably. However, from a developmental point of view, we see each phase as a time when a qualitatively different contribution is made to the individual's psychological growth. The normal autistic phase serves postnatal consolidation of extrauterine physiological growth. It promotes postfetal homeostasis. The normal symbiotic phase marks the all-important phylogenetic capacity of the human being to invest the mother within a vague dual unity that forms the primal soil from which all subsequent human relationships form. The separation-individuation phase is characterized by a steady increase in awareness of the separateness of the self and the "other" which coincides with the origins of a sense of self, of true object relationship, and of awareness of a reality in the outside world.

Normal autism and normal symbiosis are the two earliest stages of nondifferentiation—the former is objectless, the latter, preobjectal (Spitz, 1965). The two stages occur before differentiation of the undifferentiated (Hartmann, Kris, and Loewenstein, 1949) or nondifferentiated matrix (Spitz, 1965); that is, before separation and individuation and *the emergence of the rudimentary ego as a functional structure* (Mahler and Furer, 1963; cf. also Glover, 1956) have taken place.

What Spitz called the "preobjectal stage" we have named the *symbiotic phase*, a name connoting the uniquely human quality of our existence. Vestiges of this phase remain with us throughout the entire life cycle.

The Normal Symbiotic Phase

The normal symbiotic phase is marked by the infant's increased perceptual and affective investment in stimuli that *we* (the adult observers) recognize as coming from the world outside, but that (we postulate) the infant does not recognize as having a clearly outside origin. Here begins the establishment of "memory islands" (Mahler and Gosliner, 1955), but not yet a differentiation of inner and outer, self and other. Here the world becomes increasingly cathected, especially in the person of the mother, but as one dual unity with the not yet clearly demarcated, bordered-off, and experienced self. The cathexis of mother is the principal psychological achievement of this phase. But here, too, there is continuity with what will come later. We know that the infant can already respond differentially to stimuli from inside and from outside. (A light, for example, will be experienced differently from a pang of hunger.) But, unless we postulate inborn ideas, it seems most reasonable to assume that the child has no concept, no schema, of self and other to which to attribute and assimilate these differing stimuli. We postulate that experience of inside and outside is as yet vague; the most highly cathected object, the mother, is still a "part-object."

The senior author (Mahler and Gosliner, 1955) hypothesizes that images of the love object, as well as images of the bodily and later the psychic self, emerge from the ever-increasing memory traces of pleasurable ("good") and unpleasurable ("bad") instinctual, emotional experiences, and the perceptions with which they become associated.

Even the most primitive differentiation, however, can only take place if a psychophysiological equilibrium can be attained (Sander, 1962*a* and *b*). This depends first on a certain matching of the discharge patterns of the mother and the young infant, and later, on their interactional patterns, behaviorally discernible in mutual cueing, as well as in the infant's earliest adaptive patterning and in his receptive capacities with the "good enough" holding behavior of his symbiotic mother (Winnicott, 1956).

Patterns of the "Holding Behavior" of Mothers

A description of various holding behaviors will suggest why we call them the symbiotic organizers of psychological birth. We observed many different kinds of holding behaviors during the symbiotic period. Breast feeding, though important, did not necessarily result in optimal closeness of the mother and her infant. One mother, for instance, proudly breast-fed her babies, but only because it was convenient (she did not have to sterilize bottles); it made her feel successful and efficient. While breast feeding her child, she supported her on her lap with the breast reaching into the baby's mouth. She did not support or cradle the baby with her arms because she wanted her arms free to do as she pleased, independent of the nursling's activity. This baby was unsmiling for a long time. When she did develop a smile, it was an unspecific, all-too-ready smiling response. This unspecific smiling response lasted well into the differentiation period and appeared in situations when, under similar circumstances, other children might show apprehension or at least sober curiosity. Another mother breast fed her little girl, but her puritanical upbringing prevented her from feeling comfortable with a nursing infant, and she did not like to be seen nursing.

On the other hand, there was a mother who thoroughly enjoyed her children when they were infants but did not breast feed them. During feeding she held them close, supporting them well. She smiled and talked to them, and even when her baby was lying on the diapering table, she had her arms underneath him to support and cradle him. This was a mother who was particularly good with her children while they were lap-babies. Her baby son was not only very happy and content, but developed first an unspecific and then a specific smiling response very early.

One of the mothers harbored unusually high ambitions for her child in all areas of functioning. Her favorite word was "success." Her sturdily endowed baby, Junie, had to cope with the stresses of the mother's narcissistically tinged symbiotic relationship to her.

The mother's characteristic interaction with the young baby seemed to be motivated by her pride in Junie's early patterns of muscular-skeletal maturation. Junie could stiffly maintain a standing position on mother's lap, and mother would clap Junie's hands as if she were already at the pat-a-cake age. Keeping the little body erect on her lap did not leave Junie's hands free to pat or explore her mother; she would undoubtedly have done so if left to her own devices. This pattern of standing Junie erect,[4] of which her mother was inordinately proud, became, of course, greatly libidinized and preferred by the young infant. The highly invested pattern of erecting herself on mother's lap and other surfaces became very marked in Junie's first motor patterns. Later, at the beginning of the practicing period, the impulse to stand up seemed to be a most prominent pattern in Junie's locomotor repertoire, *interfering* (that is, competing) for a relatively long time with the desirable, more mature motor pattern of *propelling oneself forward toward a goal* (which dominates most infants' subsequent motor behavior). Junie's inclination to stand up interfered with her ability to move her arms and legs forward, to make them work together to approach the mother, to crawl forward. Crawling was one of the motor achievements that Junie's mother impatiently encouraged and expected her baby to attain.

In observing that favorite patterns of mothering were taken over by the infant (see Tolpin, 1972), we noted that this seemed to be especially true if the pattern signified some frustration or some particular gratification. For example, during the weaning process, after a period of happy breast feeding, Carl's mother warded off and tried to deny her infant's

[4] This is also a glaring example of what Phyllis Greenacre (1959) emphasizes, namely, that the child's body represents a penis in the mother's unconscious. We seem to have seen this in our mothers time and again, but we did not choose to point it out in each particular instance of our study.

clamoring for her breast, his clawing and tearing at her blouse to get to the breast. She comforted him by bouncing him up and down in her lap. The little boy later actively took over this bouncing up and down pattern and eventually converted it into a peekaboo game (see Kleeman, 1967). In this case, the mother's "bouncing pattern" was subsequently used by the boy in a game that was related to his mother, and later he sought social contact with his parents and visitors through his own rendition of the lovely peekaboo pattern that became the hallmark of his socializing rapprochement behavior. Thus, in Carl's case, the pattern served a constructive, adaptive, developmental purpose.[5]

Another little girl actively took over her mother's rocking pattern. The mother was an immature, highly narcissistic woman whose caretaking patterns had a mechanical quality. She would rock the baby in her lap in a tense, unrelated way. When the pattern was taken over by the child, it was not used in the mother-child relationship. The rocking was used in this case for self-comforting and for autoerotic self-stimulation, as if the child were playing mother to herself. During the subphase of differentiation, this little girl would try to augment the pleasure of rocking herself by rocking in front of a mirror, thereby adding a visual feedback to the kinesthetic pleasure. In contrast to Carl's case, the pattern taken over by this little girl served no adaptive, developmental purpose, but only contributed to her narcissism.

[5] When father came home or when guests arrived, Carl, even at 16 months of age, would hide behind a chair or bannister, ducking his head or crouching; suddenly he would lift his head and stand up, indicating with sounds and grunts that he wanted the adults to exclaim, "Here he is!"

CHAPTER 4

The First Subphase: Differentiation and the Development of the Body Image

AT about 4 to 5 months of age, at the peak of symbiosis, behavioral phenomena seem to indicate the beginning of the first subphase of separation-individuation, namely *differentiation*. During the symbiotic months —through that activity of the pre-ego which Spitz has described as *coenesthetic receptivity*—the young infant has familiarized himself with the mothering half of his symbiotic self, as indicated by the unspecific, social smile. This smile gradually becomes the specific (preferential) smiling response to the mother, *which is the crucial sign that a specific bond* between the infant and his mother has been established (Bowlby, 1958).

Freud emphasized that internal perceptions are more fundamental and more elementary than external ones. (The young infant mainly responds to internal perceptions, as noted also in Spock's baby book.) These are the responses of the body to itself and to the internal organs. Greenacre (1960) maintains that the changing states of tension and relaxation "would seem . . . to form a kind of central core of dim body awareness" (p. 207). Greenacre says:

> I have had the idea that the process of birth itself is the first great agent in preparing for awareness of separation; that this occurs through the considerable pressure impact on and stimulation of the infant's body surface during birth and especially by the marked changes in pressure and thermal conditions surrounding the infant in his transfer from intramural to extramural life.

In our observational research we could clearly see the infant-mother interaction patternings, but we could as yet only guess and extrapolate the internal patterning that contributed to the "coreness" of the primitive body image at its inception (cf. also Kafka, 1971).

Greenacre's patterning of "coreness" is not available to observational research, but behaviors which, through the mutual mirroring mechanism, serve the demarcation of the self from the "other" are amenable to observational research. Jacobson notes that the ability to distinguish objects develops more rapidly than the ability to distinguish "self" from objects. We can watch the infant molding to the mother's body and distancing from it with his trunk; we can watch him feel his own and the mother's body; we can watch him handle transitional objects. Hoffer emphasized the importance of touch (1949, 1950*a*, 1950*b*) in the boundary-formation process as well as the importance of the libidinization of the infant's body by the mother. Greenacre emphasizes the "approximation of a sense of oneness by dint of the warm body of mother or nurse [which] represents a relatively small degree of difference in temperature, texture, smell, resilience," i.e., "turgor" (cf. also Bak, 1941). Probably these relatively slight differences can be readily assimilated by the infant's preordained sensorimotor schemata (in Piaget's sense).

One would expect that when inner pleasure, due to safe anchorage within the symbiotic orbit (which is mainly enteroceptive-proprioceptive and contact perceptual) continues and pleasure in the maturationally increasing outer sensory perception (vision or looking, and possibly hearing or outward listening) stimulates outward-directed attention cathexis, these two forms of attention cathexis can oscillate freely (Spiegel, 1959; Rose, 1964). The result should be an optimal symbiotic state, out of which smooth differentiation—*and expansion beyond the symbiotic orbit*—can take place.

Hatching

The "hatching process" is, we believe, a gradual ontogenetic evolution of the sensorium—the perceptual-conscious system—which enables the infant to have a more *permanently alert* sensorium whenever he is awake (cf. also Wolff, 1959).

In other words, the infant's attention, which during the first months of symbiosis was in large part *inwardly* directed, or focused in a coenesthetic vague way *within the symbiotic orbit*, gradually expands through the coming into being of outwardly directed perceptual activity during the child's increasing periods of wakefulness. This is a change of degree rather than of kind, for during the symbiotic stage the child has certainly been highly attentive to the mothering figure. But gradually that attention is combined with a growing store of memories of mother's comings and goings, of "good" and "bad" experiences; the latter were altogether unrelievable by the self, but could be "confidently expected" to be relieved by mother's ministrations.

Observing the infants in our set-up, we came to recognize at some point during the differentiation subphase a certain new look of alertness, persistence and goal-directedness. We have taken this look to be a behavioral manifestation of "hatching" and have loosely said that an infant with this look "has hatched." This new gestalt was unmistakable to the members of our staff, but it is difficult to define with specific criteria. It is probably best described in terms of state (cf. Wolff, 1959). The child no longer seems to drift in and out of alertness, but has a more permanently alert sensorium whenever he is awake.

At about 6 months, tentative experimentation at separation-individuation begins. This can be observed in such behavior on the part of the infant as pulling at mother's hair, ears, or nose, putting food into the mother's mouth, and straining his body away from mother in order to have a better look at her, to scan her and the environment. This is in contrast to simply molding into mother when held (cf. Spock, 1963). There are definite signs that the baby begins to differentiate his own from the mother's body. Six to seven months is the peak of manual, tactile, and visual exploration of the mother's face, as well as of the covered (clad) and unclad parts of the mother's body; these are the weeks during which the infant discovers with fascination a brooch, a pair of eyeglasses, or a pendant worn by the mother. There may be engagement in peekaboo games in which the infant still plays a passive role (Kleeman, 1967). These explorative patterns later develop into the cognitive function of checking the unfamiliar against the already familiar.

Transitional Objects and Transitional Situations

As Greenacre (1960) said:

> The transitional object itself described by Winnicott (1953) is a monument to the need for this contact with the mother's body, which is so touchingly expressed in the infant's insistent preference for an object which is lasting, soft, pliable, warm to the touch, but especially in the demand that it remain saturated with body odors.[1]. . . The fact that the object is usually

[1] Dr. Greenacre recently went on record to correct her previously held opinion that this last factor was important in the constitution of the transitional object.

pressed against the face close to the nose probably indicates how well it substitutes for the mother's breast or soft neck" (p. 208).

We observed that the mother's preferred soothing or stimulating pattern is taken over, that is, assimilated, by the infant in his own way and so becomes a transitional pattern, examples of which are the stroking of the face or certain repetitious movements described in the previous chapter.

Greenacre (1960) feels that "vision is not only an adjunct but an indispensable one in establishing the confluence of the body surface and promoting awareness of delimitation of the self from the nonself. 'Touching' and taking in of the various body parts with the eyes (vision) helps in drawing the body together, into a central image beyond the level of mere immediate sensory awareness" (p. 208). Observational research with our methodology did not focus sufficiently upon the details of the structuralization, as it were, of the transitional object, but impressionistically it gave us rich material from which future studies may benefit, for example, our follow-up studies.

One of the main differences between the normally developing infant and the extreme disturbance in psychosis and possibly also in later borderline pathology seemed to us to be represented by the same circumstances by which Winnicott (1953) gauged the normalcy and pathology of the transitional object (cf. also Furer, 1964; Kestenberg, 1968; Roiphe and Galenson, 1973; Bak, 1974).

Be this as it may, it is during the first subphase of separation-individuation that all normal infants take their first tentative steps toward breaking away, in a bodily sense, from their hitherto completely passive lap-babyhood—the stage of dual unity with the mother. One can observe individually different inclinations and patterns, as well as general characteristics of the stage of differentiation itself. All infants like to venture and stay just a bit of a distance away from the enveloping arms of the mother; as soon as they are motorically able to, they like to slide down from mother's lap, but they tend to remain or to crawl back and play as close as possible to mother's feet.

The Checking-Back Pattern

From about 7 to 8 months we have found the visual pattern of "checking back to mother"—at least in our setting—to be the most important fairly regular sign of beginning somatopsychic differentiation. In fact it appears to be the most important normal pattern of cognitive and emotional development.

The baby begins comparative scanning (see Pacella, 1972). He becomes interested in "mother" and seems to compare her with "other," the unfamiliar with the familiar, feature by feature. He seems to familiarize himself more thoroughly, as it were, with what *is* mother, what feels, tastes, smells, looks like, and has the "clang" of mother. *Pari passu* as he learns the "mother *qua* mother" (Brody and Axelrad, 1966), he also finds out what belongs and what does not belong to mother's body—a brooch, the eyeglasses, and so forth. He starts to discriminate between mother and he or she or *it* that looks, feels, moves differently from, or similarly to, mother.

Stranger Reactions and Stranger Anxiety

We believe that in psychoanalytic child development literature the group of behavioral phenomena indicating the learning about the "other than mother" is described rather one-sidedly and incompletely as "stranger anxiety." But already in Spitz and Wolf's classic film on stranger anxiety, one of the outstanding features we could observe was the curiosity of the infants: their eagerness to find out about "the stranger" as soon as the stranger had averted his gaze.

Our intimate knowledge, based on our detailed and multifaceted observational studies over a long period of time, has taught us that there are individual differences, tremendous variations in timing, quantity, and quality of what is lumped together as "8-month anxiety" in general and "stranger anxiety" in particular (something that the late John Benjamin began to scrutinize in his careful studies).

To illustrate this, let us compare two children of the same mother cross-sectionally at approximately the same ages: Linda and her brother, Peter, 16 months her elder.

We saw Linda soberly and thoughtfully examine without fear, both visually and tactilely, the faces of participant observers who were fairly unfamiliar to her. Her usual happy mood persisted for a few seconds after a stranger took her out of the crib. She then became soberly aware of the "not mother" and began that which Sylvia Brody (Brody and Axelrad, 1970) calls "customs inspection," a term used for the thorough visual and tactile exploratory activity of the differentiating infant (see Mahler and McDevitt, 1968).

When on such occasions her mother took Linda into her arms, we saw that Linda no longer had a need to inspect the familiar face of the mother; instead, in her excitement, she pulled and "rough handled" her mother's neck.

Linda's happy mood and her confidence originated primarily from her closeness and from the predominantly pleasurable interaction with her mother.

In contrast to Linda's "basic trust" and lack of any *marked* stranger anxiety at any age, we observed marked stranger anxiety in Linda's brother, Peter, at 7 and 8 months. Following a latency, a lapse of 1 or 2 minutes perhaps, during which he reacted to the "stranger's" cautious and mild overtures, and during which his *wonderment* and *curiosity* were also quite definitely discernible, Peter's apprehension of the stranger seemed to overwhelm him. Even though he stood near his mother, on the same wicker chair on which she sat, and could lean on mother's body if he wanted to, he burst into tears while looking at the stranger, precisely at the moment when his mother began to stroke his head.[2]

Such comparative observations demonstrated the important differences in the specific outcome of the tense and unpredictable interaction between Peter and his mother as compared with that of the predominantly pleasurable and harmonious climate that prevailed during Linda's symbiotic phase, as well as after "hatching."

We have tried to understand these variations, taking into account the siblings' different endowment and the prevalent emotional climate of the particular mother-infant relationship as observed in their interaction (and in our interviews with the mother).

From this and many similar observations, we have come to view the development of the reactions to strangers in the following wider context: once the infant has become sufficiently individuated to recognize the mother's face—visually and tactilely and perhaps in other ways—and once he familiarizes himself with the general mood and "feel" of his partner in the symbiotic dyad, he then turns with more or less wonderment and apprehension to a prolonged visual and tactile exploration and study of the faces and the gestalt of others. He studies them from afar or at close range. He appears to be comparing and checking the features of the stranger's face with his mother's face, as well as with whatever inner image he may have of his mother (not necessarily and not even predominantly visual). He also seems to check back to his mothers' gestalt, particularly to her face, in relation to other interesting new experiences.

In children for whom the symbiotic phase has been optimal and in whom "confident expectation" has prevailed (Benedek, 1938), curiosity and wonderment, discernible in our setup through the checking-back

[2] We were able to illustrate this behavior on film.

pattern, are the predominant elements of their inspection of strangers. By contrast, among children whose basic trust has been less than optimal, an abrupt change to acute stranger anxiety may occur; or there may be a prolonged period of mild stranger reaction, which transiently interferes with pleasurable inspective behavior. This phenomenon and the factors underlying its variations constitute, we believe, an important aspect of our evaluation of the libidinal object, of socialization, and of the first step toward emotional object constancy. This inverse relation between basic confidence and stranger anxiety needs to be emphasized and further verified (see Mahler and McDevitt, 1968).

Delayed and Premature Hatching

In cases where the symbiotic process, the creating of the common "shielding" membrane of dual unity, has been delayed or disturbed, the process of differentiation seems to be delayed or premature. We have described in the preceding chapter the little girl whose mother responded to her mechanically by rocking her, but without apparent warmth and interest. In the symbiotic phase, this little girl had a bland quality and did not seem to mold to and become a quasi-part of her mother. She smiled indiscriminately and did not respond to her mother as a unique person. At an age when other children started to take a more active part in approaching mother or distancing from her, she turned autoerotically back to her own body for pleasurable stimulation; she indulged in prolonged rocking, rather than in active distancing or approach behaviors.

In another case, the symbiotic relationship was unsatisfactory for different reasons. The mother of this little boy was depressed during his early infancy. He was her third child and she was rather overburdened; they lived in modest circumstances and crowded quarters. Shortly after the birth of this child, the mother's father, with whom she had had a very close relationship, died. Furthermore, her older child had a serious accident when her third child was only a few months old. The combination of all these circumstances made the mother inadvertently ignore her new child. He was bottle fed, and often fed with his back toward mother. In general, she avoided eye contact with him. Still, the mother basically cared deeply about him, as she did about all her children. Like the little girl mentioned above, this little boy was late in recognizing mother as a special person. The specific smiling response was delayed. He was also late in using the visual modality, which is the first instrument to allow active distancing by simultaneously enabling the child to bridge the gap of space, that is, to keep distance-perceptual contact. Although he was late in this development, he never showed the bland, mechanical quality characteristic of the little girl's symbiotic and differentiation behaviors.

We also observed children who had a rather unsatisfactory symbiotic relationship because of the mother's great ambivalence toward her child and toward her own role as a mother. In these children disturbed symbiosis was not caused by indifference or depression on the part of the mother, but by her unpredictability. These infants, as if compensatorily, knew their mothers rather early; their relationship improved when greater distance made it more comfortable and when new sources for pleasure in their growing autonomy and in the outside world became available. What we seem to see, then, is a very early adaptive ability on the part of the infant.

We believe that the little girl whose mother was narcissistic and ungiving differentiated late because she could not rely on mother to be a symbiotic partner and had to do too much of the "job" by herself; that is, she had to play mother to herself. Thus, when she did differentiate, she may have shown some signs of developing a "false self" (cf. James, 1960). This seems to be a way of utilizing her own resources to the greatest possible extent. We later learned that her father's truly motherly attitude from a very early age on helped to keep her from turning away from the human object world. The little boy who received insufficient symbiotic supplies for very different reasons apparently prolonged the period of symbiosis as if to give himself and mother more time to catch up. He emerged from the symbiotic orbit when he, and perhaps also his mother, was ready.

Baby Peter was one of the children who had an intense but uncomfortable symbiotic relationship. *He began to "hatch" early.* He rapidly moved into the phase of differentiation, extricating himself from the uncomfortable symbiosis. Peter was a child who developed intense *stranger reaction and stranger anxiety.* This seems to have been one of his early defensive patterns. Long after he had overcome the original stranger reactions, they would recur, although to a considerably attenuated degree, whenever Peter underwent some period of crisis. It seems as if the unsatisfactory symbiotic phase had prevented Peter from accumulating a sufficient reservoir of that basic trust, of that normal narcissism, which provides the solid base from which to reach out confidently into the "other-than-mother" world. Furthermore, having differentiated—that is, having begun to separate—very early, Peter was easily overwhelmed by anxiety and distress because his autonomously developing ego capacities were precocious and, therefore, vulnerable. We found repeatedly that children who seemed to have an unusually difficult time with separation from mother had histories of unusually early awareness of their mother as different from other caretaking adults.

These earliest differentiation patterns seem not only to have a great deal of rationality, both in terms of the mother-child relationship and the particular endowment of each child, but they also seem to set in motion patterns of personality organization which seem to remain consistent in the further development of the separation-individuation process and possibly beyond. The birth of the child as an individual comes about when, in response to the mother's selective response to his cueing, the child gradually alters his behavior. "It is the specific unconscious need of the mother that activates out of the infant's infinite potentialities, those in particular that create for each mother 'the child' who reflects her own *unique* and individual needs. This process takes place, of course, within the range of the child's innate endowments" (Mahler, 1963; see also Lichtenstein, 1964).

We found that those infants whose mothers enjoyed the symbiotic phase without too much conflict, those infants who were saturated, but not oversaturated, during this period of important oneness with the mother, seemed to start at the average time to show signs of active differentiation by distancing slightly from the mother's body. On the other hand, in cases in which there was ambivalence or parasitism, intrusiveness, "smothering," on the mother's part, differentiation showed disturbances of various degrees and forms. In some cases where the mother acted clearly out of her own symbiotic-parasitic need, rather than out of regard for the infant, differentiation set in almost vehemently. This happened in the case of a little boy, as early as 4 to 5 months of age, because his mother was symbiotically too enveloping. For quite a while this child actually preferred to be held by adults other than his mother, adults who could provide him with greater opportunity to explore the environment visually while being held. He seemed to push away from his mother physically, much more defensively, to stem his feet and arms vigorously against the mother's body (and even arch back in a slightly opisthotonic way). This in his case seemed to fulfill a dual purpose: (1) it served, as it did with the other "more average" symbiotic infants, to put him in a position from which he could better explore the other-than-mother environment, to gain a new perspective on mother from a better vantage point, to relate to her visually from a greater distance; and (2) it achieved the goal of reducing the body surface contact with mother. What surprised us most was that in these (symbiotically) tightly enveloped children, this active process of distancing began earlier than we expected. In another child of a similar mother, close physical contact was avoided.

The seeking of distance during the differentiation subphase seemed to be accompanied by greater awareness of mother as a special person, even if this awareness, as in the above case, was negative (cf. also the differential scanning and "checking back" patterns.)

Let us illustrate further some of these phenomena of the first subphase (differentiation) in selected children, all of whom (like all "normal" children) show the general phase-related developments, along with highly individualized variations dependent upon the relation to the mother, the innate endowment, and the specific history (Weil, 1970).

Bernie had had a blissful early relationship with his mother, who seemed to find great fulfillment in breast feeding him. Because of her guilt feelings toward her older son, and also because he bit her nipple (cf. Spock, 1965), she abruptly and impulsively weaned Bernie to the bottle. The weaning brought about a marked change in the atmosphere of the symbiotic relationship. At first, the infant insistently and fretfully rooted about for the lost breast, while the mother desperately denied his obvious reaction to the weaning trauma. The radiance and contentment that his mother had exhibited during the breast-feeding gave way to listlessness and apathy, while the infant in turn became fretful, listless, and apathetic. The happy, smiling, well-molding infant at the breast became temporarily a passive, nonmolding, sacklike baby in one's arms.[3]

Then, for a short while, the generally difficult interaction between Bernie and his mother seemed favorably affected by each maturational spurt in the infant. Bernie showed great interest in locomotion: he practiced crawling and pulling up with great pleasure and persistence. As he became able to engage others with his eyes and to give signs of differential recognition of his mother, and as he gained gratification from his own developing partial motor functions, his scope of exploration expanded to include the entire playroom area (and the entire apartment at home). His mother seemed to feel relieved by the lessening of her son's symbiotic demands and total dependency, and Bernie, in turn, was able to use every bit of encouragement and protection during the practicing period.

As we said earlier, a strikingly different transition from the symbiotic

[3] In the years 1960–1962 we experimented briefly with the molding pattern (cf. Mahler and La Perriere, 1965). We not only observed the infant's body contour in relation to mother's, but we ourselves registered the nature of the young infant's molding in our arms. We described this coenesthetic sensation as: "molding well," "melting," "boardlike-stiff," "sack-of-potato kind," and so forth.

to the separation-individuation phase was observed in the other little boy who had a close and prolonged symbiotic relationship with his mother. Both of this child's parents had symbiotic-parasitic needs, overvalued their child as a vegetative being, and kept him in a state of continued symbiotic dependency (cf. Parens and Saul, 1971). This clearly slowed down his libidinal investment in his motor functions (see below), in which, perhaps, he was also constitutionally weakly endowed. Whereas Bernie entered the separation-individuation phase with a preferred modality of motor exploration, this little boy's preferred modality involved use of the tactile, prehensile and visual sense organs for a prolonged period. This preference seemed to be the outcome of several factors. Both parents insisted that his tension be relieved as soon as he manifested it, so that he did not need to exert himself in the least to get what he wanted. His mother displayed to us, and communicated in a nonverbal way to the child, her desire that he remain sedentary and accede to being handled in the reclining position, even though he especially objected to this.

This same little boy, by endowment, was a child slow to mature in motor functions. His musculature was flabbier, his large body movements more cautious and less energetic than those of other children of the same age. (A noticeable exception was his vigorous kicking whenever he was excited.) Confined to a small area by his lack of locomotor ability, he made the most extensive use of his visibly emerging perceptive-cognitive and prehensile faculties in order to occupy and amuse himself for long periods of time with "making interesting spectacles last" (Piaget, 1936). At the same time, he remained extremely visually alert to happenings around him; he willingly engaged others and accepted their comforting.

These two children illustrate two different ways of entering the first subphase of separation-individuation: differentiation. It may be worth noting that they were equally matched in overall performance on developmental tests.

We had the impression that the latter's mother, who had intensely enjoyed the symbiotic relationship with her breast-fed baby, belonged to that group of mothers who could not endure the gradual disengagement of the infant at the beginning of the separation-individuation phase. They attach, "appersonate," (cf. Sperling, 1944) the infant to themselves and discourage his groping for independent functioning, instead of allowing and promoting gradual separation. On the other hand, as we described elsewhere (Mahler, 1967*a*), there is quite a large contingent of mothers who, unlike the overly symbiotic mothers, at first hold on to their infant and then push him precipitously into "autonomy" (cf. Greenson, 1968; Mahler, 1968*b*, 1971).

As important as intrinsic variables are for eventual harmonious personality development, so a favorable mother-child interaction affects subphase adequacy. Coleman, Kris, and Provence (1953) drew attention, many years ago, to the variations of the mother's attitudes during the first years of life of the child. The mother's attitude has also to adapt in the entire course of the separation-individuation process—but especially at certain crucial points or crossroads of that process![4]

The Two Developmental Tracks of Separation and Individuation

Phenomena of normal development can best be understood when elements of the process are somewhat out of kilter. It is at the end of the first year and in the early months of the second year that one can see with particular clarity that the intrapsychic process of separation-individuation has two intertwined, but not always commensurate or proportionately progressing, developmental tracks. One is the track of individuation, the evolution of intrapsychic autonomy, perception, memory, cognition, reality testing; the other is the intrapsychic developmental track of separation that runs along differentiation, distancing, boundary formation, and disengagement from mother. All of these structuralization processes will eventually culminate in internalized self-representations, as distinct from internal object representations. The behavioral surface phenomena of the process of separation-individuation can be observed in countless subtle variations as the accompaniment of the *intrapsychic* onward development. Optimal situations seem to be those in which awareness of bodily separation in terms of differentiation from mother goes parallel with (that is to say, neither lags far behind nor runs literally far ahead of) the toddler's development of independent autonomous functioning—cognition, perception, memory, reality testing, and so on; in short, those functions of the ego which serve individuation.

In our observational research study, the progressions and regressions and the gradual integration of these two tracks of development—

[4] While we are convinced that the lion's part of adaptation must come from the pliable, unformed infant, that does not mean that mothering does not have to follow the changing requirements of the separation-individuation process; there must be a measure of adaptation on the mother's part, too.

namely, separation and individuation—can be studied by way of the back-and-forth movements between child and mother. We were able to follow this development by means of the mother-infant interaction, and particularly by observation of the vivid affectomotility, gestures, and vocalizations of the child himself.

We find it instructive to compare children who were slow in locomotor development with precociously walking toddlers. For example, two of our little boys were at the opposite ends of the spectrum of the two tracks of the separation-individuation process: *maturation* versus *development, separation* versus *individuation.* The one came to us already walking at the age of 9 months; the other took his first unaided steps only 2 days before he was 17 months old—fully 8 months apart!

The impact of such discrepancy on the separation-individuation process will be explicated and illustrated in the next chapters.

CHAPTER 5

The Second Subphase: Practicing

The Early Practicing Period

THE differentiation subphase is overlapped by the practicing period. In the course of processing our data we found it useful to think of the practicing period in two parts: (1) the early practicing phase, ushered in by the infant's earliest ability to move away physically from mother by crawling, paddling, climbing, and righting himself—yet still holding on; and (2) the practicing period proper, phenomenologically characterized by free, upright locomotion.

At least three interrelated, yet discriminable, developments contribute to the child's first steps toward awareness of separateness and toward individuation. These are the rapid *body differentiation* from the mother; the establishment of a *specific bond* with her; and the *growth and functioning of the autonomous ego apparatuses in close proximity to the mother.*

These developments seem to pave the way for the infant's interest in the mother to spill over (much more definitely than hitherto) onto inanimate objects, at first those provided by her—a blanket, a diaper, a toy which she offers, or the bottle with which she parts from him at night. The infant explores these objects visually with his eyes and investigates their taste, texture, and smell with his contact perceptual organs, particularly the mouth and the hands. One or the other of these objects may become a transitional object. Moreover, whatever the sequence in which these functions develop during the differentiation subphase, it is characteristic of this early practicing stage that, while there is interest and absorption in these activities, interest in the mother definitely seems to take precedence.

The maturation of locomotor and other functions during the early practicing period had the most salutary effect on those children who had an intense but uncomfortable symbiotic relationship. It would seem possible that this was connected at least in part with a simultaneous satisfactory disengagement process in the mothers. Those mothers who had been most anxious because they could not relieve their infant's distress during the symbiotic and differentiation phases were now greatly relieved when their children became less fragile and vulnerable and somewhat more independent. Those mothers and their children had been unable to take undisturbed pleasure in close physical contact, but they were able to enjoy each other now from a somewhat greater distance. These same children became more relaxed and better able to use their mothers to find comfort and safety.

By contrast, another mother-child interaction pattern during the early practicing period was observed in those children who most actively sought physical closeness to mother, children whose mothers had the greatest difficulty in relating to them during the process of active distancing. These mothers liked the closeness of the symbiotic phase but once this phase was over, they would have liked their children to be "grown up" already. Interestingly, these children found it relatively difficult to grow up; they were unable to enjoy the beginning ability to distance and very actively demanded closeness.

Expanding locomotor capacity during the early practicing subphase widens the child's world; not only does he have a more active role in determining closeness and distance to mother, but the modalities that up to now were used to explore the relatively familiar environment suddenly expose him to a wider segment of reality; there is more to see, more to hear, more to touch. How this new world is experienced seems to be subtly related to the mother, who still is the center of the child's universe from which he only gradually moves out into ever-widening circles.

Recently, one of us (A. B.) had the opportunity to observe closely a 7-month-old baby during this period of beginning active locomotor functioning, coinciding with a 2-week separation from his parents, and the subsequent reunion. The baby had been described as particularly easygoing and relaxed. He greeted every new person with curiosity and delight. He thoroughly examined every new person visually and tactilely. During his parents' absence he was left with his grandparents whom he knew well. This coincided in time with his rapid change from a babe-in-arms to a separating one. He began to crawl and to pull himself up to a standing position. These new acquisitions of skill, however, brought him pain rather than pleasure. He fell frequently and cried hard after every fall. Nevertheless, he insisted on repeating the painful experience, and this very quiet, easy-going child seemed suddenly quite driven. We see here clearly the powerful momentum of the innate given, the thrust for individuation. He retained his positive relationship to people around him and liked being carried, sung to, and soothed by them. When his mother returned, he at first had a rather severe crisis of reunion, crying unconsolably for quite a while and not allowing her to either feed him or put him to sleep. However, by the next day he was his old smiling and tranquil self. This reaction to brief separations, which is peculiarly specific to mother-infant reunions in the second half of the first year, might be understood metapsychologically in terms of the split that still exists in the internal part-images of the mother. This split is easily activated by such brief absences; the mother of separation must be reintegrated as the "all good" symbiotic mother so as not to hurt or destroy the good object. While the little boy continued practicing his new skills, the driven quality and the frequent falls diminished rapidly. With mother as an anchor, a center to his world, the frustrating part of the new experiences and explorations became once again manageable, and the pleasurable part of exploring predominated. This bit of personal observation fits in well with observations in our study—namely, that early explorations serve the purpose (1) of establishing familiarity with a wider segment of the world and (2) of perceiving, recognizing, and enjoying mother from a greater distance. We found that those children who had the best "distance contact" with their mothers were the ones who would venture farthest away from her. In cases where there was too much conflict about the separating process or too much reluctance to give up closeness, the children showed less pleasure during this period. But simple rules are not applicable in these processes either.

The little boy, for example, whose mother really could accept him only as a symbiotic part of herself and who actively interfered with his attempts to move away, seemed altogether to lose contact with his mother when he was at a distance from her. On the other hand, another child whose mother enjoyed closeness very much was well able to maintain contact with her mother at some distance; in fact she was especially well able during this period to use her mother and was reassured if she could just look at mother or hear her voice. At the same time, this little girl showed rather precociously a general lowering of mood when her mother was not in the room, that is, when the source for reassurance from a distance was cut off.

We also observed in this early period of practicing that the "would-be fledgling" likes to indulge in his budding relationship with the "other-than-mother" world. For instance, we observed one child at 11 months who, during this phase, had to undergo hospitalization of a week's duration. It seems he was frustrated most by his confinement to a crib, so that he welcomed *anyone* who took him out of it. When he returned from the hospital, the relationship to his mother had become less exclusive, and he showed no clinging reaction or separation anxiety; now his greatest need in the Center and at home was to be walked, with someone holding his hand. While he continued to prefer that mother do this—with and for him—he would readily accept substitutes.

Margie and Matthew (just 1 week apart in age) had progressed smoothly through the symbiotic phase as well as through the first subphase (differentiation). Both children could "confidently expect" their mothers to relieve their instinctual tensions, to be emotionally available. At 10 months of age, both infants were observed entering the practicing period with great investment of interest in their emerging motor functions and other autonomous functions of the ego. For long periods of time, they happily occupied themselves with exploring the physical environment on their own, showing what Hendrick (1951) has described as pleasure in mastery (*Funktionslust* of C. Buhler). They returned to their mothers from time to time for emotional refueling. Both mothers accepted the gradual disengagement of their infant-toddlers and fostered their interest in practicing. They were emotionally available, according to the child's needs, and provided the kind of maternal sustenance necessary for optimal unfolding of the autonomous functions of the ego.

Anna's mother, on the other hand, was unable to provide optimal availability, so that her child's capacity for confident expectation was severely taxed. The maturation of Anna's emerging ego functions took place on time, but it was as though her difficult struggle to get the attention she needed from her mother left her with insufficient libidinal energy adequately to cathect the other-than-mother world, her autonomous ego functions, and probably also her own body, with sound (secondary) narcissism. She was therefore unable to devote herself to pleasurable exploration and mastery of her expanding reality. In any event, the child was seen during the first subphase and the early practicing period sitting at her mother's feet, imploring and beseeching her mother with her eyes. The differentiation subphase lasted much longer with Anna than with her contemporaries, Margie and Matthew, although her ego functions themselves matured.

Anna's practicing period was characterized by brief, tentative forays on her own, in which she absented herself from her mother's feet only for short periods. The practicing period—the time when toddlers invest so much libido in their own autonomous functions and in their expanding reality testing—was transient and abbreviated in Anna's case and lacked a full-scale emotional development. Its relative absence highlights the central feature of this subphase as we see it: the elated investment in the exercise of the autonomous functions, especially motility, to the near exclusion of apparent interest in the mother at times. It is this, and not the development of motor skills per se, that characterizes the normal practicing subphase.

As the child, through the maturation of his locomotor apparatus, begins to venture farther away from the mother's feet, he is often so absorbed in his own activities that for long periods of time he appears to be oblivious to the mother's presence. However, he returns periodically to the mother, seeming to need her physical proximity from time to time.

The optimal distance in this *early practicing subphase* would seem to be one that allows the moving, exploring quadruped child freedom and opportunity for exploration at some physical distance from mother. It should be noted, however, that during the entire practicing subphase mother continues to be needed as a stable point, a "home base" to fulfill the need for refueling through physical contact. We saw 7- to 10-month-olds crawling or rapidly paddling to the mother, righting themselves on her leg, touching her in other ways, or just leaning against her. It is this phenomenon that was termed by Furer "emotional refueling."[1] It is easy to observe how the wilting and fatigued infant "perks up" in the shortest time following such contact; then he quickly goes on with his explorations and once again becomes absorbed in his pleasure in functioning.

The phenomenon of refueling seemed to undergo different stages and had different modalities in each child, modalities which we believe were closely connected with the preferred modality of the mother. One mother, for example, who placed great stakes on independent functioning, was particularly good in maintaining contact with her child by refueling him from a distance. When her children came to her, it was usually for brief periods of physical contact. This mother rarely rose from her chair, where she sat comfortably doing the family mending

[1] Personal communication.

and chatting with the other mothers. She seemed constantly attuned to her small children's needs, even at a distance.

In the case of Jay, a child whose locomotor ability developed very early so that the refueling capacity of mother would have been of special importance, we observed the following: Jay's mother thought that any limit set on Jay would interfere with his budding personality and independence. She watched in terror while Jay got himself into dangerous situations. She could not remain in contact with him by talking to him, as she did not want to interfere with his "independence." Although his mother watched him anxiously from a distance, Jay felt, and in a way actually *was*, deserted by her, even in her presence. Over and over again he got himself into dangerous situations that he could neither judge nor master; even while he was doing just the ordinary, he was particularly prone to hurting himself. Once he had fallen and was crying, his mother felt free to help him.

Mark was one of those children who had the greatest difficulty establishing workable distance between himself and mother. His mother became ambivalent toward him as soon as Mark ceased to be part of herself, her symbiotic child. At times she seemed to avoid close body contact; at other times she might interrupt Mark in his autonomous activities to pick him up, hug him, and hold him. She did this when *she* needed it, not when *he* did. This lack of empathy on mother's part may have been what made it difficult for Mark to function at a distance from her.

During the early practicing subphase, following the initial pull and push away from mother into the outside world, most of the children seemed to go through a brief period of increased separation anxiety. The fact that they were able to move away independently, and yet remain connected with mother—not physically, but through the distance modalities of seeing and hearing—made the successful use of these distance modalities extraordinarily important for a while. The children did not like to lose sight of mother; they might stare sadly at her empty chair or at the door through which she had left.

The Practicing Subphase Proper

With the spurt in autonomous functions, such as cognition, but especially upright locomotion, the "love affair with the world" (Greenacre, 1957) begins. The toddler takes the greatest step in human individuation. He walks freely with upright posture. Thus, the plane of his vision changes; from an entirely new vantage point he finds unexpected and changing perspectives, pleasures, and frustrations. There is a new visual level that the upright, bipedal position affords.

During these precious 6 to 8 months (from the age of 10 or 12 months to 16 or 18 months), the world is the junior toddler's oyster. Libidinal cathexis shifts substantially into the service of the rapidly growing autonomous ego and its functions, and the child seems intoxicated with his own faculties and with the greatness of his own world. Narcissism is at its peak! The child's first upright independent steps mark the onset of the practicing period par excellence, with substantial widening of his world and of reality testing. Now begins a steadily increasing libidinal investment in practicing motor skills and in exploring the expanding environment, both human and inanimate. The chief characteristic of this practicing period is the child's great narcissistic investment in his own functions, his own body, as well as in the objects and objectives of his expanding "reality." Along with this, we see a relatively great imperviousness to knocks and falls and other frustrations, such as a toy being grabbed by another child. Substitute familiar adults within the setup of our nursery are easily accepted (in contrast to what occurs during the next subphase of separation-individuation).

The smoothly separating and individuating toddler finds narcissistic solace for the minimal threats of object loss—which probably each new step of progressive development entails—in his rapidly developing ego functions. The child concentrates on practicing and mastering his own skills and autonomous (independent of other or mother) capacities. He is exhilarated by his own abilities, continually delighted with the discoveries he makes in his expanding world, and quasi-enamored with the world and his own grandeur and omnipotence. We might consider the possibility that the elation of this subphase has to do not only with the exercise of the ego apparatuses, but also with the elated escape from fusion with, from engulfment by, mother. From this point of view we would consider that, just as the infant's peek-a-boo games seem to turn from passive to active, the losing and regaining of the need-gratifying object and then the love object, so too does the toddler's constant running off until he is swooped up by his mother turn from passive to active the fear of being reengulfed by mother. This behavior also reassures him that mother will *want* to catch him and swoop him up in her arms. We need not assume that such behavior is intended to serve these functions when it first emerges, but only that it produces these effects and can then be intentionally repeated.

The Importance of Free Upright Locomotion: Walking

The importance of walking for the emotional development of the child cannot be overestimated. Walking gives the toddler an enormous increase in reality discovery and testing of the world at his own control and magic mastery. As Greenacre says, it is "also associated with an upsurge of general body exhilaration and sensory responsiveness that accompany the gaining of the upright position and walking" (1968, p. 51).

The boy's discovery of his penis must be mentioned briefly here, although we will discuss it in more detail in the context of gender identity (see p. 104). The penis usually is discovered a few weeks earlier—an exquisitely sensuous, pleasure-giving organ whose movement is, however, not subject to the ego's mastery. Having assumed the upright position, the boy may view the penis "from more angles and positions than before, and the increased interest in urination gives it an added stimulation and importance as a body part" (Greenacre, 1968, p. 51).

We found in boys and girls alike that in the very next month following the attainment of active free locomotion, great strides were made toward asserting their individuality. This seems to be the first great step toward identity formation.

The mother's renunciation of possession of the body of the infant boy and girl alike at this period is mostly quasi-automatic, even though it is sometimes freely verbally expressed as a deplored necessity. Barney's mother said, "When he runs away from me in the park and I have to carry that heavy little body back home, I tell myself, 'You better enjoy this—it won't last long, you won't be carrying him in your arms much longer.' "

It was E. J. Anthony (1971) who recognized the pertinence of Kierkegaard's beautifully expressed insights into the human child's need for his mother's emotional support at the point when he starts to walk freely. He cites the following passages to illustrate that "the influence of a disturbed and disturbing mother on the individuation of her child is in sharp contrast to that of the ordinary 'good enough' mother" (p. 262):

> The loving mother teaches her child to walk alone. She is far enough from him so that she cannot actually support him, but she holds out her arms to him. She imitates his movements, and if he totters, she swiftly bends as if to seize him, so that the child might believe that he is not walking alone. . . . And yet, she does more. Her face beckons like a reward, an encouragement. Thus, the child walks alone with his eyes fixed on his mother's face, *not* on the difficulties in his way. He supports himself by the

arms that do not hold him and constantly strives towards the refuge in his mother's embrace, little suspecting *that in the very same moment that he is emphasizing his need of her, he is proving that he can do without her,* because he is walking alone (Kierkegaard, 1846, p. 85).

But in the other mother, it is very different:

> There is no beckoning encouragement, no blessing at the end of the walk. There is the same wish to teach the child to walk alone, but not as a loving mother does it. For now there is fear that envelops the child. It weighs him down so that he cannot move forward. There is the same wish to lead him to the goal, *but the goal becomes suddenly terrifying* (Kierkegaard, 1846, p. 85).

Anthony continues in his own words:

> The fearfulness, the ambivalence, the unconscious hostility, the need to encapsulate hinder the child from stepping off on his own. With his delicate insight, Kierkegaard crystallizes the moments of development when the toddler feels the pull of separation from his mother and at the same time asserts his individuation. It is a mixed experience of enormous developmental significance, the child demonstrating that he can and cannot do without his mother, and his mother demonstrating that she can and cannot let him walk alone (Anthony, 1971, p. 263).

Speaking about *folie à deux* situations, Anthony goes on to say: "The psychotic mother fills these moments with apprehension so that the child not only has nowhere to go, but he is afraid to get anywhere."

Quite late in our study, we came to realize that it is the rule rather than the exception that the first unaided steps taken by the infant are in a direction away from the mother or during her absence; this contradicts the popular belief (reflected by Kierkegaard, among other poets) that the first steps are taken toward mother. The significance of this phenomenon bears further study.

Many of the mothers seemed to react to the fact that their infants were moving away by helping them move away, that is, by giving them a gentle or perhaps less gentle push, as the mother bird would encourage the fledgling. Mothers usually became very interested in, but sometimes also critical of, their children's functioning at this point. They began to compare notes, and they showed concern if their child seemed to be behind. Sometimes they would hide their concern in a pointed display of non-concern. In many mothers, concern became especially concentrated in eagerness for their children to walk. Once the child was able to move away some distance, it was as if suddenly the mother began to worry about whether the child would be able to "make it" out there in the world where he would have to fend for himself. Upright free locomotion seems to become for many mothers the supreme proof of the fact that the infant has "made it."

In the course of the practicing period proper, we were impressed by the tremendously exhilarating, truly dramatic effect that *upright locomotion* had on the general mood of the hitherto also very busy quadruped infant. We became aware of its importance for the achievement of the "psychological birth experience," the "hatching," through unexpected, regularly occurring observations of behavioral sequences, and by comparing them with Phyllis Greenacre's work (1957) on the childhood of the artist. It seemed to us that most practicing toddlers had "a love affair with the world" as well!

In those cases where the ascendancy of the child's free locomotor capacity was delayed, the obligatory exhilaration occurred later than usual. Thus, this phenomenon seemed to be definitely connected with, and dependent on, the function of free locomotor activity in relation to the developmental stage of other autonomous partial functions of the ego.

In summary, walking seems to have great symbolic meaning for both mother and toddler: it is as if the walking toddler has proved by his attainment of independent upright locomotion that he has already graduated into the world of independent human beings. The expectation and confidence that mother exudes when she feels that the child is now able to "make it" out there seems to be an important trigger for the child's own feeling of safety and perhaps also the initial encouragement for his exchanging some of his magic omnipotence for pleasure in his own autonomy and his developing self-esteem.

Low-Keyedness

Most children in the practicing subphase proper appeared to have major periods of exhilaration or at least of relative elation. They were impervious to knocks and falls and became what we term *low-keyed* only when they became aware that mother was absent from the room. At such times, their gestural and performance motility slowed down, their interest in their surroundings diminished, and they appeared to be preoccupied with inwardly concentrated attention, with what Rubinfine (1961) called "imaging."

Our inferences about the low-keyed state derive from two recurrent phenomena: (1) if a person other than mother actively tried to comfort the child, he lost his emotional balance and burst into tears; and (2) the child's "toned-down" state visibly terminated at the time of his reunion with the briefly absent mother, although sometimes not before a short crying spell released the accumulated tension. Both these phenomena heightened our awareness that up to that point, the child *had been* in a special "state of self": this low-keyedness and inferred "imaging" of mother is reminiscent of a miniature anaclitic depression.[2] We tend to see in it the child's effort to hold on to a state of mind that Joffe and Sandler (1965) have termed "the ideal state of self," very much akin to that which Kaufman and Rosenblum (1968) have termed "conservation withdrawal" in monkeys.

Some children transiently appeared quite overwhelmed by fear of object loss, so that the *"ego-filtered affect of longing"* was in danger of very abruptly turning into desperate crying. This was the case with Barney during that brief period when his "individuation" had not yet caught up with his maturational spurt of locomotion, serving separation. For a while, he was unable to cope emotionally with the experience of the self-induced separations from mother in space. He was visibly bewildered when he hurt himself and noticed that his mother was not automatically close by.

Our data, in their rich detail, have unmistakably shown regularly occurring combinations of factors from which we conclude that there was a dawning awareness that the symbiotic mothering half of the self was missed. The ensuing behavior of low-keyedness had different shadings in individual children compared with each other and with themselves over time.

We found this longing for the state of well-being and unity or closeness with mother to be peculiarly lacking in children whose symbiotic relationship had been unduly prolonged or had been a disturbed one: for example, in the child who had an exaggeratedly close, parasitic symbiosis with his mother, and in a little girl whose mother-infant relationship was what Robert Fliess (1961) termed *asymbiotic*. It seemed diminished and irregular in children in whom the symbiotic relationship with mother was marred by the unpredictability and impulsivity of a partly engulfing and partly rejecting mother.

[2] Though different in form, this recapturing of the absent mother in a waking, low-keyed, imaging state has parallels to Lewin's (1946) and Isakower's (1938) discussions of the conjuring up of old "lost worlds" in dreams and the state of falling asleep.

CHAPTER 6

The Third Subphase: Rapprochement

General Considerations

WITH the acquisition of upright, free locomotion and with the closely following attainment of that stage of cognitive development that Piaget (1936) regards as the beginning of representational intelligence (which will culminate in symbolic play and in speech), the human being has emerged as a separate and autonomous person. These two powerful "organizers" (Spitz, 1965) constitute the midwives of psychological birth. In this final stage of the "hatching" process, the toddler reaches the first level of identity—that of being a separate individual entity (Mahler, 1958*b*).

By the middle of the second year of life, the infant has become a toddler. He now becomes more and more aware, and makes greater and greater use, of his physical separateness. However, side by side with the growth of his cognitive faculties and the increasing differentiation of his emotional life, there is also a noticeable waning of his previous imperviousness to frustration, as well as a diminution of what has been a relative obliviousness to his mother's presence. Increased separation anxiety can be observed: at first this consists mainly of fear of object loss, which is to be inferred from many of the child's behaviors. The relative lack of concern about the mother's presence that was characteristic of the practicing subphase is now replaced by seemingly constant concern with the mother's whereabouts, as well as by active approach behavior. As the toddler's *awareness* of separateness grows—stimulated by his maturationally acquired ability to move away physically from his mother and by his cognitive growth—he seems to have an increased need, a wish for mother to share with him every one of his new skills and experiences, as well as a great need for the object's love.

As we described in the previous chapter, the need for closeness had been held in abeyance, so to speak, throughout the practicing period. For this reason we have given this subphase the name of *rapprochement.*

One cannot emphasize too strongly the importance of the optimal emotional availability of the mother during this subphase. "It is the mother's *love* of the toddler and the acceptance of his ambivalence that enable the toddler to cathect his self-representation with neutralized energy" (Mahler, 1968*b*). The specific additional importance of the father during this period has also been stressed by Loewald (1951), Greenacre (1966), and Abelin (1971).

The "refueling" type of bodily approach that had characterized the practicing infant is replaced, during the period from 15 to 24 months and beyond, by a deliberate search for, or avoidance of, intimate bodily contact. This is now compounded by interaction of toddler and mother at a much higher level: symbolic language, vocal as well as other types of intercommunication, and play become increasingly prominent (Galenson, 1971).

During the rapprochement subphase, we observed separation reactions in all our children. We ventured the hypothesis that it was among those children whose separation reactions had been characterized by moderate and ego-filtered affects in which the libidinal valence (love instead of aggression) predominated that subsequent development was more likely to be favorable.

The Shadowing and Darting-Away Patterns

Two characteristic patterns of the toddler's behavior—the "shadowing"[1] of mother and the darting away from her, with the expectation of being chased and swept into her arms—indicate both his wish for reunion with the love object and his fear of reengulfment by it. One can continually observe in the toddler a "warding-off" pattern directed against impingement upon his recently achieved autonomy. On the other hand, his incipient fear of loss of love represents an element of the conflict on the way to internalization. Some toddlers of rapprochement age already seem to be rather sensitive to disapproval; still, autonomy is defended by the "No," as well as by the increased aggression

[1] By "shadowing," we mean the child's incessant watching of and following every move of the mother.

and negativism of the anal phase. (One is here reminded of Anna Freud's classic paper on negativism and emotional surrender, 1951*a*).

In other words, at the time when the junior toddler of 12 to 15 months has grown into the senior toddler of up to 24 months, a most important emotional turning point has been reached. Now the toddler begins to experience, more or less gradually and more or less keenly, the obstacles that lie in the way of what he evidently anticipated at the height of his "practicing" exhilaration would be his "conquest of the world." Concomitant with the acquisition of primitive skills and perceptual cognitive faculties, there has been an increasingly clear differentiation, a separation, between the intrapsychic representation of the object and the self-representation. At the very height of mastery, toward the end of the practicing period, it had already begun to dawn on the junior toddler that the world is *not* his oyster, that he must cope with it more or less "on his own," very often as a relatively helpless, small, and separate individual, unable to command relief or assistance merely by feeling the need for it, or even by giving voice to that need (Mahler, 1966*b*).

The quality and measure of the wooing behavior of the toddler toward his mother during this subphase provide important clues to the normality of the individuation process. Fear of losing the love of the object (instead of fear of object loss) becomes increasingly evident.

Incompatibilities and misunderstanding between mother and child can be observed, even in the case of the normal mother and her normal toddler; these are to a great extent rooted in certain contradictions of this subphase. The toddler's demand for his mother's constant involvement seems contradictory to the mother: while he is now not as dependent and helpless as he was only a half year before, and seems eager to become less and less so, nevertheless he even more insistently indicates that he expects the mother to share every aspect of his life. During this subphase, some mothers cannot accept the child's demandingness; others, by contrast, are unable to face the child's gradual separation—the fact that the child is becoming increasingly independent of, and separate from, her and can no longer be regarded as a part of her (cf. Masterson, 1973; Stoller, 1973).

In this third subphase, that of rapprochement, while individuation proceeds very rapidly and the child exercises it to the limit, he also becomes more and more aware of his separateness and employs all kinds of mechanisms in order to resist and undo his actual separateness from mother. The fact is, however, that no matter how insistently the toddler tries to coerce the mother, she and he can no longer function effectively as a dual unit—that is to say, the child can no longer maintain his delusion of parental omnipotence, which he still at times expects will restore the symbiotic status quo.

Verbal communication becomes more and more necessary; gestural coercion on the part of the toddler or mutual preverbal empathy between mother and child will no longer suffice to attain the goal of satisfaction—that of well-being in Joffe and Sandler's sense (1965). The junior toddler gradually realizes that his love objects (his parents) are separate individuals with their own personal interests. He must gradually and painfully give up the delusion of his own grandeur, often by way of dramatic fights with mother—less so, it seemed to us, with father. This is the crossroads that we term the "rapprochement crisis."

The Mother's Attitude in the Toddler's Rapprochement Period

Depending upon her own adjustment, the mother may react to the child's demands during this period either with continued emotional availability and playful participation or with a gamut of less desirable attitudes. It is, however, the mother's continued emotional availability, we have found, that is essential if the child's autonomous ego is to attain optimal functional capacity, while his reliance on magic omnipotence recedes. If the mother is "quietly available" with a ready supply of object libido, if she shares the toddling adventurer's exploits, playfully reciprocates, and thus facilitates his salutary attempts at imitation and *identification*, then internalization of the relationship between mother and toddler is able to progress to the point where, in time, verbal communication takes over, even though vivid gestural behavior —that is, affectomotility—still predominates (Homburger, 1923; Mahler, 1944, 1949*a*). Predictable emotional involvement on the part of the mother seems to facilitate the rich unfolding of the toddler's thought processes, reality testing, and coping behavior by the end of the second or the beginning of the third year. On the other hand, as we learned rather late in our study, the emotional growth of the mother in her parenthood, her emotional willingness to let go of the toddler—to give him, as the mother bird does, a gentle push, an encouragement toward independence—is enormously helpful. It may even be a sine qua non of normal (healthy) individuation.

Danger Signals in the Rapprochement Subphase: Increased Separation Anxiety

The toddler's so-called "shadowing" of the mother (or the opposite "darting away" phenomenon often encountered in the beginning of this subphase) seems obligatory to a degree. (Some mothers, by their protracted doting and intrusiveness, rooted in their own anxieties and often in their own symbiotic-parasitic needs, become themselves the "shadowers" of the child.) In normal cases, shadowing by the toddler gives way to some degree of object constancy toward the second half of the third year. However, the less emotionally available the mother is at the time of rapprochement, the more insistently and even desperately does the toddler attempt to woo her. In some cases, this process drains so much of the child's available developmental energy that, as a result, not enough energy, not enough libido, and not enough constructive (neutralized) aggression are left for the evolution of the many ascending functions of the ego.

The vignettes that follow illustrate not only behavioral patterns peculiar to this subphase, but also behaviors we have come to recognize as danger signals of the rapprochement period.

Barney's rapprochement needs set in much earlier than usual and manifested themselves with particular poignancy. This could be traced back to his precocious locomotor development during the preceding subphase. He is the same little boy who had a typical, although quite early, "love affair with the world." During the course of his "practicing," between 9 and 11 months, he would often fall and hurt himself but would always react with great imperviousness. Gradually, by the end of the eleventh and during the twelfth month, he became quite visibly perplexed to find that his mother was not on hand to rescue him from dangerous situations. From about 11 months on, he began to cry whenever he fell. To the extent that he became cognitively aware of his separateness from mother, his calm acceptance of knocks and falls began to disappear.

During the chronological age of rapprochement, he displayed to an exaggerated degree the opposite of "shadowing." He would challenge mother by darting away from her, confidently (and correctly) expecting her to run after him and sweep him into her arms, thereby momentarily undoing the physical separateness. The mother made an increasingly frantic response to this dangerous darting behavior, so that for a while she despaired of being able to cope with Barney's "recklessness." She would then alternate between restricting Barney and, out of sheer exhaustion, relinquishing her usual alertness to his needs and attunement to his cues. She would either rush to him in every situation, whether or not his expressed need was real, or she would keep away from him when she was really needed. In other words, her immediate availability became temporarily unpredictable. The disturbance in their relationship during this period was not total, however; it did not lead in Barney either to hostility or to splitting of the object world, nor even to increased ambivalence. There were many positive aspects to Barney's rapprochement subphase. Frequently he would bring everything within reach to his mother, filling her lap; he would stand quietly near her and do jigsaw puzzles in her lap with her help or look at picture books with her. The relationship between Barney and his mother became more consistently satisfactory with the advent of the fourth subphase (consolidation of individuation and of object constancy), when he became a patient, well-functioning and, within normal limits, more sedentary child.

We viewed Barney's exaggerated "darting-away" behavior of his rapprochement subphase as a result of precocious maturation of the child's locomotor function during his practicing subphase. At that time, he had been confronted with the fact of physical separateness from mother before his emotional and intellectual functions had prepared him to cope with it. The developmental track of individuation was lagging behind that of separation. As a result, he could not properly evaluate the potential dangers of his locomotor feats (see Frankl, 1963). A set of overdetermining factors later led to a consolidation of this accident-proneness into a lasting personality trait. The origin of this trait lay demonstrably in a developmental imbalance during the second and third subphase. (The subphases of practicing and rapprochement were rather intermingled in Barney's case.) One important additional factor contributing to Barney's "darting-away" was his very early identification with and mirroring of his veritably hero-worshipped father. His children were permitted to watch, to admire and, at times, to participate in their father's highly risky athletic feats.

A different manifestation of the rapprochement subphase was observed in children whose mothers were unable to adjust to the progressive disengagement and/or the increased demandingness of the growing child. Maternal unavailability made the practicing and exploratory period of such children rather brief and subdued. Never certain of their mother's availability and thus always preoccupied with it, they found it difficult to invest libido in their surroundings and in their own functioning. After a brief spurt of practicing, they would return to their mother, with ever greater intensity and attempt by all possible means to engage her. From such relatively direct expressions of the need for mother as bringing a book to be read to them or hitting at the books or needlework their mothers were habitually preoccupied with, they turned to more desperate measures, such as falling or spilling cookies on the floor and stamping on them in temper tantrums—always with an eye to gaining their mothers' attention, if not involvement.

The very good innate endowment of one of these children helped her in terms of the rapidity of her language development; the usual period of baby talk was almost entirely omitted. This early acquisition of verbal communication may have taken place precisely because her mother could communicate with her better by verbal means than by any other; this mother addressed and even "consulted" her daughter verbally, as if the child were her equal in age.

This child then showed that which we have come to regard as a danger signal in the third subphase. She was overly sensitive in her concern with her mother's whereabouts at all times and tended to "shadow" her whenever her mother moved about or left the room. She displayed marked separation anxiety and could not easily be comforted in her mother's absence. The relationship was at that early stage beset by many precursors of serious developmental conflicts, giving rise to marked ambivalence and the splitting of "good" and "bad" objects and probably also of self-representations. In short, this little girl showed the characteristic disturbances or crises of rapprochement in a highly exaggerated way.

It may be of interest to relate some details of the developmental history of this child in the course of the fateful "second 18-month period of her life."

It had already been observed by us that the play of this little girl had a quality of early reaction-formation. The mother reported that her daughter had shown disgust when she gave her a portion of her older brother's clay to play with, and this had been as early as 18 or 19 months. The child's toilet training started at about 20 months, seemingly without pressure. She was already saying the word "do-do" at that age and at first her mother was quite well attuned to cues from her daughter concerning her toilet needs. She praised her whenever the child produced either urine or feces. From her twentieth month on, she was repeatedly heard saying, "Bye-bye, wee wee," as she pulled the chain to flush the toilet. Soon, however, many observers noted that she was beginning to request bathroom trips whenever she wanted her mother's attention or whenever she wanted to prevent mother from leaving the room for an interview—in any event, more frequently than she could actually have had a bowel or urinary urge.

This little girl was bowel trained by 22 months and at that age was able to go for days without wetting. At the beginning of toilet training (particularly bowel training), we saw that she was willing and able to oblige her mother so that both mother and daughter found in the toileting an emotionally positively charged meeting ground. But within 2 months, toileting had been drawn into the conflictual sphere of this mother-child interaction. At around 23 months of age, the toddler used wetting all across the room as a weapon. Her mother was then pregnant and as time went on, her pregnancy caused her to become naturally narcissistically self-absorbed. She had fewer and fewer positive reactions to her daughter's demands to accompany her to the upstairs bathroom at home. In fact, she told us that she asked her then 4-year-old son to substitute for her in taking his sister to the toilet. The boy, we later learned, did not miss the opportunity to display his manly prowess, his penis, to his little sister. Her penis envy thus gained momentum, as did her defiance of mother.

A battle around toilet training ensued between daughter and mother. At around 2 years of age, the child started to use her sphincter control to challenge her mother; severe constipation developed in the wake of her deliberately withholding her feces.

We did not see this little girl for about 3 months (from her twenty-fifth to her twenty-eighth month), during which time a sister was born.

She returned at 29 months of age, following close behind her mother, who was carrying the new baby. The mother looked harassed and tired as she entered the room. She complained that her daughter was driving her crazy. The child had indeed been very difficult, whining and demanding, but, in addition, for the past 2 or 3 days had been withholding her feces and had not had a bowel movement. According to her mother, she was in pain most of the time and actually very uncomfortable. The pediatrician, she reported, had assured her that this was a normal occurrence after the birth of a new baby and that she should take it calmly and pay no attention to the toileting at this time. She said with a hopeless gesture, "But I simply can't do it."

We observed this little girl in the toddler's room playing with water. This, however, was not the kind of play that children her age usually enjoy, and it appeared to us to be of a rather "compulsive" nature. She began to scrub a bowl to which flour had stuck and was very determined to scrub it clean, becoming annoyed when she could not do so. She looked up at the observer and said, "Bowl not clean." All this while she seemed most uncomfortable. She obviously needed to defecate and was under continual bowel pressure. Beads of perspiration appeared on her forehead and the color would come and go from her face. Twice she ran to the toilet. She sat on the toilet and urinated; then she got up and became preoccupied with flushing the toilet. She went back to the toddler room and listlessly played with dough, but again, and all during her play, she was in discomfort and kept jiggling and jumping, with the color repeatedly draining from her face. Finally, she jumped up and ran to the toilet, sat down on it, and said to the observer, "Get me a book." Sitting and straining, she looked up at the observer with a rather painful expression on her face and said, "Don't let Mommy in." The observer encouraged her to talk about this some more, and she said, "Mommy hurt me."[2] She then looked at the

[2] Here we see the child's utter confusion between externally inflicted pain and pain deriving from somatic (inside the body) sources. In her 29-month-old mind the pain seems to come from the "bad" introject; the inner painful sensations are then externalized, attributed to the "bad" mother.

book, at the pictures of baby cats and baby horses. As the observer was showing the pictures of the baby farm animals to her, the child began to look more and more uncomfortable. She looked down at her panties, which had become stained, and asked for clean ones. Finally, in extreme discomfort, she seemed unable to hold back the feces any longer and called out, "Get me my Mommy, get me my Mommy." Her mother came quickly, sat down beside her, and was asked by her daughter to read to her.[3]

The participant observer watched from the booth and noted that the mother was reading the same book about farm animals that the first observer had read to the child. Pointing to the animals, the toddler was heard to say, "My Poppy has a piggy in his tummy." Her mother looked perplexed and asked, "What?" The child repeated the sentence. The mother seemed distraught, as her daughter was now talking gibberish. She felt the child's forehead to see whether she was feverish, but the toddler smiled, pointed to the book again, and said, "No, it's a baby horse." At this point, with a blissful expression on her face, she defecated. After her bowel movement, she got up from the toilet seat; she seemed relaxed and began playing peek-a-boo with the swinging door, asking the observer to stand behind it.

In this episode, the sequence of behaviors and verbalizations enabled us to draw conclusions, to reconstruct the precursors, as it were, of the development of this little girl's infantile neurosis *in statu nascendi*. With deficient emotional supplies from mother, neither the libidinal investment in her self-representation nor her excellent development of autonomy had been enough to replace gradually the obligatory early infantile symbiotic omnipotence. The child could not progressively and gradually identify with the "good" mother image; she could not make a soothing, comforting mothering function her own by assimilation (internalization). In spite of her excellent endowment, she was unable to ward off the onslaught of separation anxiety and the collapse of self-esteem. Her anger at mother for not having given her a penis was unmistakable in her verbal material. She coveted those gifts that mother received from father. The child turned in her disappointment to father, and when mother became pregnant, in a perplexed way she obviously equated gifts with baby, with feces, and with a penis. She showed great confusion about the contents of the body; her own pregnancy fantasies were quite evident, but she was unclear as to who had what in his or her belly. She seemed to expect a baby in the belly of her father, as well as in her mother's.

The mother-toddler relationship was such that the child had to defend the good mother against her own destructive rage. This she did by splitting the object world into "good" and "bad" in order to keep good and bad apart. The good was always the absent part-object, never the present object. To clarify this, let us describe another sequence of events and verbalizations in this child's third year. Whenever her mother left, she had temper tantrums and would cling to her beloved and familiar play teacher, but not

[3] As soon as the pain gets unbearable, the symbiotic mother is the only one who is invoked to help in the painful delivery of the stool.

without verbally abusing her while still keeping her arms around her neck. When they read a book together, the child found fault with every picture and every sentence that the playroom teacher offered; she scolded the teacher; everything was the opposite of what the teacher said, and she was "Bad, bad, bad."

The senior author watched this behavior from the observation booth and ventured quietly into the playroom where she sat at the farthest corner from the little girl and her loved and hated teacher. The toddler immediately caught sight of the "intruder" and angrily ordered her out. She softly interpreted to the child that she understood: the child really wanted no one but her Mommy to come back in through that door and that was why she was very angry. She was also very angry because not Mommy, but the observer, was reading to her. The senior author went on to say that she knew that Mommy would soon come back. With this quasi-interpretation, some libidinal channels seemed to have been tapped; the child put her head on the observer's shoulder and began to cry softly. Soon, the mother came back. It was most instructive to see, however, that not a flicker of radiance or happiness was noticeable in the daughter at that reunion. Her very first words were, "What did you bring me?" and the whining and discontent started all over again.

For quite a while this little girl did not succeed in attaining a unified object representation or in reconciling the good and bad qualities of the love object. At the same time, the integration of her own self-representation and her self-esteem suffered.

By contrast, what we saw in Barney's case was merely a transient developmental deviation in the form of a rapprochement crisis. In the case described at length above, we observed a symptom-formation, constipation that lasted well into her sixth year, developing on the basis of a rather unsatisfactory mother-child relationship yet activated and, to a great extent, produced by accumulated stress and probably by shock traumata, as well.

Until way beyond the fourth subphase, this little girl's relationship to her mother remained full of ambivalence. Her school performance was excellent, however. Her social development was good. Our follow-up study will tell us more about the fate of her infantile neurosis.[4]

A seemingly very harmonious relationship appeared to characterize the mother-child interaction between Matthew and his mother during the entire practicing subphase. The mother was adept at encouraging inde-

[4] The follow-up study is being conducted by John B. McDevitt, M.D., with Anni Bergman, Emmagene Kamaiko, and Laura Salchow, and with the senior author of this book serving as consultant. It is sponsored by the board of the Master's Children's Center, and to a limited extent by the M. S. Mahler Research Fund of the Menil Foundation.

pendence and autonomy in her children, while at the same time she seemed libidinally fully available to them; that is, she gauged her response to Matthew with great intuitive understanding of his changing needs. His mother's ability to do this, we believed at that time, would ensure Matthew's smooth progression into the beginnings of the rapprochement subphase. Despite his mother's pregnancy and the arrival of a new sibling when he was 19 months old—a time when the toddler's renewed need for the mother increases in intensity—Matthew seemed to remain self-sufficient. He was able to use other adults as mother substitutes and seemed to have achieved some identification with his mother, as shown by his interest in other babies and in his little brother—an interest in which the aggressive element at first seemed amazingly well controlled. We observed that Matthew also had a good relationship with his father. He seemed able, in sum, to sustain a prolonged interest in the world, even into the rapprochement subphase, while at the same time sharing whatever his mother was ready to share with him. Only toward the end of the rapprochement subphase, when we ordinarily expect rapprochement behavior to give way to libidinal object constancy, did we realize that the task of becoming independent so early and abruptly was apparently too much for Matthew.

During the beginning of the rapprochement subphase, Matthew underwent an emergency hernia operation. (This happened during summer vacation.) Matthew's mother told us that she had to leave Matthew at the hospital, where he was very unhappy. However, he was said to have recovered quickly once he returned home. When he returned to us at the age of 18 months, he showed no signs of undue stress, although we observed that he had adopted a pattern of climbing into precarious positions. Interaction between Matthew and his mother remained pleasurable, even though his mother now had to leave Matthew by himself at our Center, while his older brother started nursery school. The mother was required to function as a "mother attendant" nursery teacher and to take turns with other mothers at the nursery school.

Matthew then started to show some signs of strain. During mother's absence, he needed to be held on the lap of an observer. He tended to become tired more easily, and toward the end of the morning he sometimes regressed to creeping, instead of walking. Only a few months after his baby brother had been born, Matthew showed conspicuous signs of disturbance by his practice of hurting himself almost habitually and by a marked increase in his readiness to cry. He frequently climbed into his mother's lap, which she would allow when the baby was not there. When mother was occupied with the baby, however, Matthew turned to other adults. He paid very little attention to the baby. While apparently continuing to be cheerful, there were subtle signs that all was not as well as it might be. As time went on, Matthew became restless and hyperactive, and he fell even more than before. He showed great interest in his mirror image, making faces at himself. (The significance of this last-mentioned behavior is difficult to interpret.)[5]

Matthew's mother needed to believe that Matthew was becoming more mature and therefore increased her expectation of his becoming more and more independent! In reality, Matthew's seemingly greater maturity—his mirroring identification with his older siblings, especially those of school age—may have also been a kind of sad resignation with depression; this would have been too painful for the mother to recognize. Another form of attempted adaptation was identification with the rival baby. Matthew showed signs of wanting to be a baby himself; like his baby brother, for instance, he would climb into the playpen. This his mother, however, could not tolerate. Matthew reciprocated by becoming less responsive to his mother's verbal instructions and began to show some diffuse aggressive activity, such as throwing things or running about aimlessly. Earlier, Matthew had been described as a happy, radiant child. At this time, Matthew still continued to smile, but there was a unanimous impression among the observers that his smile lacked its former radiance. It had become strained, more a grimace than a smile, as though it were in compliance with his mother's expectations of him, as well as an appeal to the world at large. Also, Matthew did not react, or probably did not permit himself to react, much to his mother's absences from the room.

At the age of 2, Matthew was sent by his mother to the toddler room without her. In fact, the demands of the rest of the family upon the mother were so great that the baby, who would have been the fourth child in the family to be observed in our study, could not be brought to us regularly by the mother.

The toddler room teacher observed Matthew masturbating in an autoaggressive way, very often by clutching his penis and pulling up his legs —that is to say, by regressing to autoerotic activity.[6] The playroom observer noted that Matthew's facial expressions did not change appropriately with changes in his situations and that he was tending to become reckless and hyperactive. Thus, it seems that the accumulation of traumata (shock and stress traumata in Kris's sense; cf. also Khan,

[5] Cf. McDevitt's studies on the mirror image (unpublished).
[6] Not in the quiet, serene way we have seen in other boys.

1963) was too much for Matthew.[7] He emerged from the rapprochement subphase with a tendency to find satisfaction in autoerotic and autoaggressive activities, as well as in hyperactivity, and with a kind of blandness in his affective life—all of which on superficial observation seemed to be in compliance with mother's wishes that he be independent and remain her happy little "big" boy.

In Henry's case, his mother's second pregnancy, as well as his weaning, occurred at the height of that stage at which the early practicing subphase overlaps the differentiation subphase. (His mother joined our project when Henry was a little over 9 months old.) At this time, he crawled to her frequently and clamored to be taken onto her lap: he seemed to need contact and steady "refueling" from her. This occurred when he began carefully practicing the preliminaries of upright locomotion short of walking. Henry's wooing approach behavior thus occurred prematurely, before the upright locomotor practicing period. It was closely tied to his mother's conspicuous emotional aloofness during her pregnancy; in this respect, Henry's case is reminiscent of the case of the little girl presented above. At 11 to 13 months, Henry was carrying out motor feats that surpassed those of the other children in his age group and which were admired by everyone, yet merely taken for granted by his mother. After he had finally mastered active upright locomotion by the age of 14 months, his mother ceased altogether to respond to his renewed active wooing. Thereupon Henry proceeded to adopt more and more exaggerated voiceless devices to appeal to her. During the hot summer months, he would perspiringly carry heavy toys in both arms over to his mother, as quasi-offerings, but to no avail. The exaggerated character and repetitiveness of this approach over a period of weeks was obviously symptomatic and overdetermined. In it were incorporated elements of the mother's practice, from the beginning, of substituting toys for her own self. It contained somatopsychic elements of identification with the mother's far advanced gravidity; it also contained elements of compliance with his mother's conscious and unconscious wish that her son be big and strong (he was rather small). Finally, it contained elements of primitive preliminaries of defense, such as identification (mirroring) and projection. All these devices having failed, we saw very early, after a period of severe depression (Mahler, 1961), how this young child gradually resorted to the mechanism of masochistic surrender.

[7] In the cramped quarters where the M.'s lived, primal scene exposure seemed to be unavoidable!

The Third Subphase

We have already referred to the phenomenon of "shadowing." In excessive amounts, it is, we believe, one of the danger signals of this subphase, one sign that the child's awareness of separateness is causing great strain: the child attempts to hold on to mother by attempting to respond to every move and every mood, as well as by making insistent demands upon her. In Tommy, the outstanding feature of the individuation process was this phenomenon of "shadowing"—his refusal to let his mother out of his sight. He followed her every move from out of the corner of his eye; he literally dashed in her direction as soon as she walked toward the door, or whenever she made a move. His widely ranging vocal communications were directed exclusively to his mother and gradually developed into predominantly petulant and poorly enunciated verbal communications to her. He was one of those toddlers (like Barney) in whom locomotion had already brought about an awareness of the self as separate from the mother before he was emotionally ready to cope with this awareness. This caused Tommy to throw temper tantrums which lasted much longer than the usual few minutes.

In general, the potential danger signals during this phase include greater than average separation anxiety; more than average shadowing of the mother or continual, impulse-driven "darting away" from the mother, with the aim of provoking her to give chase; and finally, excessive sleep disturbances. (Transient sleep disturbances are a normal characteristic of the second year of life.)

Culling from our data and their processing, we found that we could subdivide rapprochement into three periods; (1) beginning rapprochement; (2) the rapprochement crisis; and (3) individual solutions of this crisis, resulting in patternings and *personality characteristics* with which the child enters into the fourth subphase of separation-individuation, the consolidation of individuation.

We arrived at these subdivisions through comparing month by month the nine most thoroughly studied children—the last group in our study —with regard to the development of their object relations, their moods, their psychosexual and aggressive trends, as well as their cognitive development. As we describe rapprochement in more detail, we shall be drawing on examples from the detailed studies of these children.

Beginning Rapprochement

At around 15 months, we noticed an important change in the quality of the child's relationship to his mother. During the practicing period as described, mother was the "home base" to which the child returned often in times of need—need for food, need for comforting, or need for "refueling" when tired or bored. But during this period mother did not seem to have been recognized as a separate person in her own right. Somewhere around 15 months, mother was no longer just "home base"; she seemed to be turning into a person with whom the toddler wished to share his ever-widening discoveries of the world. The most important behavioral sign of this new relating was the toddler's continual bringing of things to mother, filling her lap with objects that he had found in his expanding world. They all were interesting to him, but the main emotional investment lay in the child's need to share them with her (see Barney, Henry, and others, pp. 80–88). At the same time, the toddler indicated to mother by words, sounds, or gestures that he wished her to be interested in his "findings" and to participate with him in enjoying them.

Along with the beginning awareness of separateness came the child's realization that mother's wishes seemed to be by no means always identical with his own—or contrariwise, that his own wishes did not always coincide with mother's. This realization greatly challenged the feeling of grandeur and omnipotence of the practicing period, when the little fellow had felt "on top of the world" (Mahler, 1966*b*). What a blow to the hitherto fully believed omnipotence; what a disturbance to the bliss of dual unity!

Parallel or concomitant with his sensing that mother was a person "out there in the world" with whom he wanted to share his pleasures, we noted that the toddler's elated preoccupation with locomotion and exploration per se was beginning to wane. The source of the child's greatest pleasure shifted from independent locomotion and exploration of the expanding inanimate world to *social interaction*. Peekaboo games (Kleeman, 1967), as well as games of imitation, became favorite pastimes. Recognition of mother as a separate person in the large world went parallel with awareness of other children's separate existence, their being similar yet different from one's own self. This was evidenced by the fact that children now showed a greater desire to *have* or to *do* what another child had or did—that is, a desire for mirroring, for imitating, for identifying to an extent with the other child. They wanted the toys or the cup of juice and cookie that were handed to the other child. Along with this important development there appeared specific goal-directed anger, aggression if the desired aim definitely could not be attained. We are not, of course, losing sight of the fact that these developments take place in the midst of the anal phase, with its characteristics of anal acquisitiveness, jealousy, and envy.

The discovery of the anatomical sexual difference during this period will be discussed in a later part of this chapter (see p. 104); suffice it to say here that for girls, the penis seems to become the prototype of a wished for, but unattainable, "possession" of other children. For boys and girls alike, this discovery enhanced a more distinct awareness in the child of his own body and its relation to other persons' bodies. Increasingly, the toddler seemed to experience his body per se as his own possession. No longer did he like it to be "handled." Most noticeably, he resisted being kept or held in a passive position while being dressed or diapered. He did not even seem to like to be hugged and kissed, unless he was ready for it. We felt that this claim to the body's autonomy was more accentuated in boys.

Social Expansion and the Importance of the Father Relationship

The child's desire for expanded autonomy not only found expression in negativism toward mother and others, but also led to an active extension of the mother-child world: *primarily, to include father*. Father, as a love object, from very early on belongs to an entirely different category of love objects from mother. Although he is not fully outside the symbiotic union, neither is he ever fully part of it. The infant, in addition, probably very early perceives a special relationship of the father to the mother, the significance of which, during the separation-individuation phase and in the later preoedipal phase, we are barely beginning to understand (Abelin, 1971; Greenacre, 1966; Mahler, 1967*a*).

But the rapprochement child develops relationships with others in the environment besides father and mother. In the children in our study we could observe that from about 16–17 months on, they liked to spend increasingly long periods away from their mothers in the toddler room, and that boys and girls alike began to seek out observers, every so often the male observers, and to form quite close attachments to them.[8]

[8] This early preference for male observers, when it occurred, seemed to have a gender specific style, which, however, we are not ready to interpret or even analyze with any degree of certainty.

Separation Reactions in the Early Rapprochement Subphase, with Clinical Illustrations

During the early rapprochement subphase, we found a most interesting change in the children's reactions to mother's being in or out of the room. They were all now increasingly aware of mother's absence and wanted to know where mother was (thereby augmenting significantly their own spatial orientation!). On the other hand, however, they were also increasingly able to remain absorbed in their own pursuits and often did not want to be interrupted. They would want to "go see" mother, but not with the intention of staying with her; rather, they would pass by her, veer away, and then return to their own occupations. This veering away seemed to be more prominent in boys than in girls. However, when mother herself was too far away for too long a time, we found different reactions from those of the previous subphases. We have already described the "low-keyedness" that is characteristic of the differentiation and the practicing subphases, as a reaction to mother's absence from the room. Now, during early rapprochement, we seemed to find a different kind of behavior: the mother's absence brought on increased activity and restlessness. It would seem that the equivalent of low-keyedness, at the time of the child's realization of his separateness, is the affect or emotion of sadness (cf. Mahler, 1961). Sadness, however, seems to require a great amount of ego strength to bear (cf. Zetzel, 1949, 1965), an investment that the child at this age seemed unable to muster; hyperactivity or restlessness might thus be seen here as an early defensive activity against awareness of the painful affect of sadness.

As the rapprochement subphase progressed, the children found more active ways of coping with mother's absences: they related to substitute adults, and they engaged in symbolic play (see Galenson 1971). They often invented forms of play that helped them to master the fact of the disappearance and reappearance of things; or their play tended to consist of social interaction. Many forms of their play revealed early identification with mother or father—for example, in the way they held on to dolls and teddy bears. Beginning internalization of the object representation appeared to be taking place. Ball play, for example, seemed to lend itself particularly well both to social interaction and to feelings and fantasies of parting with and refinding an object (see Freud, 1920). Donna would throw away the ball and then take special pleasure in finding it again; another little girl would lose the ball and then need the observers to retrieve it for her; Wendy, who liked exclusive one-to-one relationships with adults, would use the ball to engage an adult observer in play.

For most children, the period of early rapprochement culminated at the age of about 17 or 18 months, in what looked like a temporary consolidation and acceptance of separateness. This went along with great pleasure in sharing possessions and activities with mother or father, as well as increasingly with the now expanding social world that included not only adults but also other children—toddlers their own age, older children, and babies. During the practicing period, the word "bye-bye" had been of great importance; the most important word of this period of early rapprochement was "hi."

During this 17–18 month age level that served consolidation, we did see, however, important harbingers of the impending struggle with the love object, adumbrated by many behaviors. The most striking of these was the occurrence of temper tantrums[9] in practically all the children. We saw many signs of greater vulnerability, of impotent rage, and of helplessness. There was a recurrence in many children of stranger reactions. As in the earlier stranger reactions (at 7 to 9 months; see pp. 56–58) we could observe a mixture of anxiety, interest, and curiosity. Now there was often a self-conscious turning away from the stranger, as if the stranger at this point constituted a threat to the already toppling delusion or illusion of exclusive union with mother. There seemed to be a threat involved in the very fact that certain people other than mother began to become genuinely important in the child's life (loyalty conflict), as if that were incompatible with the hitherto exclusive, very special relationship with mother (cause and consequence seemed to be confused, and projective or externalization mechanisms seemed to prevail).

In our sample of the most systematically observed children, there were several in whom the period of the first consolidation of separateness either did not seem to have occurred in the ordinary way or else had been cut short. In each case, this seemed to be connected with difficulties during the earlier subphases of the mother-child relationship. Let us illustrate this with our observations on two of these children.

During the first part of the 17–18 month period, Mark continued to be interested in an increasing variety of people and activities. He was attracted by the toddler room; he was able to leave mother and return to her and generally had a happy relationship with his mother. At about the middle of the 17–18 month period, however, Mark started to become very de-

[9] Some explanation of the psychodynamics of temper tantrums was offered by the senior author in her "tic" studies (Mahler and Luke, 1946; Mahler, 1949*a*).

manding. He constantly needed the mother's attention, but he did not seem to be at all certain what he really wanted from her. He began to show a pattern of rapid alternation of extreme approach behavior and excessive aggression or withdrawal from his mother. This "ambitendency" spread to other people and other goals as well. For example, Mark would typically insist on being picked up by his mother but as soon as he was in her arms he would angrily demand to be let down. He clung to his mother anxiously, as if he were afraid that she would leave him or would withdraw her love forever. All this was due, we felt, to an unusual perplexity in both mother and child concerning the reading of each other's cues—a miscarriage of "mutual cueing." (This calls to mind the mother's perplexity about cues from her older child, described by Mahler and Furer, 1963*a*, pp. 4–5; cf. also Spitz, 1964, the "derailment of the dialogue.")

Harriet also showed somewhat deviant behavior during this period: she did not cling to her mother, but rather ignored her; in fact, she paid much less attention to her during her eighteenth month than during the previous month. She took little note when her mother left or returned. She did not show the great pleasure in social give-and-take that was seen in other children; she seemed, during this month, to have withdrawn into herself. This little girl was described as being self-contented, but generally not interested in people. Typically, she would play with toys, dolls, and teddy bears and babble to herself, giving us the feeling that she was involved in a world of her own, in her own fantasy life. She seemed to satisfy her need for physical closeness by behavior that was quite peculiar to her: by using inanimate objects. Also, when in distress, she would lie flat against the surface of the floor, or on the mattress on the floor, or would squeeze herself into a narrow space; it was as if she wanted to be enclosed (held together) in this way, which would afford her some of the sense of coherence and security that she was missing in the relationship with her mother.

On Structuralization of the Ego and the Establishment of a Cohesive Self

We should emphasize that the child's first awareness of separateness had brought with it pleasurable discoveries of beginning autonomy and social interaction, expressed in a number of the important words and gestural communications of that period. One of these was finding that one could *ask* to have one's wish fulfilled, through employing the words and gestures of demand or need. For example, "cookie" was an important early word for all children. With the discovery that one could call mother and command her attention, the words, "Look, Mommy," also became used very often. Further, there was the discovery that one could find mother and others, and exclaim one's delight; this was denoted by the now typically used word, "hi!" Also important at this point was the discovery that one was praised and admired if one performed motor and other feats of skill. It seemed important to the rapprochement toddler that he could provide pleasure to mother; this he expressed, from the very beginning of this period, by bringing toys to her.

The more painful aspects of separateness had barely begun to dawn on the toddler during these months, except in those children in whom various circumstances, in part intrinsic and in part experiential, promoted premature separation crises.

The Rapprochement Crisis: 18–20 to 24 Months and Beyond

Grandeur and Fear of Loss of Love

Around 18 months our toddlers seemed quite eager to exercise their rapidly growing autonomy to the hilt. Increasingly, they chose not to be reminded that at times they could not manage on their own. Conflicts ensued that seemed to hinge upon the desire to be separate, grand, and omnipotent, on the one hand, and to have mother magically fulfill their wishes, without their having to recognize that help was actually coming from the outside, on the other. In more cases than not, the prevalent mood changed to that of general dissatisfaction, insatiability, a proneness to rapid swings of mood and to temper tantrums. The period was thus characterized by the rapidly alternating desire to push mother away and to cling to her—a behavioral sequence that the word "ambitendency" describes most accurately. But already at that age there was often a simultaneous desire in both directions, that is, the characteristic *ambivalence* of children in the middle of the rapprochement subphase.

It was characteristic of children at this age to use mother as an *extension of the self*—a process in which they somehow denied the painful awareness of separateness. Typical behavior of this kind was, for example, pulling mother's hand and using it as a tool to get a desired object or expecting that mother, summoned by some magical gesture alone, rather than with words, would guess and fulfill the toddler's momentary wish. An unexpected and strange phenomenon appeared, seemingly a forerunner of the projection of one's negative feelings: this was the child's sudden anxiety that mother had left, on occasions when she had not even risen from her chair! There occurred, more or less frequently, moments of a strange, seeming "nonrecognition" of mother, after a brief absence on her part.

How were we to understand this tendency suddenly to "lose" the feeling of the presence of mother, at a time when, with increased separateness, she had become a person in the outside world? Was it regression in the face of too much strain, caused by the need to recognize that one had to function separately? Or was it caused by the conflict between the wish to manage by one's own self and the wish to partake in mother's omnipotence? The desire to function by one's own self may be particularly threatening to the child at the very point in development when one's own feelings and wishes and those of mother are still poorly differentiated. The wish to be autonomous and separate from mother, to leave her, might also mean emotionally that the mother would wish to leave him (introjective-projective period of Ferenczi, 1913). Conceptualization of these rapprochement phenomena was made even more complicated and puzzling by the fact that this blurred identity of mother in the outside world coincided, quite frequently, with a tendency on the mother's part to react adversely to her separating, individuating toddler. The mother's reaction at that time was quite often tinged with feelings of annoyance at the toddler's insistence on his autonomy, at his wanting, for example, to tie his shoelaces without help, and so on. "You think you can manage on your own? All right, I can leave you to your own devices, see how you fare." Or, "A moment ago, you did not want to be with me. Well, now I don't want to be with you" (see Mahler, Pine, and Bergman, 1970, pp. 257–274).

As we mentioned earlier, we found in many toddlers a *powerful resurgence of stranger reaction*. This was every so often referred to by the observers as "shyness." The renewed stranger reaction occurred especially toward people in the outside world who at an earlier point in the infant's life had been regarded as special friends. We quote only one of the typical behaviors from the records of our observations:

> Frankie's relationship to adults other than mother expressed itself in the following behaviors. He would sometimes approach them in a friendly way from a distance; however, as soon as *they* would approach *him*, he would flee to his mother. Once he rolled a ball to an observer who used to be his best friend; when she rolled it back to him, however, he ran away to his mother.

Indecision was a typical behavior of this period. Several of the children at this time would stand for many minutes on the threshold of the toddler room, unable to decide whether or not to join the activities inside. Standing on the threshold would seem to be the perfect symbolization of conflicting wishes—the wish to enter the toddler world away from mother and the pull to remain with mother in the infant room. (This is somewhat reminiscent of the doubting and indecision of obsessive-compulsive neurosis.)

The Third Subphase

There were some children who could practice their growing autonomy and wish for independence with relatively little apparent conflict. Again an example from our records:

Linda had had an unusually trusting relationship to her mother, and her mother had enjoyed Linda all along. But Linda now protested against being carried upstairs by her mother, something which up to then had delighted her. She now seemed to need less physical contact with mother. She wanted to explore "the world" away from mother and became increasingly involved in social interaction with others. When her mother was out of the room, Linda was able to play for long periods independently. Even if she seemed to miss her mother, she could become so involved in her activities that she would look for her only for a moment and then go on with what she had been doing.

In some cases, on the other hand, where the mother was either dissatisfied with her child, terribly anxious about him, or aloof, normal rapprochement patterns became greatly exaggerated. In the two contrasting behaviors of approach and distancing, this ambivalence conflict had been acted out in either extreme shadowing of mother or darting away from her (in the late practicing and in the early rapprochement subphase), or else it had caused excessive wooing of mother, alternating with extreme negativism.

Widening of the Emotional Range and the Beginning of Empathy

During this period, the range of affects experienced by the toddler seemed to widen and become quite differentiated. In describing the preceding period, we talked about the hyperactivity and restlessness that seemed to be a defense against sadness over loss of the previous symbiotic unity. Now, the need to deal with the affects of sadness and anger, disappointment in mother, or the realization of one's own limited abilities and relative helplessness could be traced in many other different kinds of behaviors. During this period, for example, observations made on many children stated for the first time that they were fighting their tears, attempting to suppress their need to cry.

Teddy's reactions to another child's crying, for example, were interesting to observe. He just could not bear to hear another child cry. This seemed somehow to stimulate his aggressive defensiveness; unprovoked, he would attack other children![10] His undeniable awareness of separateness and vulnerability seemed, however, to have given rise to a new

[10] Whether this affective reaction could or should be regarded at such an early age as identification with the aggressor or as projective identification we do not know.

capacity for empathy, which was expressed in positive ways as well. Teddy, who often showed this aggressive reaction when he heard another child cry, at other times reacted quite sympathetically to the moods of the other children. For example, he would bring his own bottle to Mark when Mark was crying, or else he would approach Harriet with great sympathy and interest on a day when she was in an obviously low mood.

We saw, at this age, many signs of identification with the attitudes of others, especially those of mother or father. This was on a higher level of real ego identification—not the introjection or mirroring characteristic of earlier periods, such as the period of differentiation, when we saw children take over patterns of their mother's caring for them in their own first steps toward individuation and separateness (Part II, Chapter 3, pp. 50–51). For example, Frankie developed at the rapprochement age a loud and demanding manner, as well as a tendency toward dramatization that was quite reminiscent of his mother's attitude. Another little boy was not only demanding, but also unwilling to share. He was intent on coercing mother into fulfilling his wishes. He was particularly unwilling to relinquish the omnipotence of the symbiotic dual unity; this was reminiscent of his mother's tendency toward a symbiotic-appersonating relationship (Sperling, 1944), which she had pursued way beyond the symbiotic stage with her much older daughter.

Another form of identification as a defense was demonstrated by children who had had to cope with the birth of a sibling during the early rapprochement period, and who now identified with their mother's care and concern for the new baby.

Partial internalization seemed to be one way of coping with, or defending against, the increasing vulnerability that the toddler felt as his awareness of separateness increased. He painfully realized not only that he was at times alone and helpless but also that even his mother could not always restore his sense of well-being, that indeed her interests were separate and distinct from his own, and that the two by no means always coincided. All these feelings were of course aggravated if the birth of a sibling intruded into the hitherto exclusive relationship with mother.

Separation Reactions during the Rapprochement Crisis (18 to 21 Months)

During the period of the most acute rapprochement crises, all the children were aware of, and at times highly sensitive to, mother's whereabouts when she was absent from the room. On the cognitive side, the ability to realize that mother could be elsewhere and could be found (cf. Piaget's "object permanence") was now well established. This knowledge did suffice at times to reassure the toddler when he experienced the emotion of missing his mother. In general, however, the toddler at this age did not like to be passively "left behind." *Difficulties with the process of leave-taking itself began to develop,* expressed in the reaction of clinging to mother. Usually these reactions were accompanied by a depressive mood and an initial inability, brief or prolonged, to become involved in play.

Often, during these times of intense emotional anguish after being left, the toddler would attach himself closely to one of the observers, wanting to sit on the observer's lap, and occasionally even regressing into sleepy drowsiness. At such times, the observer was clearly neither another love object nor merely some person in the other-than-mother world, but rather a kind of symbiotic mother substitute, an extension of the self. Yet splitting the object world had also begun (see Kernberg, 1967). The "observers" lent themselves particularly well to the child's exercise of this defense, becoming the target of his impotent rage reactions, in order to protect the good mother image from his destructive anger. This was observable particularly in those children who had had a less than optimal relationship with their mothers during the earlier subphases.

Splitting mechanisms (see pp. 82–84; 117) at this time could take various forms. If the observer in mother's absence became the "bad mother," she could not do anything right, and a mood of general crankiness prevailed. The "good mother" was longed for, yet she seemed to exist in fantasy only. When the actual mother returned, she might be greeted with "What did you bring me?" as well as with a spectrum of angry, disappointed, and other negative reactions. Or else the observer, as the substitute mother, might become temporarily the "good symbiotic mother," and the toddler might passively sit on her lap and eat cookies, like a small infant. Yet when the actual mother returns, there might be the impulse to get to her as fast as possible, and at the same time an impulse to avoid her, as if to ward off further disappointment. The toddler might ignore mother upon her return, or go toward her and then veer away, thereafter rejecting mother's overtures. In the latter instances, it would seem that the absent mother had become the "bad" mother and thus was to be avoided. Another variation was that the mother substitute was treated ambivalently as both the "good" and the "bad" mother, like the ambivalently loved mother herself when she was present.

We saw struggles of this kind in many different degrees and variations. One could see with special clarity during this period the roots of many uniquely human problems and dilemmas—problems that sometimes are never completely resolved during the entire life cycle.

Transitional Phenomena

We saw other mechanisms as well for coping with separation during the rapprochement crisis. One little girl who had entered this part of the rapprochement phase later than the other children—probably because her mother managed to fulfill her needs and remain "omnipotent" for such a long time, instead of giving her the gentle push that is needed by the fledgling—transferred the demand for exclusive possession of mother to mother's chair. When mother left the room, she would at once sit in mother's chair. If the child did get up from the chair, she would not permit anyone else to sit in it. The word "mine" became important to her at this time; she would not share mother with anyone and could bear mother's absence only if she maintained exclusive possession of mother's chair. The chair became for her a kind of organ-object used as a bridge to mother in Kestenberg's sense (1971).

Other children showed a variety of transitional phenomena that were less clearly related to their mothers. For example, they would consume large quantities of pretzels and cookies, or else insist on carrying their bottles about. Some children could not stand remaining in the playroom without their mothers, but would wander into the room where mothers and children hung up their coats when they arrived at the Center. We became used to regarding the coat room as a "transitional room," because it was located between the infant room—the world of mother and infant—and the toddler room—the world of toddler autonomy. This dressing room, in addition, had a floor-to-ceiling window to the outside world; furthermore, as the place where the coats were hung, it represented the room of transition between home and Center.

The reading of storybooks became another transitional activity of particular importance: many toddlers liked to be read to while mother was out of the room. Storybooks would seem to be of a transitional nature, since they satisfied the need for distancing and for exploring the wider world (by way of symbolization and fantasy); on the other hand, the situation served the purpose of closeness, of getting near the person who was reading.

While the toddlers during this period needed to know where mother was, and did not in general like being passively left (as they reacted to the leave-taking by mother), they became increasingly able to leave mother *actively and on their own.* The toddler room itself took on greater importance: it seemed to become for many toddlers a refuge from the conflictual relationship with mother. The children tended to be content there; they became absorbed in play with toys and materials, and with each other. They began to form a relationship with their play teacher, who was "optimally available" to all of them. This relationship was not to a mother substitute, but to a new adult, who could be helpful in promoting the child's interests in the outside world. In addition, this new adult could offer alternative satisfactions and thus channelize discontent and promote incipient sublimations.

Individual Patterning of Rapprochement: The Optimal Distance

By the age of 21 months, a general diminishing of the rapprochement struggle could be observed. The clamoring for omnipotent control, the extreme periods of separation anxiety, the alternation of demands for closeness and for autonomy—all these subsided, at least for a while, as each child once again seemed to find the optimal distance from mother, the distance at which he could function best. In our setting, this optimal distance was usually represented by the nearby, yet separate, toddler room, which offered stimulation, the opportunity to exercise autonomy, and growing pleasure in social interaction.

The growing individuation that seemed to make possible this ability to function at a greater distance, and without mother's physical presence, are as follows: (1) The development of language, in terms of naming objects and expressing desires with specific words. The ability to name objects (Katan, 1961) seems to have provided the toddler with a greater sense of ability to control his environment. Use of the personal pronoun "I" also often appeared at this time, as well as the ability to recognize and name familiar people and oneself in photographs;[11] (2) the internalization process, which could be inferred both from acts of identification with the "good," providing mother and father, and from the internalization of rules and demands (beginnings of superego); and (3) progress in the ability to express wishes and fantasies through symbolic play, as well as the use of play for mastery.

By about the children's twenty-first month, we made the important observation in our month-by-month comparisons that it was no

[11] At the writing of this book, we have not been able to analyze our data sufficiently to be able to determine unequivocally the timing and the contextual factors of the appearance on the nonsyncretic "I."

longer possible to group the toddlers in accordance with the general criteria hitherto used. The vicissitudes of their individuation process were changing so rapidly that they were no longer mainly *phase specific, but individually very distinct, and different from one child to the other.* The issue in question was not so much that of realization of separateness, but rather how this realization was affected by, and in turn affected, the mother-child relationship, the father-child relationship (the latter now being clearly different from the former), and the integration of the individual child's total personality. We also observed that there seemed to develop at this time a rather significant difference in the development of the boys as compared with the girls. In our comparatively small sample of cases, the boys, if given a reasonable chance, showed a tendency to disengage themselves from mother and to enjoy their functioning in the widening world (see Greenson, 1968). The girls, on the other hand, seemed to become more engrossed with mother in her presence; they demanded greater closeness and were more persistently enmeshed in the ambivalent aspects of the relationship. This seemed connected with the realization of the sexual difference. Very importantly, the narcissistic hurt experienced by the girls of not having a penis was almost without exception blamed on the mother (see p. 106).

For example, the mother of one little girl felt that her child was becoming more and more demanding and imperious. She would demand whatever it was she wanted and would become quite angry if she could not get it. In the park, mother said, the child would insist that mother swing her interminably. She continued to go to her mother for help in any difficult situation, rather than make any attempt to find her own solutions. Once, following a struggle over mother's absence from the room, she looked at a picture book in which she identified all kinds of pictures, but she would not identify the picture of "the mother" (mechanism of disavowal).

At 22 months, another little girl became much more stubborn and negativistic. She particularly objected to wearing the kind of clothes that her mother picked out for her and had tantrums about having her hair combed. At the same time, she became more clinging to her mother. At the Center, where from a very early age on she had distinguished herself by her dislike of the other children, she became even more wary of them and expressed intense dislike if anyone tried to "usurp" her mother's attention. She found it increasingly difficult to go to the toddler room; when her mother finally took her there, the child returned to the infant room, leaving her mother behind. She was not very interested in toys, except as objects for social interaction with mother and other adults. She often went back to her mother for close contact. We understood this behavior as a displaced competition with her siblings for her mother's exclusive attention, wanting it for herself as the baby daughter. Most of the time, she did not object to her mother leaving the room, but would run to her when the latter returned. On one such occasion, she ran to her with a doll and showed her excitedly just how the doll made "pee-pee."

A third little girl in her twenty-second month showed a wish for closeness to her mother, as well as a need for physical stimulation by her. Mother responded to this by often holding her on her lap, stroking and stimulating her in a rather sensuous way. When mother was not there, the child would stimulate herself by masturbating. She continued to enjoy the play in the toddler room, but went to the infant room more often, obviously because of a greater need to be near mother. Often she approached mother with a peekaboo game, or somehow enticed her mother to chase her. She showed direct jealous reactions to her little sister and even tried to take the bottle away from her. In her twenty-second month, this little girl started to use the word "Mommy" for the first time. Also, she would wake during the night and call out for her mother. She looked for her mother and asked for her when mother was out for an interview. While mother was absent, she seemed to play alternately at being the baby and at being mother to babies. This situation of course was particularly multidetermined, and it could be understood only through our intimate knowledge of the preceding subphase developmental history and through our knowledge of the mother.

The boys, on the other hand, seemed to cope with the sight of the penislessness of the girls in a much less overt way; their apperception became confused with anal concerns, and later on with phallic castration anxieties expressed in the symbolism of their play.

By the children's twenty-third month, it seemed that the ability to cope with separateness, as well as with actual physical separation, was dependent in each case on the history of the mother-child relationship, as well as on its present state; it was certainly much less phase-specific. We found it hard to pinpoint just what it was in the individual cases that produced more anxiety in some and an ability to cope in others. Each child had established by this time his own characteristic ways of coping. When periods of crisis occurred, it was not always easy to see what the crisis was related to. Sometimes, it seemed related to the *child's* anxiety about his own rapid individuation (every so often this resulted in heightened ambivalence and aggression) or to bodily pressures not unrelated to simultaneous disappointment in mother; at certain times, the crisis seemed definitely related to bodily pressures (oral, anal, and phallic, that is, zonal) in Greenacre's sense (1945). Sometimes it seemed related to the degree and nature of the mother's availability, sometimes to the mother's own feelings of anxiety as the child started to become more individuated.

In short, this very important "final phase" of rapprochement as intrapsychic development seemed to be the summation of the solution of the many maturational developmental tasks that each individual child had arrived at during the course of his particular subphase development, up to the beginning of the fourth subphase.

The Beginning of Gender Identity

Mothers often commented that the bodies of their girl babies felt different from those of the boys, that the girls were softer and more cuddly. We do not wish to argue whether this feeling of the mothers was culturally determined, or whether it was due to the fact that baby girls actually mold in a more pliable way than do boys; probably both. In any case, the feeling of the mother about her child's body may well have some early patterning influence. On the whole, we did observe boys to be more motor-minded than girls and more stiffly resistant to hugging and kissing, beyond and even during differentiation; we also saw that the boys were interested earlier in moving objects, such as cars and trains.

Whatever sexual differences may have preexisted in the area of innate ego apparatuses and of early ego modes, they certainly were greatly complicated, and generally compounded, by the effects of the *child's discovery of the anatomical sexual difference*. This occurred sometimes during the 16 to 17 month period or even earlier, but more often in the twentieth or twenty-first month.

The boy's discovery of his own penis usually took place much earlier. The sensory-tactile component of this discovery may even date back into the first year of life (see Roiphe and Galenson, 1972, 1973); but there is uncertainty as to its emotional impact. Around the twelfth to fourteenth month, however, we have observed that the upright position facilitates the visual and sensory-motor exploration of the penis (p. 72). Possibly in combination with a maturational advance in zonal libidinization this led to a greater cathexis of this exquisitely sensuous, pleasure-giving organ.

Incidentally, it is hardly noted in psychoanalytic developmental psychology that the discovery of the penis, and particularly the important experience of its involuntary erection and detumescence, parallel the acquisition of voluntary free locomotion of the body. Except for Löfgren (1968), we did not find any reference to the little boy's noticing his highly cathected organ, his penis, moving (that is, erecting) on its own. This passive experience is probably very important. It would seem that the little boy becomes aware of the involuntary movement of his penis at the same time that he develops mastery of his own body movement in the erect position (see Mahler, 1968*a*).

At any rate, the little boy's exploration of his own penis during the practicing subphase seemed at first an experience of unmitigated pleasure; several mothers reported their boy's frequent quiet masturbation at home. This differed from our observation later in the separation-individuation phase (at the end of the second and the beginning of the third year) of boys clutching their penises for reassurance.

The girls' discovery of the penis confronted them with something that they themselves were lacking. This discovery brought on a range of behaviors clearly indicating the girls' anxiety, anger, and defiance. They wanted to undo the sexual difference. Therefore, it seemed to us that in girls, masturbation took on a desperate and aggression-saturated quality more often than in boys and at an earlier age. We have already mentioned that this discovery coincides with the emergence of the affect of envy (p. 91); in some of our girls, early penis envy may have accounted for the persistent predominance of this affect.

The discovery of the anatomical sexual difference took different forms in different children. One little boy (who talked early) discovered his mother's navel, and called it her "pee-pee." Other examples are scattered throughout this book.

The most dramatic (and yet the most typical) reaction to the rather sudden discovery of the anatomical sexual difference was acted out and put into words by Cathy at the tender age of 14 months. This we found to be singularly poignant, because of the circumstances of this little girl's life at that time. Cathy was then particularly vulnerable because her father was temporarily away. She was an unusually bright, charming, eminently verbal, precocious little girl, who was everybody's favorite and a great comfort to her mother. The latter took unusual pride in her little girl's feminine qualities, always dressing her with particular care. She was, so to say, her more beautiful and feminine alter ego. During the father's absence, the mother took a part-time job, and during that part of the day Cathy was taken care of by the mother of one of the little boys in our study. Cathy, who was precocious in all ways, was already partially toilet trained. One day we noticed that she did not want to sit on the toilet; instead, she started to whine and hold on to her genital area. The mother had previously told us that on several occasions Cathy had been bathed with her little boy friend. Upon being asked whether Cathy had noticed her little friend's penis, the mother told us that Cathy had commented that her boy friend had *two* belly buttons. A period of extreme crankiness ensued, and this hitherto charming little girl became impossible to satisfy in our nursery group. A while later, Cathy started to become not only cranky but aggressive toward the other children. Her particular form of aggression (from which nothing could deter her) was pulling the hair of boys and girls alike. Eventually, the mother told us that because Cathy hated to have her hair washed, she had been taking her into the shower with her to wash her hair. In the shower, Cathy had grabbed at her mother's pubic hair, obviously searching for the "hidden penis." Because of Cathy's verbal precocity we had the opportunity to follow the ups and downs of her attempts to come to terms with the narcissistic injury of not having a penis. This might have hit her so hard because of the absence of the father, and perhaps also because until then she had been such a perfect cherished love object to her mother, to herself, and to everybody else. She had displayed a blooming optimal, even maximal, self-esteem. There was another little girl who was similarly very hard hit by the discovery of the sexual difference. She, too, was very clearly for her mother a perfect child and a completion of her own self (see Stoller, 1973; Galenson and Roiphe, 1971).

In short, we found that the task of becoming a separate individual seemed, at this point, to be generally more difficult for girls than for boys, because the girls, upon the discovery of the sexual difference, tended to turn back to mother, to blame her, to demand from her, to be disappointed in her, and still to be ambivalently tied to her. They demanded from mother that she settle a debt, so to say. As the girl is hit with her own imperfection, she may become imperfect in the unconscious of the the mother as well. Boys, on the other hand, seemed to become faced with castration anxiety only later; during the second and third year, they seemed to find it more expedient than girls to function separately; they were better able to turn to the outside world, or to their own bodies, for pleasure and satisfaction; they also turned to father as someone with whom to identify. They seemed somehow to cope with their castration anxiety in a phase of quasi-preoedipal triangulation (Abelin, 1972); in our setup, this could not be easily followed.

Discussion of the Third Subphase

In our observational study, we saw why the rapprochement crisis occurs, as well as why, in some instances, it may become—and remain—an unresolved intrapsychic conflict. It may set an unfavorable fixation point, thus interfering with later oedipal development; at best, it may add to the difficulty of the resolution of the oedipus complex and lend a peculiar cast to it.

The developmental task at the very height of the separation-individuation struggle during the rapprochement subphase is a tremendous one. Oral, anal, and early genital pressures and conflicts meet and accumulate at this important crossroad in personality development. There is a need to renounce symbiotic omnipotence, and there is also heightened awareness of the body image and pressure in the body, especially at the points of zonal libidinization. Belief in mother's omnipotence seems to be shaken.

While the fear of object loss and abandonment is partly relieved, at this developmental stage, it is also greatly complicated by the internalization of parental demands; this not only indicates the beginning of superego development, but also expresses itself in fear of *losing the object's love*! In consequence, we observe an intensified vulnerability on the part of the rapprochement toddler. Fear of *loss of the love of the object* goes parallel with highly sensitive reactions to approval and disapproval by the parent. There is greater awareness of bodily feelings and pressures, in Greenacre's sense. These are augmented by awareness of bowel and urinary sensations during the toilet-training period, even in quite normal development. Children often display, in some instances quite dramatically, a reaction to the discovery of the anatomical sex difference.

The persistence and degree of the rapprochement crisis indicate premature internalization of conflicts, developmental disturbances that were precursors of infantile neurosis, but may even decisively stand in the way of the development of infantile neurosis, in the classical sense! As we said before, conflict is at first acted out, that is to say, indicated by coercive behaviors directed toward the mother, designed to force her to function as the child's omnipotent extension; these alternate with signs of desperate clinging. In other words, in those children with less than optimal development, the ambivalence conflict is discernible during the rapprochement subphase in rapidly alternating clinging and negativistic behaviors. These alternating behaviors are the ingredients of the phenomena we designate as "ambitendency"—that is, as long as the contrasting tendencies are not yet fully internalized. This phenomenon may be in some cases a reflection of the fact that the child has split the object world more permanently than is optimal into "good" and "bad." By means of this splitting, the "good" object is defended against the derivatives of the aggressive drive.

These two mechanisms—coercion and splitting of the object world—if excessive, are also characteristic of most cases of adult borderline transference (Mahler, 1971; see also Frijling-Schreuder, 1969). We were able to study the possible antecedents of this in the verbal, primary-process material of a few children at the end of their second year of life and during their third year. These mechanisms, along with the problem of finding what the late Maurice Bouvet (1958) described as the "optimal distance," may prevail as early as in the fourth subphase of separation-individuation, at a time when "libidinal object constancy" should begin to be achieved and separation reactions should be diminishing.

Disturbances during the rapprochement subphase are likely to reappear in much more definite and individually different forms during the final phase of that process in which a unified self-representation should become demarcated from a blended and integrated object representation.

The clinical outcome of these rapprochement crises will be determined by: (1) the development toward libidinal object constancy; (2) the quantity and quality of later disappointments (stress traumata); (3) possible shock traumata; (4) the degree of castration anxiety; (5) the fate of the oedipus complex; and (6) the developmental crises of adolescence—all of which function within the context of the individual's constitutional endowment.

CHAPTER 7

The Fourth Subphase: Consolidation of Individuality and the Beginnings of Emotional Object Constancy

FROM the point of view of the separation-individuation process, the main task of the fourth subphase is twofold: (1) the achievement of a definite, in certain aspects lifelong, individuality, and (2) the attainment of a certain degree of object constancy.

As far as the self is concerned, there is a far-reaching structuralization of the *ego*, and there are definite signs of internalization of parental demands indicating the formation of superego precursors.

The establishment of affective (emotional) object constancy (Hartmann, 1952) depends upon the gradual internalization of a constant, positively cathected, inner image of the mother. This, to begin with, permits the child to function separately (in familiar surroundings, for example, in our toddler room) despite moderate degrees of tension (longing) and discomfort. Emotional object constancy will, of course, be based in the first place on the cognitive achievement of the permanent object, but all other aspects of the child's personality development participate in this evolution as well (see McDevitt, 1972).[1] The last sub-

[1] J. B. McDevitt, in his as yet unpublished papers and discussions, has significantly elaborated the criteria for libidinal object constancy in the sense used in this book.

phase (roughly the third year of life) is an extremely important intrapsychic developmental period, in the course of which a stable sense of entity (self boundaries) is attained. Primitive consolidation of gender identity seems to take place in this subphase as well.

But the constancy of the object implies more than the maintenance of the representation of the absent love object (cf. Mahler, 1965*a*; Mahler and Furer, 1966). It also implies the unifying of the "good" and "bad" object into one whole representation. This fosters the fusion of the aggressive and libidinal drives and tempers the hatred for the object when aggression is intense. Our view of libidinal object constancy is most closely similar (we believe identical) with Hoffer's, even though differently formulated. Hoffer (1955) stated that object constancy has to be regarded as the last stage in the development of a mature object relationship. It has a special bearing on the fate of the aggressive and hostile drives. In the state of object constancy, the love object will not be rejected or exchanged for another if it can no longer provide satisfactions; and in that state, the object is still longed for, and not rejected (hated) as unsatisfactory simply because it is absent.

The slow establishment of emotional object constancy is a complex and multidetermined process involving all aspects of psychic development. Essential prior determinants are (1) trust and confidence through the regularly occurring relief of need tension provided by the need-satisfying agency as early as in the symbiotic phase. In the course of the subphases of the separation-individuation process, this relief of need tension is gradually attributed to the need-satisfying whole object (the mother) and is then transferred by means of internalization to the intrapsychic representation of the mother, and (2) the cognitive acquisition of the symbolic inner representation of the permanent object (in Piaget's sense) in our instance to the unique love object: the mother. Numerous other factors are involved, such as innate drive endowment and maturation, neutralization of drive energy, reality testing, tolerance for frustration and for anxiety, and so forth.

It is only after object constancy is well on its way, which according to our conceptualization does not seem to occur before the third year (see Mahler, 1965*b*), that the mother during her physical absence can be substituted for, at least in part, by the presence of a reliable internal image that remains relatively stable irrespective of the state of instinctual need or inner discomfort. On the basis of this achievement, temporary separation can be lengthened and better tolerated. The establishment of object permanence and of a "mental image" of the object in Piaget's sense is a necessary, but not a sufficient, prerequisite for the establishment of libidinal object constancy. Other aspects of drive and ego maturation and development take part in the slow transition from the more primitive ambivalent love relationship, which exists only as long as it is need satisfying, to the more mature (in the ideal and rarely attained instance postambivalent) *mutual give-and-take love-object relationship* of the schoolchild and the adult.

Before we go on, a further word is in order about the Piagetian work on "object permanence" (Piaget 1937; see also Gouin-Decarie, 1965) and our own use of the term *object constancy*. Piaget's work (1937) has made clear that the development of object permanence takes place at about 18 to 20 months of age and is reasonably established at that time. But his studies focus on inanimate, transiently cathected, physical objects. Does this development take place at the same rate vis-a-vis the libidinal object, the mother? From our findings, we must decisively answer this question in the negative. There are at least two major differences between the libidinal object and those objects studied by Piaget: (1) the child is in continual contact with the libidinal object, that is, the mother; and (2) these contacts often take place under conditions of high arousal—of longing, frustration, gratification, excitement. The mother, an "object" in the psychoanalytic sense, that is, something through which drive gratification is achieved, is far more than an "object" in the merely physical-descriptive sense. We expect that repeated contact and high arousal make for differences in the rate of acquisition of a concept of permanence (see Bell, 1970; Fraiberg, 1969; McDevitt, 1971, 1972; Pine, 1974).

But the effect of the libidinal status of the object upon the rate of acquisition of a concept of its permanence is by no means unequivocal. One of us has suggested that "the heightened learning and recording of memories that may take place under conditions of optimal arousal (that is, a drive state that does not reach traumatic dimensions) and under conditions of repeated encounter may solidify aspects of the internal representation of the libidinal object even before 18 to 20 months" (Pine, 1974). McDevitt (1972, unpublished); on the other hand, speaking of the period even after 18 to 20 months, suggests that "the mental representation of the mother may be so buffeted by violent and angry feelings that the stability of this image, at least from the libidinal as opposed to the cognitive side, is disrupted" (see also Chapters 5 and 6, pp. 65–108). Interestingly, Bell (1970) has shown experimentally that infants with harmonious relationships with their mothers develop "person permanence" prior to "object permanence," while the reverse is true where the relationship is disharmonious. (Our studies have amply illustrated this.) Thus, "the presence of intense libidinal and aggressive ties to the object may . . . make for *more rapid* and *less fixed* attainment of a permanent representation of a permanent object" (Pine, 1974; see also L. Kaplan, 1972).

All of this suggests that the development of libidinal object constancy is a complex process. In general, however, libidinal object constancy is sufficiently permanent in the normal 3-year-old, represented socioculturally in the choice of age 3 as a common point of readiness for entry into nursery school (cf. A. Freud 1963).

This fourth subphase of the separation-individuation process is not a subphase in the same sense as the first three, since it is open-ended at the older end.

We see a prominent, though still only relative, shift from phenomena of the rapprochement subphase with more or less difficulty in leavetaking, and increased capacity to play separately from mother, with indications that the child can increasingly hold on to the image of her ("the good mother") automatically in her absence. But these changes reach no single, definite terminal point.[2]

We have found that as this subphase proceeds, the child is in general able gradually to accept separation from the mother once again (as he did in the practicing period); in fact, when he is engrossed in play, he seems to prefer staying in the toddler room without the mother to leaving the toddler room with her. We regard this as a sign of the beginning achievement of emotional object constancy. Yet many complex conflictual and conflict-free processes seem to go on in the child in the course of the third year, rendering object constancy a still rather fluid and reversible achievement. It is still, as Hartmann has communicated to one of us (Mahler), a matter of degree.[3] It is dependent on the context of many other developmental factors, the prevailing ego state, and the environmental affective response of the moment. An illustration of this follows.

Let us describe the behavior of three children on the day that the mothers, with adequate explanation, were asked to retire to their area of the infant room and leave their toddlers more systematically under the care of the playroom teacher in the toddler room. Here, as in our previous illustrations, phase-related behavior and marked individual variation characterize each case.

Three senior toddlers (26 to 28 months old) had graduated to the

[2] Among psychoanalytic writers, Jacobson (1964) is one who makes clear the continuance of problems of merging of self and object images well into the third year.

[3] Personal communication.

toddler room, which had become quite familiar to them. Its appeal had lured them for many months, but they had been in conflict about leaving mother behind in the infant room, and they required her presence in the toddler room. When the mothers were asked to retire to the adjoining, readily accessible, infant room, we were able to observe, on the one hand, the toddlers' reaction to this mild separation, and on the other, the mothers' readiness for, and manner of, separating from their now more independently functioning children (Chapter 2, pp. 26–28).

The first little girl, whose mother had been optimally—in retrospect we would say rather maximally—available emotionally during the course of the earlier subphases, *seemed* to have progressed further than the other children in terms of object constancy. We believed that the inner image of the mother was positively and unambivalently cathected; indeed this child *understood where* mother was and could manage quite well during mother's brief absence (whether in another room or away from the Center) from about the age of 25 to 26 months. On the day the mothers were asked to stay in the infant room, the senior worker in charge of the toddler room described the first little girl's reaction as follows. She stayed close to her mother while mother was sitting in the toddler room with her. When her mother left, she allowed herself to become more and more interested in the play initiated by the worker and for a short while was not even concerned about her mother's whereabouts. As a matter of fact, when the mother left the room, she did not immediately notice her departure. She became aware of it only as she was drawing and growing very pleased with herself, at which point she asked several times, "Where's Mommy?" We believe that at this moment she wanted to share her drawing with her mother (rapprochement), but when no one answered her call, she was able to continue her drawing, and even to become more involved in it. (In our description of the third year, however, we shall see in greater detail how delicate, complex, and open-ended the vicissitudes of emotional object constancy still are at that age period.)

In contrast to the first little girl, who had apparently achieved a high degree of libidinal object constancy at this point, one little boy had suffered early disappointments in his mother. He acted that day, as he had on many previous days, as though he held a conflictual, ambiguous inner image of mother, to the point of generally wishing to avoid her. On this day, he was very quiet and subdued from the time he arrived at the Center. As usual, he busily engaged himself in activities, but from the time his mother left the toddler room, his mood became more and more low-keyed, perhaps even slightly depressed. He expressed his unhappiness by the solemn way in which he stood by the sink listlessly, uninterested in water play, usually one of his favorite activities. He did not ask for his mother, however, and did not appear to notice her absence, but he had a rather distant look in his eyes.

The second little girl exhibited still another kind of behavior. In general, her tolerance of being left by mother was very poor, even if the separation was very brief. She responded to her mother's leaving both immediately and intensely. When she noticed that her mother was about to leave, she ran to her, clung to her, whined, and cried. The worker suggested that she take a baby doll which she had enjoyed playing with enormously the previous week. For a moment she stopped crying, clasped the doll close to her body, and seemed to be on the verge of playing with it; but when she realized that her mother was *in fact* not staying, she was unable to play with the doll. Instead, she clung to it and cried as she ran after her mother. Finally, she noticed the familiar figure of one of our staff, whose presence seemed to comfort her somewhat. However, she remained subdued during the time her mother was absent. In other words, she could maintain her emotional equilibrium for a short time in mother's absence by substituting a one-to-one child-adult relationship. It should be emphasized that the rapprochement crisis still casts its shadow upon the developmental progress towards emotional object constancy; progression ever so often is punctuated by regression, ambivalence interfering most noticeably in the process of leavetaking, when the "mother in the flesh" is still potentially there.

It is typical that when there is a great deal of ambivalence in the relationship, mother's leaving stirs up considerable expressed or unexpressed anger and longing; under such conditions, the positive image of the mother cannot be sustained. The reactions of the three children upon reunion with their mothers also revealed strikingly different patterns in the development of object constancy. The first little girl, who seemed to have retained the positive image of her mother during the latter's absence, and who had been able to utilize the play and her involvement with familiar people to ease her concern, greeted her mother with smiles; she made welcoming gestures with the toys she brought her and in general seemed genuinely pleased to see her. The little boy exhibited an absence of appropriate affect: no show of pleasure at his mother's return. The mother commented that her son didn't miss her, that he "didn't care." When the second little girl saw her mother return, she reacted with visible ambivalence. She grimaced, then tried to smile, but looked hurt and angry at her mother.

The behavioral referents, indicators of these variations in the development of emotional object constancy, are intelligible through the study of the infant-toddler's relationship to his mother during the previous subphase of separation-individuation.

The first little girl had the good fortune of having optimal, that is, flexible and progressive mothering, according to the changing needs in the previous subphases. Her mother was patient, understanding, and consistently emotionally available in the first *two* subphases, and when developmentally appropriate—so we thought at the time—she slowly encouraged her daughter's developing independence and autonomous functioning. Partly by endowment and partly as a consequence of the optimal mother-child interaction in the symbiotic phase and in the first two subphases of the separation-individuation process, this little girl had developed in her second year of life the following characteristics: basic trust, confidence in mother and others, and a sound secondary narcissism with good self-esteem. She definitely was more advanced than any of her contemporaries in her secondarily autonomous ego functioning.

As we observed in the instance cited above, this child at 25 and 26 months of age coped with mother's absences extremely well. When she asked for her mother, a simple explanation of mother's whereabouts was clearly understood by her and satisfied her. It seemed that she had a sound and satisfying inner image of her mother and an intrapsychic representation which was positive and invested with confidence. This permitted excellent autonomous ego functioning, despite some slight distress and "longing" caused by mother's absence.

We will see, however, that even this little girl's well-developing libidinal object constancy could not be maintained vis-à-vis unusually severe and accumulated shock traumata (pp. 143–145).

We were suprised to see, on the day the mothers were asked to remain in the infant room, how reluctantly this little girl's mother heeded the principal investigator's carefully explained request that mothers retire to the adjoining, readily accessible room and let their children come and go at their will. (For the first time it became clear to us that this first little girl's mother made herself not only optimally but also phase-unspecifically "available" to an excessive degree.)

In contrast to this mother, who made herself *too* readily available not only in the rapprochement subphase but way beyond, the little boy's mother (whom we described briefly earlier) could not help but be unpredictable in her emotional attitudes and tendencies toward her son. As we watched him after his mother had left the toddler room, he seemed to be completely involved in fantasy play, had at times a sober and at times a sad facial expression, lacked the vivaciousness characteristic of that age, and did not become involved with people. Even so, his autonomous ego functioning was excellent. In other words, he had to and did rely too predominantly and too precociously on his own autonomy, seemingly suppressing his emotional need for the mother's sustenance.

The second little girl continued to react to her mother's leave-taking with much anxiety; she would become sad, forlorn, and withdrawn. On days when she was not too disturbed, she could cope partially by actively mothering the doll baby, that is, through identification with mother. Otherwise, she became the helpless baby herself, constantly eating, seeking out and leaning against her favorite (male) observer as a need-satisfying mother substitute, or seeking autoerotic and narcissistic gratifications such as violent rocking on the rocking horse or frequently glancing at herself in the mirror. Her separation anxiety and her anger toward her mother resulted in marked regression of the narcissistic variety.

The Achievement of Individuality

Because the child learns to express himself verbally during this period, we can trace some of the vicissitudes of the intrapsychic separation process from the mother, and the conflicts around it, through the verbal material that we get from him, along with the phenomenology of his behavior. Verbal communication, which began during the third subphase, develops rapidly during this, the fourth subphase of separation-individuation, and slowly replaces other modes of communication, although gestural language of the whole body and affectomotility still remain very much in evidence. Play becomes more purposeful and constructive. There is a beginning of fantasy play, role playing, and make-believe. Observations about the real world become detailed and are clearly included in play, and there is an increasing interest in playmates and in adults other than mother. A sense of time (and also of spatial relations) begins to develop and with it, an increased capacity to tolerate the delay of gratification and to endure separation. Such concepts as "later" or "tomorrow" are not only understood but also used by the child of this age: *they are experimented with, polarized by his mother's comings and goings.* We see a lot of active resistance to the demands of adults, a great need and a wish (often still unrealistic) for autonomy (independence). Recurrent mild or moderate negativism, which seems to be essential for the development of a sense of identity, is also characteristic of this subphase. (The child is still mainly in the anal and early phallic phase of zonal development.)

Thus, the fourth subphase is characterized by unfolding of complex cognitive functions: verbal communication, fantasy, and reality testing. During this period of rapid ego differentiation, from about 20 or 22 months to 30 or 36 months, individuation develops so greatly that even a cursory description of it exceeds the scope of this book (Escalona, 1968). Suffice it to say that establishment of mental representations of the self as distinctly separate from representations of the object *paves the way* to self-identity formation.

In ideal cases, during the second half of the third year, the libidinal investment persists regardless of the absence of immediate satisfaction and maintains the child's emotional equilibrium during the object's temporary absences.

During the period of normal symbiosis, the narcissistically fused object was felt to be "good"—that is, in harmony with the symbiotic self—so that primary identification took place under a positive valence of love. The less gradually, the more abruptly, intrapsychic awareness of separateness occurs, or the more intrusive and/or unpredictable the parents are, the less does the modulating, negotiating function of the ego gain ascendancy. That is to say, the less predictably reliable or the more intrusive the love object's emotional attitude in the outside world has been, the greater the extent to which the object *remains* or *becomes* an unassimilated foreign body—a "bad" introject, in the intrapsychic emotional economy (cf. Heimann, 1966). In the effort to eject this "bad introject," derivatives of the aggressive drive come into play; and there seems to develop an increased proclivity to identify the self-representation with the "bad" introject or at least to confuse the two. If this situation surfaces during the rapprochement subphase, then aggression may be unleashed in such a way as to inundate or sweep away the "good object," and with it, the good self-representation (Mahler, 1971, 1972*a*). This would be indicated by early severe temper tantrums, by increased attempts to coerce mother and father to function as quasi-external egos. In short, great ambivalence may ensue which continues to mar smooth development toward emotional object constancy and sound secondary narcissism. These are the consequences for those children in whom the too sudden and too painful realization of their helplessness has resulted in a too sudden deflation of their previous sense of their own omnipotence, as well as of the shared magical omnipotence of the parents, in Edith Jacobson's (1954) sense. These are the toddlers who, in the third year in particular, show a tendency to split the object world into "good" and "bad," and for whom the "mother in the flesh" (Bowlby, 1958), "the mother after separation" (Mahler, 1971), is always disappointing, and whose self-esteem regulation is most precarious.

We have observed many of our normal children recoiling from mother or showing other signs that had to be interpreted as a kind of erotized fear upon being cornered by the mother who wanted playfully to seek bodily contact with the child. At the same time, romping games with the father were often sought and enjoyed. These behaviors, we feel, were signs of the fear of reengulfment by the narcissistically invested, yet defended against, dangerous "mother after separation," in whose omnipotence some of these children still appeared to believe, although they felt that their mothers no longer let them share in her magic powers (Mahler, 1971).

The principal conditions for mental health, so far as preoedipal development is concerned, hinge on the attained and continuing ability of the child to retain or restore his self-esteem in the context of relative libidinal object constancy. In the fourth open-ended subphase both inner structures—libidinal object constancy as well as a unified self-image based on true ego identifications—should have their inception. However, we believe that both of these structures represent merely the beginning of the ongoing developmental process.

The "internal mother," the inner image or intrapsychic representation of the mother, in the course of the third year should become more or less available in order to supply comfort to the child in mother's physical absence. The first basis for the stability and the quality of this inner representation is the actual mother-child relationship as we saw it unfolding in the day-to-day interaction between mother and child. It seemed to be the result of the preceding three subphases. This, however, is by no means an end point. We will show in Part III, in our more detailed descriptions of five children's separation-individuation vicissitudes, how this new little being, in his third year, ready to put into action his independent functioning in his relatively greatly widened world, tries to weather, without the physical presence of his mother, the new storms which at times threaten or even do sweep away that delicate, newly formed inner structure of relative emotional object constancy.

The threats to libidinal object constancy and separate individual functioning originate from various sources. First of all, there is the pressure of drive maturation, which confronts the child with new tasks as he goes through the anal phase with the demands that toilet training entails. Then upon entering the phallic phase, the child becomes much more aware of the sexual difference, and along with it he experiences castration anxiety of varying intensity.

Psychoanalysts are well aware of the great variety of negations, fantasies, accusations, and fears with which the child tries to cope with these problems. For us, it is important here to see how these affect a budding, libidinal object constancy and libidinal investment of the individuating self.

We have described how castration anxiety, from as early as the second part of the second year on, may counteract the development and sound integration of self-representations (probably the body image in the first place) and may also counteract the libidinally cathected identificatory processes. Cumulative (developmental) traumata (cf. Khan, 1964) in the anal and especially in the phallic phase may constitute a roadblock in the way of object constancy, as well as in the way of a preliminary consolidation of the child's individuality.

These preceding and ongoing events decisively determine the 3-year-old's style and degree of integration of his individuality. Both achievements—consolidation of individuality and emotional object constancy—are easily challenged by the struggle around toilet training, and by the awareness of the anatomical sexual difference, a blow to the narcissism of the little girl and a great danger to the little boy's body integrity.

By the third year, there is in the life of each child a particular constellation that is the result of the hitherto experienced optimal or less than optimal empathic personality of the mother, her mothering capacity, to which he responds. This response branches out to the father and to the entire psychosocial constellation of the child's family. His reactions are greatly influenced by accidental, but sometimes fateful, happenings such as sicknesses, surgical interventions, accidents, separations from mother or father, that is to say, by experiential factors. Accidental events of this sort in a sense constitute each child's fate and are the substance from which are formed the endlessly varied, but also endlessly recurring, themes and tasks of his particular life.

As we describe the waxing and waning movements toward and away from emotional object constancy of the five children whose development we have followed through the rapprochement conflicts up to the end of the third year, we will see each child's conflicts and struggles over gaining and maintaining libidinal object constancy during the fourth subphase. We shall try to determine to what extent, if any, the characteristic struggle of the rapprochement subphase comes to an end, and/or how the resolution of the rapprochement crises fosters or hinders progress toward sound individuality (self-identity) and toward object constancy. We will also try to show each child's characteristic beginning and gradually solidifying defensive structure, as well as each child's adaptive style, that is, his ways of coping with his individual problems (see Mahler and McDevitt, 1968).

Part III

Five Children's Subphase Development

INTRODUCTION

HAVING followed so many children through their separation-individuation process, we have found infinite variations in subphase development depending on the child's innate endowment, the mother-child relationship and experimental circumstances of each subphase. In this part we shall follow five children epigenetically through their subphase development. The case histories that follow illustrate the exquisitely complex and self-repeating constellations of variables, the kaleidoscopically permutating patternings, the alternations of progressive and regressive steps in the individuation process, and the characteristic waxing and waning of the children's newly acquired drive and ego positions (in interactions with their mothers and their expanding environment).

CHAPTER 8

Bruce

WE saw in Bruce a well-endowed child coping with a considerably difficult mother-child relationship. From birth on, mother imparted to the young infant her anxiety about his intactness. Bruce's case represents an example of a remarkably successful individuation against considerable odds. Adverse circumstances at the chronological age of symbiosis were noted by all the observers. The developmental examination that took place between his fourth and fifth month indicated that the fit of this mother-infant pair—their mutual cueing—was precarious. Both mother and infant were anxious, tense, restless, and seemed uncomfortable with each other.

Bruce's Mother

Mrs. A.'s anxiety seemed to exceed the usual apprehension of mothers with their first babies. Since we did not analyze her and, therefore, do not have thorough knowledge of her underlying conflicts about motherhood, we do not wish to describe here what we surmised about her fantasies concerning her child. Suffice it to say that Mrs. A. had an anxious compulsion to convince herself that her baby was born intact. The first months of pregnancy were fraught with adversities; that Bruce was born by spontaneous delivery, with normal birth weight, in excellent condition, and that he was extremely active from the moment he was born, did not dispel his mother's anxieties. Neither mother nor baby enjoyed the short time of breast feeding. In the early months of the symbiotic phase, Bruce seemed more easily soothed by a pacifier than by the feeding process.

Bruce's Subphase Development

Bruce was a very tense, hypertonic, and restless baby who had difficulty molding. He cried himself into quite severe "tantrums" with which his mother had difficulty dealing. This fact, and his persistent sleep disturbance at night and at naptime, had an exhausting effect on Bruce's mother. Bruce could neither be calmed nor fed in the horizontal position; he did not allow himself to be cradled before his fifth month.

Inasmuch as Bruce was such a restless sleeper, Mrs. A. became preoccupied with and always concerned about his "not getting enough sleep." Every so often she interpreted his fretting and fussing as sleepiness, and she would rather awkwardly and deliberately put him to sleep, although we all felt that he was alertly watching his surroundings. Bruce's remarkable alertness and interest in the goings on at the Center were counteracted by his mother's concern over his not getting enough sleep.

Bruce developed an early social smile which, by 5 months of age, grew into a specific preferential smiling response for his mother. By that time, he had grown into a rather robust, chubby little boy who was much calmer. He maintained his favorite vertical position by virtue of his particularly well developed thigh and calf muscles; he liked to brace his legs on his mother's lap. He was described as very alert and interested in toys, and this made his mother somewhat more relaxed and happy.

Bruce had been described as a very restless baby, sucking on the pacifier with great intensity, but by 5 months of age his motor activity became gradually more goal-directed and less in the service of discharge of internal discomfort. He was able to play happily by himself for longer periods and had developed the ability to wait for his meals. He began to use his mouth for exploring as well as for sucking. The degree of his lack of tolerance for disruption from without showed in his startle reactions to certain noises. But although he showed this hyperalertness to abrupt loud noises, he seemed to have developed an increased tolerance to internal stimuli. Whereas from 4 to 5 months, Bruce showed excited pleasure at the sight of his bottle, gradually this excitement lessened, and by 5 to 6 months he showed similar excitement when looking at toys. We learned that he responded with excitement, smiles, and gurgles when he *heard* his father coming home. By the age of 5 months, he also showed a particular attachment to his blanket, which had become a true transitional object. He gurgled and cooed with delight whenever it was given to him. His receptivity was notably an auditory one, that is, he preferred or was geared particularly to the auditory modality. At 5 months of age, Bruce started to mold more comfortably when his mother cradled him. Although Bruce had been a relatively unsmiling baby during his first few weeks with us, he now became friendly and smiling.

Comparative scanning of people and "checking back" to mother was reported in the beginning of Bruce's sixth month, as was the fact that he still cried and fretted a great deal before suddenly falling asleep.

During the differentiation and early practicing subphases, Bruce vigorously turned to the outside world. He seemed to derive great pleasure from his expanding motor capacities. But the fact that he, like every normal child, was relatively independent in the early practicing period seemed to make his mother feel rejected; in consequence, she could not offer herself to Bruce for emotional refueling. She again tended to interpret his fretting when tired out and in need of *her* as a need for *sleep*. Unwittingly, she tended to put a distance between him and herself.

At this time, around 6 or 7 months of age, Bruce developed severe stranger reactions. He could be comforted only by his mother. Although Mrs. A. was pleased by this, she was at times unable to comfort him when he was upset. The optimal distance for Bruce and his mother, in the course of the differentiation and early practicing periods, was one in which Bruce would play with toys in the playpen while Mrs. A. watched him across the room. Bruce would frequently look at his mother, and she said that she would never have thought that "watching a little baby could be so much pleasure."

During the early practicing period, Bruce took great delight in his explorations. His growing interest in the world around him seemed to have helped him overcome the earlier stranger reaction. He was in an elated mood. At first he still needed to sit on mother's lap to get used to a stranger, but his interest in the world took over more and more. He needed little physical contact with his mother; he was reassured from a distance by looking at her and by vocalizing.

When Bruce was 9 months old, his mother became pregnant again. At the same time, she seemed impatient with Bruce, especially if he wiggled while she diapered him. The announcement of her pregnancy closely followed Mrs. A.'s conversation about wanting to go back to work. The new unplanned pregnancy seemed to arouse further conflict and anxiety in the mother, and this was reflected in her relationship with her son. Mrs. A. now complained that she never knew what Bruce wanted; she often gave him *food*, instead of herself. Around 9 months, Bruce developed a transient, but rather severe, disturbance in his food intake. Mrs. A. complained about her difficulties bathing, diapering, and dressing him. He seemed to struggle to avoid being put into the reclining position or being made to be still, that is, passive. Mrs. A. would yell at him, and then she would feel guilty about her anger. We felt that Mrs. A.'s behavior toward Bruce was a displacement onto him of the anger she felt about the new pregnancy, about which she complained repeatedly, and which caused her to feel physically rather poorly and continually nauseous.

At this time, when Bruce was 9 to 10 months old, she felt compelled to teach him the meaning of the word, "No." It seemed that at this time during her own crisis, she found it difficult to let Bruce be an individual in his own right; she wanted him to remain passive, a controllable appendage of his parents.

Bruce reacted to the change in his mother by losing the earlier joy in his practicing. Rather than crawling about and manipulating objects, he started to pull himself to a standing position (reminiscent of his earliest lap-baby pattern). At this age, the standing position generally contributes to the child's pride and feeling of well-being. However, in Bruce's case, the standing position seemed to contribute to a lowering of mood. We may speculate that because he was unable to revert without help to the sitting or quadruped position, the standing posture may have made him feel more vulnerable in terms of his body image and his bodily feelings. This, no doubt, contributed to Bruce's renewed wariness of strangers and his decreased enjoyment of independent play. However, in spite of this temporary disturbance, when he moved somewhat later into the *practicing period proper*, Bruce *did show* the general characteristics of this subphase. He very much enjoyed the world around him, was delighted with his developing functions, and from 10 to 14 months of age was able to tolerate short separations from his mother.

Actually the height of the practicing period proper coincided with our summer recess, and we saw Bruce only on one home visit. When he returned after the vacation, at 14 months of age, he was beginning to show behavior typical of the period of *early rapprochement*, very prematurely indeed. His awareness of mother's whereabouts became very keen; he took pleasure in sharing his possessions with her, particularly his food. Again there was a return of stranger and strangeness reactions, and he needed a period of sitting in his mother's lap before becoming involved in the activities of the other children in the room. Because rapprochement started so early, we saw in his case a far too great (non-optimal) overlapping of practicing and rapprochement features of the separation-individuation process.

By now Mrs. A. seemed to accept her new pregnancy, and so she became better attuned to Bruce's needs. At the same time, she became anxious and hovered over him whenever he became venturesome in his walking and climbing.

As the rapprochement period progressed, Bruce became more aware of mother's absences from the room. He would play near her empty chair and would sometimes cry when the door opened and someone other than mother entered the room. On the whole, the mother-child relationship during the early months of the rapprochement period was quite positive. However, just as in Bruce's early practicing subphase, when the first flowering of a good relationship with mother was impeded by the advent of mother's pregnancy, so now again, toward the end of her pregnancy, Mrs. A. became increasingly tired, depressed, and irritable. She again started to feel unduly burdened with Bruce. She compared him unfavorably with the other children at the Center, and she reduced contact with him. At first Bruce seemed to react by trying to help himself; for example, he started to feed himself. He would make appeals in an indirect way; he would get into dangerous situations, thus forcing his mother to rescue him. But finally a quality of passive surrender crept into his behavior. He became more clinging and depressed.

Bruce was 16 months old when his baby sister was born. Initially he tried to cope with this event by avoiding the sight of his mother with the baby, by literally looking away. But by the time his sister was 1 month old, his avoidance mechanism no longer worked; he became more depressed, was unable to enjoy himself, and was quiet and subdued. He anxiously clung to his mother and would not let her out of sight, as if he feared that she might abandon him. At this point, Mrs. A. realized Bruce's depression; she became worried about him and was more patient and giving with him.

The intermittent progression and regression in Bruce's relationship with his mother seemed to come to a halt when, in his nineteenth month, there was a turning point in his development. He overcame his depression and started to find much pleasure in play and in his relationships to other people. Bruce *began to be able to use language*. This ability to use words seemed to be a great help to him, as he could now put into words his active curiosity and interest in the world. It is not quite clear in this child's case whether his early acquisition of language was a maturational achievement that then made turning to the outside world much easier, somewhat similar to the model of precocious maturation of locomotion, or whether his turning to the outside world and to other people made it possible for him to learn to talk. It seems to have been a circular process.

In his nineteenth and twentieth months, Bruce overcame his earlier strong separation reactions. He became extremely, perhaps reactively, independent. He seemed less disturbed by the presence of the baby sister, found a name for her, and took some pleasure in helping to care for her; in other words, he seemed to be able to "identify with the active mother." At the Center he became very much attached to the toddler room and to many people, enjoyed relationships with both adults and the other toddlers, and eagerly participated in all activities.

Bruce's rapprochement crisis had received its particular flavor from the birth of his baby sister, as well as from the mother's periodic turning away from him because of the pregnancy and her periods of impatience with him.

Bruce resolved his rapprochement crisis suddenly and for the time being rather successfully. It seemed he had done this not so much by coming to terms with his mother (even though he had identified with the active mother), but rather by disidentifying from her, in Greenson's sense, (cf. Greenson, 1968), by turning to his father. We were, of course, unable to observe this directly in our set-up, but we were soon able to reconstruct it from Bruce's symbolic play and verbalizations. (He "cooked" for his father, had imaginary telephone conversations with his father, and so forth). His relationship with his mother was often too ambivalent, and he coped with this by ignoring his mother every so often and by turning away from her. He was, for example, intent on sharing the pleasurable aspects of his life with people other than mother. We felt that this turning away from mother could, after all, be only a temporary solution and that the earlier separation struggle might well recur at a later time.[1]

Bruce's resourcefulness and inmate endowment helped him to adapt to the difficulties in the mother-child relationship. His liabilities, on the other hand, seemed to have derived at least in part from the conflicts inherent in that relationship, the need for turning away so early (18 to 19 months) from closeness with her, and his tendency to rely on his own resources to such a large extent by the chronological end of the rapprochement subphase.

[1] We happen to know that intense separation reactions did indeed occur, not immediately upon his entry to nursery school, but a few months later (see Speers et al. 1971; Speers, 1974).

Bruce's Third Year

At the beginning of his third year, Bruce was a serious little boy who was intent on what he was doing. Even though he sometimes seemed subdued, he was nevertheless always active and continuously busy and occupied. He loved the toddler room and was well adjusted to playing there. His attention span was considerable. Play seemed extremely important to him, not only as the symbolic (re)enactment of his own reality, but also as a vehicle through which he related to people. When he liked someone, he was not content only to be near that person, but he would also want to play with that person. As far as his mother was concerned, he wanted to play with her or to have her read to him.

Bruce's mood at the beginning of his third year seemed relatively unaffected by his mother's absence or presence. He did not pay much attention to her when she was in the toddler room. When she was not there and he seemed to show signs of needing her or thinking about her, he seemed to ward off this longing by quickly becoming involved in play.

Bruce was especially fond of being read to. In this way it seemed that he could be close to someone (sitting next to the person or in his or her lap) and at the same time exercise his continuously active cognitive interest in the world. His cognitive development was most promising; he became very interested in the sequence of things and events. He seemed to have a definite feeling for the time and rhythm of the morning in the playroom, with one activity following another (developing sense of time). He usually started out the day quietly, but as he became involved in activities, he gradually became more animated. Occasionally he was exuberant, engaging in lively play with the other children, including imitating noisy activity. He took pleasure in painting; he would often slap the paper with the brush or move the brush up and down vigorously in the paint pot, thereby expressing his active aggressive drive.

Bruce detected his penis in his tenth month and seemed to touch and handle it without conflict. In the third year, however, there were indications that he was beginning to be concerned about castration, and certainly he had some anal conflicts. Sometimes he sought closeness to mother when having a bowel movement, but at other times he resisted mother's interference, her handling his stool or changing his diapers. He showed interest in things being broken or having parts come off, and in things being fixed.

Play seemed to have had a reassuring quality for Bruce; it seemed to help him cope with what disturbed him. He liked to play with trains, especially to make the train go through a tunnel. In this way he apparently was able to work out his interest and concern about things coming and going, things and people disappearing and reappearing.

The following example shows how careful, psychoanalytically oriented observation of behavior and play sequences allows us to infer inner processes, in this case, concern about giving up of feces, about loss of parts of a whole object, about loss of body parts, and probably also concern about temporary loss and recovery of the love object—all symbolically acted out in play and expressed with words.

One morning, after having had a bowel movement in his diaper, Bruce looked for his mother. When he could not find her, he picked up a book on trains, his favorite book; he pointed to a picture and talked about the coal car, which happened not to be in this particular picture. He knew the train had a coal car, even though it was not shown. Similarly, he had just looked for his mother but could not find her. Also, he had moved his bowels, which he felt in his diaper, but which he could not see. Subsequently he found another book and looked at the picture of a family. He pointed to and named the father and the boy, but he did not name the girl and the mother who were also in the picture. Then he went to the toy mail box, pointed to the flap that had come off it, and then clearly enunciated: "doo-doo" (bowel movement). Subsequent to this he played with hollow blocks, putting a small one into a big one (quasi hiding it) and then putting them in order. Then he looked out the window, where he had often seen boys playing in the yard and said, "boy," even though nobody was in the play yard at this point. He called the observers' attention to all these parts that belong to a "syncretic whole," which at that moment, however, were missing or invisible. Thus, with his free associative sequence of words and actions, he disclosed his concern about missing part-objects or whole-objects, particularly the absent love object, his mother.

Bruce could not easily express his needs directly; he touched his mother while avoiding looking at her. Many signs indicated that both mother and child were trying to improve their relationship, but their attempts were tentative and feeble.

Bruce showed his need to be taken care of and his "identification with the active mother" by playing with the toy animals; he fed them play dough, imitating the way his mother fed his little sister, himself, and his father. He often played at cooking for daddy or played telephoning with him; he was also able to show his need for his mother more openly by seeking her out in the infant room.

In the early part of his third year, Bruce showed practically no signs of jealously toward his sister when he was with her; on the contrary, he seemed pleased to see her when she came into the toddler room. He also enjoyed playing with her when he went "visiting" into the infant room, where she usually was (she was less than 12 months old). He seemed almost eager to share his possessions with her. Instead of directly competing with his little sister, Bruce showed rivalry with his playmates. In the toddler room he insisted on the exclusive attention of the teacher, particularly when she was engaged with another child. If she was reading a book to him, for example, and then was temporarily called away to another child, Bruce would indirectly clamor for her return by pretending to read very loudly from the book that had been left with him. Although formerly he had been very generous with his playmates in the toddler room, he now refused to share. The inhibition of his aggression toward his sister had begun very early in his rapprochement subphase and seemed to have the structure of a true defense mechanism of repression (see Mahler & McDevitt, 1968). This inhibition of aggression eventually extended to the other children as well; whereas for a while he had been able to hold his own in struggles over possessions, he now passively let things be taken away from him.

Bruce's mother seemed on the whole to be pleased with her son at this juncture. In some areas of interaction, however, she still tended to treat him like a passive baby rather than as a growing little boy. We noted this particularly when she was diapering him: unlike other mothers of boys his age, she continued to put Bruce into the horizontal passive position rather than change his diaper while he was standing or at play.

We felt that Bruce's good autonomous ego functioning, as observed in his speech, his handling of objects, and his constructive goal-oriented activity, resulted from his very good innate endowment, as well as from his relationship to, and identification with, his father. Bruce looked forward to his father's return in the evening long before his usual homecoming time. After father came home, they spent much time together and father taught Bruce a lot. As mentioned before, the good relationship with the father seemed to have helped Bruce in his subsequent attainment of the second level of identity formation, that of gender identity (Mahler, 1958*b*; Stoller, 1973) (see also Chapter 6, p. 104). Mrs. A. continued to extricate herself from the bond with her son. Now, by her son's third year, she openly segregated maleness (or masculinity) from femaleness (or femininity): she said that Bruce and his father were both compulsive and intellectual, whereas she and her daughter were emotional.

To summarize, Bruce's rapprochement crisis had reached its peak during the second year at the time of the birth of his baby sister. He then went through a period of intense unhappiness and clinging. Subsequently, he seemed to "resolve" his rapprochement crisis by repressing his hostile feelings toward his little sister (disavowal) and by disregarding his mother's comings and goings (Mahler & McDevitt, 1968). He turned instead to other people—mainly to his father, but also to playmates and to observers at the Center—and to the pursuit of ego activities such as constructive and symbolic play. This was the picture we found at the beginning of Bruce's third year.

This somewhat precarious balance in Bruce's emotional life could not consistently hold under the impact of demands and inside pressures arising during the third year. In part, these pressures were psychosexual, having to do with increased awareness of the anatomical difference between the sexes and with the struggle over toilet training. Pressures came from another area as well—from the vicissitudes of the relationship between Bruce and his mother. Mrs. A. went back to work on a part-time basis as a teacher when Bruce was 27 months old. He begged her to stay home and cried when she left. The sitter reported that although after the mother's departure Bruce's crying did not last long, he would ask to take a nap (regression), something he rarely did otherwise. This behavior was reminiscent of the fact that Mrs. A. often had interpreted Bruce's bids for attention during the differentiation subphase (5 to 10 months of age) as signs of sleepiness and would then very deliberately put him to sleep.

In the months following her return to work, Mrs. A. reported that Bruce seemed ornery, unhappy, and often angry at home. She could do nothing to satisfy him; she felt provoked. She attributed this behavior to Bruce's dissatisfaction with himself over toilet training.[2] From the point of view of separation-individuation, Bruce's behavior seemed to have the character of the rapprochement subphase, when the child yearns at times for a return to the symbiotic phase. Of course, this is impossible to attain beyond the chronological age of symbiosis. The child now functions on a higher ego level. The very fact that he is able to yearn for "paradise lost," to form a wish, in Max Schur's sense (the ego filtered affect of longing [Mahler]) establishes him forever as a separate being.

His sibling situation added further distress to his fourth subphase of separation-individuation. In the beginning of his third year, his little sister grew into a toddler and began to walk; she came into the toddler

[2] Mrs. A. generally tended to underplay her importance to her son. Typically, she attributed his difficulties to toilet training, rather than to the fact that he had difficulty accepting her return to work.

room, as a toddler would, demanding and receiving a great deal of attention. Bruce was not happy about this and reacted to her presence by attempting to ignore her (denial), just as he had ignored his mother. Furthermore, as his sister began to leave mother as "home base" and began to prefer the toddler room, Bruce rushed to reoccupy the vacated "home base." He went to mother very directly, and both of them enjoyed affectionate interchange.

For Bruce, the teacher in the toddler room had always been clearly the most important person at the Center. But when his sister would come into the room, go directly to the teacher, and climb into her lap with the determined expectation of being accepted there, Bruce's reaction was to turn back to mother instead of competing with his sister for the teacher's favors. At the same time, Bruce's ability to avail himself of mother's vacated lap helped him to get additional libidinal supplies from her at that point, and this may have been a factor in helping him overcome the intense reactions to her return to work.

Between 32 and 33 months, Bruce had started to reconcile himself to the presence of his sister in the toddler room. On coming into the toddler room after arriving at the Center, he developed a most interesting and telling ritual; it had to do with showing his pride in whatever he was wearing, especially his pants. He indicated in no uncertain terms that he wanted the teacher to admire him before he would cross the threshold. This wish to be admired, especially for his clothes, for his pants, for his boyishness, seemed to fit in with his tendency to defend himself and his possessions in a more active phallic way and to hit back at other boys in his group when they were aggressive toward him. Still his main struggle was with anal conflicts. Under the impact of toilet training and castration anxieties, the rapprochement crisis became reactivated and culminated in temporary disturbances in object constancy, particularly in a peculiar confusion about his mother's whereabouts.

Bruce knew that at times his mother went downstairs to the basement to have coffee with the other mothers. At the time of his temporary confusion, Bruce might say, "I want to go down (to the basement) to see Mommy," even though he knew his mother was upstairs where he had just seen her a minute before. Another time he asked to see his mother in the infant room on a day when he knew his mother was not at the Center.

Still another observation of similar kind was made on one occasion when Bruce's mother asked him to go home with her and the baby, whom she was holding. A few minutes later, when he was ready to go home, Mrs. A. was not holding the baby in her arms anymore. Bruce looked bewildered because he still expected the baby to be there. He immediately began a frantic search for his sister as if he feared that she had vanished. His bewilderment in regard to her whereabouts shows clearly that it was Bruce's aggressive feelings and fantasies that were responsible for his temporary disturbance of orientation. Bruce usually succeeded in denying and, we felt, even in repressing his aggression.

An inordinate vacillation ensued: at times Bruce ignored his mother, and at other times he was not ready to separate from her at all. He also reacted in unpredictable ways to his play session observer. At times he seemed to feel very close to her, to have a good time with her, and to look forward to her playing with him. At other times he would suddenly behave as if he did not know her at all.

By the age of 33 months, Bruce developed a tendency to hold on to what he coveted. The way he held on to certain possessions, things that clearly had symbolic meaning, allowed us to infer that he was preoccupied with holding onto his bowel movements, which in turn was connected with castration anxiety. Bruce liked to poke holes in the play dough, then cover them up, and say with great relief: "Hole all gone." He became particularly attached to certain toys or objects, which at least for that period of time became treasured possessions. He carried these with him everywhere and would not let anyone take them away from him. He was particularly interested in opening and closing the closets of the doll house, in putting things inside them and taking them out again. Bruce was very reluctant to go to the bathroom, thus following his pattern of avoiding situations that were anxiety producing. He seemed to be undergoing a partly internalized struggle as far as toileting was concerned. He would tell his mother only after he had wet or soiled his diaper and then would insist on being changed. One morning after Mrs. A. brought Bruce to the Center, she reported that he had neither urinated nor defecated since the evening before. Bruce appeared to be straining; he seemed preoccupied and unresponsive. Finally, he had a bowel movement, and after mother changed his diaper, he was smiling, free, and sociable.

Following this episode, Bruce had his bowel movements in the toilet at his own request for one weekend at home. But he once again returned to diapers and for a short while still insisted upon having his diapers changed. Then repeatedly he had a bowel movement in his diaper, but denied that it was there, although he walked stiffly all morning. When his mother wanted to change his diaper, he objected strenuously, although he did not physically struggle with her. (Observers were repeatedly struck by Bruce's passive demeanor when his mother picked him up.) For the rest of the month, Bruce did not want to have his diapers changed after wetting or soiling. It seems that at this point his conflict between passivity and activity became partly internalized. This conflict around toilet training was brought about by two factors: (1) Bruce did not get sufficient approval from his mother in toilet training, and (2) his mother handled his body rather roughly, thus reinforcing Bruce's general fear of being handled by her.

There was indication in Bruce's play that his interest in the appearance and disappearance of objects was at least in part determined by his concern over the loss of body parts. This seemed to be a combination of castration anxiety and concern over loss of the feces. Toward the end of the third year, Bruce still would not go to the bathroom and was not toilet trained. Although he was generally fairly tolerant of other children and was willing to share with them, there was one occasion when he was quite passionately determined not to share three boxes of crayons. He needed to have them all: he would take them out of the boxes, put them back in, and eventually put them all inside the milk truck. When all the crayons were in the milk truck, Bruce said, "All gone." Then he opened the door to reassure himself that they were still there.

One play sequence was of special interest. The play session observer offered to make something for Bruce out of play dough. He wanted her to make a zebra. When she asked what a zebra was, he said first that it had a tail, then that it had an udder, and eventually that it had stripes. He pretended and acted out that the zebra would bite her; then he comforted her by holding her hand inside his armpit. Here he acted out in play the conflicting feelings of wanting to hurt, maybe wanting to get rid of, and then wanting to be close and hold on. The play seemed to encompass two aspects of oral activity, biting (oral aggression) and incorporation (which served in part to soothe and to comfort).

In spite of his intense conflicts, and the occasional conspicuous uncertainties in regard to object permanence, *toward the end of the third year* Bruce definitely seemed to have entered the phallic phase. This attainment was, however, very precarious. Whereas he became much more assertive and much more active, he no longer was able to play as consistently and constructively with toys as he had in the past. He tended to throw things around and to become very excited. Formerly, he had an outstandingly long attention span, which was not true during this period. The new features in his play and other behavior seemed now clearly connected with the fact that play would often touch on painful, partly internalized conflicts. As soon as his play activities stirred up those conflicts, he seemed to abandon the activity; for instance, he did not like to be reminded of the "mommy-baby" situation, nor did he like to face the fact that something could be broken. The avoidance of the painful situation was very similar to Bruce's earlier avoidance of quarrelsome (conflictual) external situations with mother.

Although in certain ways Bruce was more assertive, he still avoided situations in which he would have to ask for attention, for fear that he would not receive it. He would then tend to ask for it in indirect ways. For example, when his observer came into the room he appeared to want to play with her; but instead of asking to play or going up to her, he would go out of the room looking back to see if she would follow him. This seemed to be an attenuated form on a higher symbolic level of the darting-away behavior of the rapprochement subphase described in Chapter 6.

One area in which Bruce definitely was more assertive by the second half of the third year was in defending his possessions when somebody else threatened to take them away. Bruce's phallic elation, which manifested itself at times in hyperactivity, seemed in part a genuine delight with his growing capacities, with an admixture of phallic excitement. Often he was outgoing and happy. He was apt to be the leader in play. He expressed himself quite precisely and seemd to enjoy words and verbal communication. It was said that he was outstanding in his awareness of his world and in his emotional participation in what he observed. At other times, though, his elated hyperactivity seemed more clearly defensive.

At the end of the third year, when Bruce was enrolled in nursery school, we were rather optimistic about his developmental potential and felt that there was a real basis for the development of his autonomy and his relation to objects, human and otherwise. We were somewhat apprehensive, however, about possible depressive potentialities and passivity.

CHAPTER 9

Donna

IN SPITE of a well-attuned symbiotic period and "perfect" mothering, Donna did not have an easy time during the separation-individuation process. Though her mother's capacities seemed to grow with the child's changing developmental needs, Donna developed earlier and greater than average separation anxiety. She gradually seemed to lose confidence in her own resources and in the "non-mother" outside world. Up to the age of about 14 months, she was in all respects the most competent of the babies in our study and functioned quite well in routine separations from her mother. However, despite the fact that she had developed adequate cognitive object constancy at an earlier age than most babies, she found the process of leave-taking from mother quite painful.

Donna's Mother

For a long time all the observers of the project considered Mrs. D. the perfect mother. The babies at the Center also picked her as a favorite mother substitute. Only in retrospect did we realize that, unlike most of the other mothers who during the period of first active distancing by the infant reacted by giving a "gentle push" to the fledgling, Donna's mother did not. Without any gentle encouragement to distance herself, Donna most probably sensed her mothers' unconscious doubt that Donna could manage alone. This definitely seemed to have contributed to a feeling of greater than usual early dependency on mother's approval and disapproval (very early superego precursors).

Donna's Subphase Development

Donna was a planned baby and both parents had wished for a girl. Mother felt comfortable with her from the beginning and breast-fed her for 2 months. At 4 to 5 months, at the height of symbiosis, Donna's mood of calm and quiet contentment was consistent. Mother and child were well attuned to each other and were matched in temperament, both being calm and somewhat serious. Donna's excellent innate endowment was observed in the way she amused herself in the playpen by babbling and studying other-than-mother people. Comparative scanning had its inception in Donna's fifth month as well. She showed her specific attachment to mother by smiling at her more often than at others. When she was tired, her energies were quickly restored by sitting on mother's lap for a short period. By contrast, when held by an observer, she seemed to become more sober. While she had this mild stranger reaction on occasion, she generally did not seem to mind being held by the observer and would "examine" the latter's chin, mouth and nose. Difficulty in falling asleep was noted at 5 to 6 months of age, and very early food fads were reported as well. Donna crawled early, and she used this skill to crawl away from mother and explore the environment. Unlike most of the other children, at the beginnings of differentiation, Donna showed no overwhelming excitement or enjoyment: there were no ups and downs in her mood; she was typically even-tempered.

In the Reduction of Data for the 7- to 8-month period, there was a comment that Donna was the kind of baby who did not make a big fuss over something she wanted. Perhaps there was a relationship between this and her mother's need for only minimal cues from Donna. Perhaps Donna did not have to be insistent or demanding to get what she wanted. Already from 6 months on, a dawning awareness of separateness was observed in Donna's behavior. She displayed mild stranger reaction!

In her seventh month, Donna used her emerging ability to crawl not only for the pleasure of the activity, but also to reach toys and to distance herself from mother. By the eighth month Donna's early stranger reaction diminished, and father and brother, as well as a boy her own age at the Center, occupied Donna's preferential interest. Low-keyedness became quite marked when mother was out of the room, and there were mild indications that in mother's absence she did not function as well. At reunion with mother she was exuberant. Mother was definitely the center from which Donna increasingly radiated out.

Around this time, Donna was interested in her mirror image and would touch it. At around 8 months, she still had difficulty going to sleep. Her mother connected this with father's returning home in the evening and Donna's wanting to play with him. Her finicky eating habits continued. Her stranger reactions were greater than in the previous months, and they were different in quality: when held by the "other-than-mother," she looked down at the floor, avoiding the person's face. Even when she was in mother's lap, "other-than-mother" persons seemed threatening to her if they came close.

When Donna was around 9 to 10 months old, the family took a trip to the country, where Donna was handled by many people. Subsequently, at the Center, Donna had intense separation reactions. When mother was out of the room, Donna frequently looked at the door and searched the room with her eyes. She was upset by reminders of mother, for instance when she saw someone other than mother coming through the door, when she saw her own mirror reflection without her mother, or when she found someone else sitting in mother's chair.[1] Looking in the face of observers produced a kind of stranger reaction in her, and when mother returned to the room, Donna would periodically look at her face, as if to reassure herself. Along with these early separation reactions, Donna also appeared precocious in her mirroring identification with her mother, both gesturally and mimetically.

In this 9 to 10 month period of early practicing, except for her separation reactions, Donna played happily and independently away from mother. Donna and mother were still always aware of each other, even when Donna pursued activities at a distance.[2] Every so often, Donna would go back to mother for brief emotional refueling.

Donna was sensitive to her mother's interference with her first attempts at autonomous functioning. She cried when her mother prevented her from going through the open doorway.

Donna learned to walk at 11½ months of age, during summer vacation. Though not fearful, she (unlike most of the other children) was cautious in her motor activities. Following summer vacation, Donna seemed at the peak of the practicing period's obligatory love affair with the world. She was fairly oblivious of mother and friendly with observers. Mrs. D. said, "She loves everyone and everything. She wants to embrace the whole world." At this time, even though she did not like her mother

[1] In actuality and in her mental image, she and mother seemed to belong syncretically together. This seemed to be a *sine qua non* for Donna to experience the "ideal state of self."

[2] The senior author called such intangible mutual attunement between an infant-toddler and his mother (even when separate in space) the "invisible umbilical cord."

leaving the room, she could cope with her absence by turning to motor activity, toys, and other people.

Donna's cognitive progress was characterized as follows under "Newly emerging ego functions" (the second of the nine "orienting questions"; see Appendix C, p. 262): "She continues to learn by imitation of the gesture, and her sensorimotor intelligence progresses. She begins to connect words with feeling states, objects, and actions [Spitz's "global words"]. Two months later, Donna began using these global words in the service of communication.

In her thirteenth and fourteenth months, however, Donna's widening activities led to greater frustration and the beginning of anger. According to her mother, when she couldn't get what she wanted, she would scream in anger. Once when Donna could not get a toy from a boy of her approximate age at the Center, she began angrily kicking her feet in the air, though still smiling. On another occasion, she butted her head against a little girl's chest and took toys away from her. She intentionally pushed another little boy aside, even though her expression did not clearly indicate anger; rather she seemed to be clowning. She tapped a little girl on the head with a wooden hammer and then seemed concerned and confused when this 15-month-old child started to cry; Donna backed away and started to mouth her fingers. Donna would appropriate a toy from another child rather matter-of-factly, but seemed upset when the child cried. On one occasion she knocked a little girl down. Mrs. D. stated that Donna got mad if frustrated, particularly when she wanted to go outdoors. In addition, if the mother spoke to Donna in an angry or scolding manner, her feelings would immediately be hurt and she might cry and look unhappy. One of the observers felt that Mrs. D. was a little slow in restraining Donna from hurting other children. Mrs. D. connected much of this kind of behavior to Donna's roughhousing play at home with her brother. The participant-observer assigned to this mother-infant pair had the impression that the mother rarely opposed Donna, was extremely patient, and that, as a result, there was rarely a direct confrontation between the two.

In her fourteenth to fifteenth month, Donna was described as a highly alert child who was more active than any of her peers and very involved in locomotion, especially climbing. When angry, she reacted with more focused and directed expressions of anger than before. She was also described as being more consistently happy and exuberant, more self-reliant, independent, and confident than ever before. She was the most self-assertive of her peers, always knowing what she wanted.

It seemed at 14 to 15 months, Donna recognized her mirror reflection as herself. She made clear progress in differentiating self-representation, and thus seemed to be aware of her separateness rather early.

Around the same age, interaction with mother changed to sharing pleasurable activities, an indication of the beginning of the rapprochement subphase.[3] Donna began to react to mother's leaving the room by crying almost immediately, but she could still be rather easily distracted. However, soon she began anxiously to anticipate mother's leaving. At this point she tried to cope with her separation anxiety by *actively practicing separations*. She would say "bye-bye" frequently and would go to the playpen. However, when mother left the room, Donna would quickly run to the door and cry. Now it was no longer as easy to distract Donna, and she became generally intolerant of frustration. Her way of coping with mother's absences was to want to go out the door also; being allowed to go out seemed to relieve her distress. Along with reports of rivalry, jealousy, and increase of *aggression* in Donna, there were for the first time reports that Donna had certain fears; the noise of the vacuum cleaner, Halloween masks, monsters, and television frightened her.[4]

When Donna was about 16 months old, her rapprochement crisis started: as she became increasingly aware of mother as separate, she wished increasingly to be close to her. She did not like to see her mother paying attention to other children. When mother sat close to a baby, Donna took the pacifier away from the baby and put it into her own mouth. She climbed onto mother's lap or buried her face in mother's skirts. Donna at this time also became more conspicuously jealous of her older brother and wanted everything he had. She was persistent in getting what she wanted. When mother went out for an interview, Donna would fuss and go to the door crying. Beginning use of the word "no" by Donna was reported and heard rather frequently. Sometimes she could be distracted by play, especially ball play. However, when she was picked up by an observer she collapsed and cried until she saw her mother. At this time, in the midst of the rapprochement turmoil, she also seemed to become aware of the sexual difference. She would pull up her skirt and look at her protruding abdomen. She would touch her

[3] One participant observed considerable anger and unusually complex jealousy reactions in Donna at that age. This is important and ought not to be glossed over. Between 14 and 15 months of age, Donna was the most aggressive and provocative of all the children.

[4] Between 14 and 15 months of age there is mention of Donna's provocative darting away from mother at the playground, but that activity is said to have lessened by 16 months.

genitals when her diaper was changed. She noticed now when she was wet, and she did not like it. We also learned from her mother that Donna "looked" at her older brother's penis when the two children were bathed together.

From about 16 to 18 months, Donna seemed to have a temporary resolution of her rapprochement crisis by way of identification with her mother. She began to play mother to dolls and babies. She now sought out her mother relatively little, and when she did, it was usually not for comfort but rather for brief contact, to play a game or to share an experience or feeling. She freely left the infant room. She was quite happy, interacted animatedly with all the observers, and was very interested in the other children. She functioned well when mother was out for an interview, comforting herself by drinking juice. She demonstrated her *precocious cognitive-affective ego development* by being the only child her age who identified persons in photographs; she could identify herself, her mother, and the other children at the Center. She also knew the names of all the other children. She displayed excellent frustration tolerance at this age, aided by her identification with mother.

Those seeming solutions of the rapprochement struggle are more often than not only temporary. The rapprochement crisis, in Donna's case, for example, reappeared within a month. At 18 months of age Donna again showed much more concern about mother's whereabouts and greater fear of the strange; in addition, she displayed increased possessiveness. Whereas Donna had gone to the toddler room freely for quite a while (from the time she could walk by herself), she now would not go there unless mother went with her. She also avoided closeness to the other children and was very distressed when her mother left the room. She was again very possessive of her mother and did not want to share her with anyone. Donna cried easily when scolded. She developed at this point a great fear of loud noises, such as the rumbling of passing trucks and drilling on the streets.

This rapid change in Donna's affect and behavior was triggered by an illness requiring a penicillin injection which her mother could not prevent. This shook Donna's belief in her mother's omnipotence and caused a wavering of her belief in mother's magic powers. Once when she woke up during the night while she was ill, she repelled her mother, did not allow her to comfort her, but insisted that her father come instead.

Donna now seemed to be quite torn between the wish for independent autonomous functioning and her need to be ever close to mother. She needed to know constantly where her mother was. During her play at home, she would often call out "Mommy." Even though mother would answer from another room, this did not suffice; she would have to go and see her mother before she could return to her play.

Likewise, whereas at times Donna would venture away from mother into the toddler room, the slightest frustration there would make her return to mother. She was observed to be very possessive in the toddler room, and was the child who used the words "I," "me," and "mine" most often, as early as 19 months of age.

It was reported that Donna was quite negativistic and stubborn. She would insist on doing things for herself, and she resisted being dressed, having her diapers changed, or being put to bed. (She was in the midst of the anal phase.) Donna's clinging behavior, however, alternated with more independent, assertive, and adventurous behavior.[5]

Around the beginning of her twenty-first month, Donna had minor surgery on her scalp. During the procedure she was wrapped in a sheet and held on a table by three nurses. She cried bitterly the entire time. After returning home she seemed quite cheerful, but she didn't want to look at herself in the mirror on the following day because she was wearing a bandage on her head. She connected a box of bubble bath, which had been given to her as a gift at that time, with the surgical procedure, and refused to be bathed.

Two weeks after Donna's operation, Donna's brother had to be taken to the hospital for a tonsillectomy. Mother stayed overnight in the hospital with him. This was the first time in Donna's life that her mother had been away from her overnight.

The penicillin shot, the operation, and the brother's tonsillectomy, with mother's absence from the house overnight, were accumulated traumata that occurred precisely at that vulnerable period of rapprochement, when internalization processes are at their height. Thus we could see in Donna's case with particular clarity how the rapprochement crisis is made more poignant by the coming together of the three main anxieties of childhood: namely, fear of abandonment (fear of object loss), fear of loss of love, and, in particular, castration anxiety.

During the remaining months of her second year, Donna continued to show what we would consider somewhat exaggerated rapprochement behavior. She continued to need to be physically close to her mother.

[5] When Donna was between 20 and 21 months of age, Mrs. D. woefully said: "She is no longer my little baby," and followed her protectively into the toddler room, not leaving her to her own devices. We noted in retrospect that this overprotection contributed to the development of a greater than average ambivalence toward mother on Donna's part.

She seemed to find it difficult to leave mother, to engage in activities on her own. After a period of separation she would seek contact with mother on a regressed level, she needed to *touch* and *feel* her mother; seeing her and knowing where mother was would not suffice.

Donna's *great ambivalence* toward her mother was demonstrated by the fact that when she was with her mother she was often most demanding and *coercive*. Even though she was described as *generally* cheerful, happy and even-tempered, she could whine and fuss at the slightest frustration. During this period Donna, who had always been a cautious child, became even more cautious and was reluctant to try new motor activities, especially those that would have caused self-stimulation, such as riding a rocking horse. She had many small fears and apprehensions, and she reacted quite negatively to attempts at toilet training. In short, at the end of the second year, Donna's rapprochement crisis was by no means resolved.

The evaluation of Donna's subphase development presented us with a puzzle. Here was a well-endowed child with a mother who was both willing and ready to respond to her every cue. Yet already during the practicing subphase Donna developed separation reactions just a bit stronger than those of the other children, as well as some reluctance to enjoy fully her early locomotor functioning, caused perhaps by her greater than average fear of object loss. Though this was not extreme in her case, it seemed just enough to establish a characteristic pattern, a behavior in Donna which clearly indicated that she felt that she could not manage without her mother, even though, or perhaps because, her mother was ever ready and ever available to her.

The accumulation of traumata Donna experienced, coupled with the early pattern of needing mother close by, her exposure to her older brother's anatomy in the closeness of the bathtub, and their roughhousing mutual overstimulation seemed to make it impossible for Donna to come to a solution of her rapprochement crisis. Interestingly, Donna's separation anxiety was greatest during the process of *leave-taking itself*. Once her mother had left her in the toddler room, she could function very well, better than when her mother was present. She then seemed to "forget" temporarily her need for mother as she became involved in age-adequate play with the other toddlers; she then appeared again to be one of the most excellently endowed children, one of those who took great pleasure in autonomous functioning.

Donna's Third Year

At the beginning of the third year, Donna seemed to be a generally even-tempered child with an expressive face. At times she was rather subdued but at other times she would become exuberant and would run around with abandon. She did, however, show a degree of fearfulness about certain gross motor activities, such as climbing. Donna was definitely sociable, engaged adults, and showed added pleasure in her activities when she received attention and encouragement from an adult. She preferred to play with people rather than by herself. It was noted that she was assertive and would push aside anyone who got in her way.

Two central themes emerged. The first involved her *clinging to her mother*. This was seen earlier and now again from 24 to 25 months on. Each day when she arrived at the Center, she clung to her mother and would not respond to any efforts to engage her in play. Each day it took a while (up to a whole hour) for Donna to disengage herself from mother. Once Donna's mother had left the room, however, Donna usually became involved in play activities, and although she would ask for mother occasionally, she was readily reassured by an explanation of where her mother was.

The other theme that emerged early during the third year had to do with Donna's *reaction to the sexual difference and preoccupation with toileting*. One day she put the mother and girl dolls on the toilet, rejecting at the same time the father and the boy dolls. When the boys in the toddler room left to go to the bathroom, Donna raised her skirt, pointed to her genitals, and said, "Momma." She then left the room herself and began to look for the "real mother." When she did not find her, she joined the children in the bathroom. When she saw one of the boys pulling up his pants, she said, "No," and again went to look for her mother, whom she eventually found in the baby room. She stayed only briefly with her mother, however, and soon started to play with the toys in the baby room. She arranged toys in patterns, put rings on pegs, played with hollow blocks; it seemed that the play with these more structured and symbolic, even though more babylike toys, helped Donna to master her feelings of anxiety. We felt that these feelings concerned to a great extent castration anxiety.

During the early months of her third year, Donna seemed to vacillate between a feminine and a masculine image of herself. This seemed to run parallel with denial of anatomical differences; that is, she would avoid looking at one of the boys who was running around without pants on, or she would say, after seeing a boy urinate, that *he* was a girl. Donna was particularly excited when one of the boys chased her with a paintbrush. In her play activities, Donna alternated between being feminine and charming or boisterous and aggressive. In her doll play she gave all the dolls the name of her older brother.

There was also fantasy play concerning a little girl in bed with daddy. Her mother sensed a new feminine quality in Donna's relationship to her father, although according to mother, Donna showed no rivalry with, or jealousy of, her mother.

In order to understand the unexpected difficult, vacillating, and problem-laden course of Donna's third-year development, it is essential to recognize the important role played by penis envy and concern about her genitals. This was inferred from behavioral as well as from verbal material, mostly during play sessions.

Donna had a urinary infection, which occurred in her twenty-eighth month. She experienced discomfort in the genital area and was examined by an unfamiliar woman doctor, her regular male doctor being out of town. This experience increased Donna's castration anxiety, and from then on, she openly expressed fear that she might hurt herself, for example, when she climbed. She could not easily say how and where she might hurt herself, but she finally indicated it by sitting on one of her hands while touching her genitals with the other hand.

There was at this time, around 28 months, also a change in Donna's toilet behavior. Donna had become toilet trained during the preceding month (between 26 and 27 months of age) and usually managed entirely by herself. When she urinated in the toilet at the Center she was proud. Now following the trauma of the urinary infection and the examination by the strange doctor, during which she had to lie on a table without mother holding her, she required help in being toileted, and she most strikingly avoided looking at herself or at her urine for quite a while. She obviously avoided the painful memories connected with the urinary infection, but she complained about her "hurt," pointing to her genital region.

A variety of material came from Donna's mother, as well as from Donna herself, relating to castration fears, to concern with the primal scene, and to fantasies of being a boy. In one of her play sessions, Donna said that she had hurt her knee, and pointed to her genitals. She also complained to her male participant observer that she had hurt her knee in the park, giving a very essential association by volunteering the statement that *it was her mother who had pushed her down*, thus clearly blaming mother for her "hurt."

At this time, Donna liked to build tall structures and then break them down. She also liked to watch other children in the bathroom, although she herself could not talk about or use the toilet at the Center. Her mother reported that while Donna occasionally used the potty chair at home, for the most part she would not (a further regression in toilet training).

Following the urinary infection, Donna began to cling to her mother more vehemently each day when they first arrived at the Center. She often cried bitterly when her mother left. Yet Donna did not follow her mother, even when the teacher offered to take her there. She actually seemed relieved by her mother's leaving; she seemed to be torn between her desire to cling to mother and her desire to function independently. Thus we could see internalization of a conflict before our eyes. Donna seemed to utilize all her resources to enable herself to make the break away from mother each day. Her mood during the period of clinging was whiny, constrained, and apprehensive, and she was described as being frequently angry at her mother. It seemed that mother was no longer the all-giving figure in Donna's eyes that she once had been. This resulted in great ambivalence toward the mother, and some splitting of the object world.

In the second half of the third year, in spite of Donna's florid castration fears and partly internalized conflicts, she began to venture into activities that she had previously feared: she went on the rocking horse, even though briefly and fearfully at first. She also began to climb readily on the large wooden blocks, an activity which she had previously been afraid to do. At the same time, however, Donna became more vulnerable and afraid of the other children's aggression.

It is of interest that in spite of this, Donna turned very actively to boys rather than to girls as playmates. She liked playing with Charlie, who bossed her much as her own brother did at home. She followed another boy in the group like a shadow; he was her favorite boy playmate. She was observed to have been quite desperate when the mother of her little "boy friend" once refused to take her along to their house, which she often visited. One of the observers remarked that Donna behaved at this point as though she expected to be able to acquire her little boy playmate's penis by closeness to him (as though by a kind of osmosis). Whether these were preliminary signs of the little girl's acceptance of her masochistically tinged gender identity, we do not know.

Donna

Certainly not unrelated to the great ambivalence described above, Donna's difficulties in entering the activities of the toddler room continued. At the beginning of the morning before becoming involved in activity, she frequently had her finger in her mouth biting and exploring her mouth. When she eventually did become involved in play activity, it was frequently doll play, usually feeding the dolls. Mother remained very patient with Donna, occasionally making efforts to involve her in activities, but at other times just waiting for Donna to move away on her own. Conditions in the toddler room also influenced Donna's need to cling to, or her readiness to separate from, mother. If there was more than usual activity there, she was apt to cling to mother more tenaciously and for a longer time.

Donna used certain behaviors to ward off anxiety. For example, she frequently showed off with certain tricks what she could do with her body. She had learned some of these tricks from her brother, some from her father; others were apparently her own inventions. These seemed to be an effort to reassure herself that her body was all right (it could even do tricks). After showing a trick she had learned from her father, she looked at her arms and said, "They are baby arms." She had a doll which she insisted was neither a boy nor a girl, but just a baby. Apparently for Donna the baby had still the potentiality to become a boy. Mother reported that when Donna was in distress, she referred to herself as a baby, whereas when she was in a good mood, she said she was a girl.

The following play sequence illustrates how dangerous the world may become when the formerly trusted symbiotic mother becomes threatening after full awareness of separateness. Donna was painting a "lion." She then painted a small spot which she said the lion bit off the mommy lion (penis bitten off by the lion?). She seemed to cope with a confusion in her fantasy life, wondering whether mother had "it" and kept it from her or perhaps was castrated as well.

Donna felt her lack of a penis as a narcissistic wound for which she blamed her mother; her main defense was regression, clinging to the symbiotic mother like a baby, and sucking her fingers at the same time. Actually her mother comforted Donna as one would a baby, by holding her in her arms. She thus appeased the aggression in the relationship, but caused Donna to inhibit, that is, to hold in and repress her aggressive impulses. Father seemed to become an increasingly important figure for Donna. While she sometimes resisted mother, she would go along with father in getting ready for bed. Once when the parents were about to go out for the evening. Donna kissed her father goodbye, but not her mother. Her favorite activity at this time was to sit in father's lap while he rocked in the rocking chair. During a home visit Donna was very pleased as she showed the observer the toys that Daddy had *fixed* for her.

While listening to a story about trains, Donna slapped her hand on the picture of a train excitedly, holding the other hand over her genital area and rocked back and forth. Then she slapped at the picture and put her hand to her mouth and pretended to gobble up the train. This may have represented an effort to undo her castrated condition by pretending to eat the train, the favorite toy of her little boy playmate whose penis she coveted so much.

One particular day around the age of 2½, Donna was in a happy mood when she came to the Center; she was able to leave her mother and go straight to the toddler room without any need to cling. This followed a visit to the zoo during which, for the first time, Donna was able to drink through a straw as her brother did. She was very proud of this accomplishment, and it may have been the key to her good mood.

In this second half of the third year Donna often imitated the play of boys as one attempted solution to her penis envy. She became freer in her gross motor activities. She started to ride the rocking horse, went up and down the stairs, and got particular pleasure from sliding down the slanted board on her stomach. It seems that this kind of activity provided her with sensual pleasure and reassured her that her body was intact.

Mother reported that at home Donna liked to go about without her pants on and that she frequently touched her genitals, saying that they hurt. Mother thought that there was no longer any physical discomfort, that the urinary infection was gone, and that Donna's complaints reflected rather her concern about this part of her body.

Donna's relationship with boys and men took on a more openly pleading character. She wanted her father to do things for her, such as dress her. At the Center, when she went to the bathroom accompanied by a male observer, she insisted that he give her much help in toileting and spread her legs apart to show him what she had made as well as to expose her "castrated" state. She also attempted to imitate her father and brother urinating. While playing, she straddled the incline board, pushed a truck up it, and then let it slide down between her legs. She verbalized that though she did not have a penis yet, she was sure that one would still grow for her.

At the same time Donna was very much interested in mothers and babies, and when she saw a picture of a large and a small airplane she described them as a mother plane and a baby plane. She seemed to shift from being the baby to identifying with mother by mothering dolls, cooking, and so on. Her manner was often described as mature, and at such times she would be officious in her dealings with other children, including her brother.

There was a change in Donna's attitude toward toilet accidents and night wetting. She became upset and cried when she wet herself on the way to the bathroom, whereas previously she had calmly accepted such accidents. In the past she often woke at night and called her mother to take her to the bathroom, but she started to do so less frequently now and remained dry at night. Sometimes she would awake during the night crying and upset, saying that she had to "pee-pee." While there was no indication that any pressure was ever put on Donna regarding toilet training, she now seemed afraid that she would wet her bed (precursors of superego development?).

Donna continued to show her concerns about harm to her body in many ways. She displaced anxiety to a large extent to her nose and, as described earlier, to her knees. Donna's mother described the following incident. Donna had had a nosebleed. She became unduly alarmed, cried excessively, and wiped some blood off on her knee; she seemed extremely frightened. Later when she told her father about it, she forgot to mention the bloody nose and told him she had hurt her knee. Once before, she had blamed her mother for allegedly pushing her down, causing her to hurt her *knee*.

By the end of the third year, Donna still fluctuated between rather mature independent behavior in many areas and behaviors in which she clung to her babyhood. Her maturity showed itself in her identification with mother: in her mothering behavior toward dolls, in her toileting herself without help (even when she was away from home), in her wanting to choose her own clothes, and so forth. But she still drank milk from the bottle, and her initial reaction to any strange or anxiety-arousing situation was to cling to her mother, pull at her clothes, or take food into her mouth. Her mother, who had always been so patient and accepting of Donna, now began to show some negative reactions; she expressed impatience and irritation with Donna's clinging behavior.

Donna, sensing her mother's growing impatience both with her difficulties in leave-taking and with her growing independence, seemed to seek new solutions on her own. At times, she rushed into the toddler room as if wishing not to give herself enough time to hesitate and let anxiety overcome her. Eventually, she arrived at a new solution: she found a ritual of leave-taking which made it easier for her to make the transition from being with mother to functioning without her. She stayed near mother for a while, while showing an observer whatever she had brought from home. She went into minute details, sometimes about a number of things, connecting the here and now with something familiar, and then she was able to let mother go (we are reminded of Bruce's similar behavior).

As a result of her superior endowment and what seemed to be superior mothering, we thought Donna was the infant and junior toddler who had the greatest chance for smooth subphase development. We expected that with the relatively even evolution of her ego and this most favorable nurturing, she would reach libidinal object constancy by the third year. We also expected that the two levels of identity formation would gradually be reached in the fourth subphase of separation-individuation with minimal developmental difficulties.

That this was not the case made us keenly aware of the intricacy and the variability of middle-range "normal development." It made us realize in particular that prediction in the realm of "normal development" is impossible beyond the statement that in all probability major pathology in the future will be precluded.

The developmental difficulties that ensued in Donna's case seemed precisely due to the lack of gradualness with which her belief in her own magical omnipotence, fed by more than optimal reliance on her mother's omnipotence, was replaced by self-esteem.

Most importantly, however, the difficulties resulted from the accumulation of "shock traumata" (Kris, 1956) between the twentieth and thirtieth month, which seemed to have prevented the gradual neutralization of aggression. Abrupt repression became necessary, which had to be reinforced by the additional defense mechanism of reaction formation. Greater than average separation anxiety and inhibition ensued and made sublimation at least temporarily difficult. However, we were confident that, despite the difficulties, through the flux of developmental energy Donna would eventually overcome these disturbances.

CHAPTER 10

Wendy

IN Wendy we saw a particularly attractive, cuddly, well-molding, generally placid and happy baby, passionately loved by her mother as her symbiotic fulfillment. Mother and infant appeared to be particularly well-attuned to each other. It is puzzling that with that kind of blissful symbiosis, Wendy showed very early signs of quasi-differentiation, which consisted of very sudden fretful crying, intensive scanning and apparent recognition of different people, and protesting mother's leave-taking. We feel in retrospect that her hyperalertness during her third and fourth months was due to a degree of hypersensitivity in Bergman and Escalona's sense (1949). She developed a very early preferential smiling response and even initiated smiles to her mother by the age of 3 to 4 months. She cried if her mother passed by without stopping to interact with her. Instead of "enjoying" premature abandonment in the symbiotic dual unity's orbit, Wendy surprised us with her early scanning of the environment. Her hyperalertness to the surroundings beyond the mother-child common orbit was due to her innate hypersensitivity. Along with the early signs of differentiation, Wendy did not seem to take advantage of the maturational growth of her own ego or of the resources of her environment. Because of her hyperalertness, we feel in retrospect that, more than the average infant, Wendy would have needed a particularly strong, protective shield of mothering for a protracted period during her earliest infancy. This might have prevented her heightened perceptions from impinging upon the "ideal sense" of symbiotic oneness. For as much as Mrs. M. enjoyed and loved Wendy as her baby, she was not able to compensate with a *protracted* protective shield of mothering. Probably no mother could. Wendy's early reactions to abruptness and sudden changes in her environment—forerunners at 3 months of later "strangeness reactions"—continued practically without interruption throughout the separation-individuation process; they changed only in form, structure, and complexity in the course of the subphases.

Wendy's Mother

On the mother's part there were components that reinforced Wendy's tendency not to use her own resources, and even less the resources of her environment, for the purpose of differentiation and individuation, or separation from mother. During and after the short symbiotic period, Mrs. M. was very emotionally involved with this, her third, child. However, at the first tentative signs of differentiation on Wendy's part, she developed a tendency to disengage herself abruptly; she could not allow her child actively to explore her face in a tactile—in addition to a close visual—way, when Wendy wanted and needed to do so. As early as 3 to 4 months, Wendy vocalized and protested with an angry voice.

Wendy's mother was a particularly beautiful woman who did not take to motherhood easily. She was insecure about herself as a mother and as a woman, and she needed to prove herself at all times. She was always busy improving herself and her home, but she always felt that she was not doing enough. She readily disparaged herself; she described herself as a bad mother, and emphasized that her children preferred their father, who gladly shared mothering functions with his wife. Mrs. M., who was so easily discouraged and impatient with her own self, tended to be the same way with her children as soon as they showed any sign of differentiation and individuation. She saw herself in them and saw them in herself. We noted that she would talk to Wendy's older sister, not more than 30 months old, as if she were an adult; she seemed to "consult" her in making decisions. This she did not to find out what the child really wanted, but because she was unable to make up her mind herself. Her children's growing-up process was threatening and uncomfortable to her. It seemed to confront her with her own problems about aging and about those sides of her own personality that she considered negative.

Once the symbiotic period had ended, Mrs. M. was characteristically less comfortable with her children. She was unable to enjoy the playfulness of the individuating child and her relationship did not grow into playful mutuality.

Wendy's Subphase Development

Wendy was breast-fed and very gradually weaned in her fourth month. She never turned to the bottle with any enthusiasm, however, and certainly she did not take the night bottle—as so many of the other children did—as a kind of transitional object. No adverse reactions to the gradual weaning process were observed or reported; in fact, at 4 and 5 months, Wendy and her mother were a very happy and well-attuned mother-child pair with a rich interaction.

Wendy was pretty, soft, and well-molding, and her mother seemed to derive great pleasure from the physical closeness with her. The baby appeared cuddly, quite placid, and content. Her mother was very much aware of Wendy's slightest need. From very early on, however, she discouraged Wendy, as we have said, from tactilely exploring her face, as well as from pulling her hair, things that Wendy wanted to do at the time when infants typically needed to familiarize themselves with mother *qua* mother (Brody and Axelrad, 1970). Mrs. M. made up for this by smiling at Wendy, cradling her, talking to her, kissing her, and so on. But the predilections and idiosyncrasies, the specific patterns of her mothering, certainly reinforced Wendy's seemingly innate preference for the visual modality. It may have added to Wendy's diminished need and wish to explore her environment through touch at a time when children acquire the ability to crawl and to handle and feel objects in their expanding surroundings.

When uncomfortable, Wendy would actively protest and make gestures indicating her needs; this was recognized by one of us as having the emotional tone of appeal and of specific *longing*. Wendy engaged her mother very actively, and it was observed that she smiled at her in such an "irresistible" way that her mother had to smile back and could not walk away or continue to read or sew.

Whereas most of the children got used to the Center and grew fond of coming, Wendy never did. It never became homelike to her. In fact, she soon seemed to have equated the Center with everything that was "bad" (unfamiliar), and mother, siblings, and home with everything that was "good" (familiar). This pervasive attitude of Wendy's stemmed to a great extent from the fact that Mrs. M. herself did not have a consistently positive attitude toward her own participation in the project; the mother's motivation itself seemed marred by ambivalence. As a consequence of her exclusive "passionate symbiosis" and her subsequent very early and intense separation anxiety, Wendy's pervasive longing for closeness and union with her mother crowded out interest in the world and counteracted progress in individuation, that is, in ego development; it prevented her from turning to her own resources.[1]

As we have noted, the visual modality was highly cathected in Wendy and remained so even when there should have been a greater investment in locomotor functioning and in exploring objects tactilely with the hands and mouth. This was true in spite of the fact that Wendy's motor abilities unfolded according to the maturational timetable. Their ascendance was rather on the early side. She started to crawl at around 6 months and to walk with support at around 11 months. However, she did not invest these abilities with any enthusiasm; she did not use them to explore the environment. Instead, it seemed that Wendy preferred to stay close to her mother; she needed continuous closeness to mother to be able to enjoy anything in the outside world. She did not seem to want to leave behind the familiar status quo of the symbiotic relationship; she apparently could not take any of the risks of separate functioning, with the inherent "minimal threats of object loss." (Mahler and Furer, 1963*a*).

Thus we did not see in Wendy many of the usual characteristics of either the early practicing period or of the practicing period proper. There seemed to be little inner pressure toward autonomous functioning. Instead Wendy continued to prefer to have things done for her rather than to do them herself. As long as she was not threatened with separation or separateness, she was a charming, delightful baby. But even the slightest threat of loss of the symbiotic closeness would upset her greatly. Any invitation to a pleasurable interchange or relationship outside the mother-infant orbit would make Wendy return to mother immediately. Whereas most of the children in the early practicing period used their developing motor function to crawl in a direction away from mother in order to practice and explore, Wendy would crawl back to mother whenever mother put her down at a distance from her. Wendy would rarely use her crawling and other motor abilities to approach anyone other than mother. (Even after the third year, Wendy related only to people who in some way could be regarded as an extension of her mother,

[1] Developmental tests indicated that Wendy had average endowment, of which she did not take optimal advantage. The tests showed that at 21 months and again at 29 months of age Wendy's language development was 4 months behind her chronological age, and that in the personal-social sector of her personality, development was lagging as well. However, by 34 months her development had rather evened out, that is to say, by the end of the second half of her third year, she had an impressive spurt in her language and personal-social development—facts that we discovered independently of the tests, through observational data as well as from Mrs. M.'s reports.

those to whom her mother had developed a positive relationship and whom she approved of or invested with sympathy.)

We knew Mrs. M. quite well, as her older daughter had also been in our study. We knew from her that she dreaded the process of separation-individuation, with its obligatory pulls and pushes, tacks, and ups and downs. She liked and enjoyed, especially with Wendy, the period of bodily closeness. But once the symbiotic stage had passed, she would have liked an independently functioning child. Wendy seemed to sense her mother's predilection for the symbiotic infant, and even though she "hatched" in the sense described above (that is, her hypersensitivity caused her to become aware of some aspects of the outside world rather early), she tried to remain symbiotic as long as possible. In fact, it seemed as if she automatically resisted separateness. She never functioned comfortably without mother in our setup, and as we said before, she did not want to or was not able to adjust to or get familiar with the Center.

In addition, we thought that Wendy may have had a somewhat diminished need to venture into the outside world. She was the youngest child in the family, and her older siblings, who very much adored her, seemed to provide her with a lot of stimulation, which she passively accepted. Thus, in a way, they brought the outside world to her.[2]

Wendy's practicing period was altogether unusual. It is most interesting and noteworthy that although Wendy learned to take her first unaided steps at 13 months of age, she took them when her mother was not present in the home. This would suggest that Wendy felt free to let her individuation take its course only if retreat into symbiosis with mother was not available: her thrust toward individuation was possible only in mother's total absence. Wendy did not begin practicing in a true, active sense until she was about 18 months old, the chronological age that is regarded as the height of the rapprochement subphase. In addition, this belated practicing period did not have the subphase-specific characteristic of exhilaration; it was probably dampened by the concomitant cognitive development of the rapprochement subphase, namely the unavoidable recognition of oneself as separate from mother. To ward off this recognition, Wendy's mood remained very dependent on mother's mood or on the atmosphere of the world around her, reflecting her use of primary identification. Her affects could not take on an individual quality of their own. Nevertheless, this belated practicing period was the time when Wendy was best able to function with mother, either at some distance

[2] On the other hand, in the sibling situation, as in the infant-mother relationship, the "bad" side was displaced, as we will see later, to the toddlers at the Center.

from her, or even when mother was out of the room. While more typical rapprochement behavior, such as increased negativism and assertiveness, did appear in Wendy toward the end of the second year, this consisted of a particular stubbornness and refusal to accept mother substitutes. Nonetheless, the overlapping pleasure of independent functioning, that is, the attributes of the practicing period, did seem to ameliorate the pains of the rapprochement period for a while.

Wendy's difficulties in the intrapsychic separation process were most probably related to difficulties in her mother as well. Her mother was not able to support her in practicing and exploring. Hence, we saw in Wendy a tendency to want to return, in fact to regress, over and over again to the closeness of the mother-baby relationship. As individuation progressed in the purely maturational sense, the obligatory drive for autonomy and separateness evoked in Wendy greater than average negativism, temper tantrums, and a tendency to passive-aggressive behavior, instead of progress toward constructive aggression, symbolic play, and other activities independent of mother. She tended to become upset or to regress as a consequence of relatively minor frustrations, and her feelings were very easily hurt.

However, we did not see any apparent struggle in the area of toilet training. In the beginning of the third year, Wendy's mother reported the remarkable fact that toilet training was progressing without difficulty. By 32 months of age, Wendy was not only toilet trained during the daytime with very few accidents, but she was also continent during the night. This is one more area in which Wendy was able to oblige her mother.

Wendy's Separation Reactions and Separation Anxiety

As mentioned before, Wendy seemed to begin differentiating quite early, in her fourth month; by the age of 6 to 7 months the relationship with her mother was even more exclusive and her stranger and strangeness reactions more intense. These consisted of startling at noises and showing puzzled expressions when looking at strangers. At 8 to 9 months, Wendy cried when she looked at herself in a mirror if she could not also see mother's image beside hers; furthermore, she cried when mother left the room as well as when mother returned.

During the next 2 months, at the chronological age of the early practicing period, we saw a continuation of this tendency which started during the preceding months; distancing from mother seemed to constitute a threat to Wendy. She preferred to sit still and visually take in her environment; her separation reactions became quite intense, and she could be comforted only by closeness to her mother. She was not willing to use her growing abilities to separate physically, that is, to crawl away from mother. When mother was out of the room, Wendy went to mother's chair. Her separation reactions did not consist only of low-keyedness, as we observed in the average child at the chronological age of early practicing, but rather of *very severe distress and sadness*, suggesting "miniature anaclitic depression" (cf. Mahler and McDevitt, 1968). However, she was friendly and interested in the world as long as mother was close by.

At 20 months of age, Wendy began to show an unusual mixture of the characteristics of the practicing period proper and of the rapprochement period. Gradually, she became more independent. She did not go to her mother as often as before, nor did she miss her as much when mother left the room. There was some attempt to work out problems on her own instead of immediately appealing to others for help. She started to approach her mother with games and especially liked to play ball with her. In mother's absence she could use various temporary substitutes.

At this time, Wendy's innate sensuality was particularly apparent; she enjoyed all kinds of autoerotic, kinesthetic, and tactile experiences. Her mother said that she liked to swing for very long times.

Then by the end of the second year, during the twenty-third and twenty-fourth months, there was once more a change, in that she again needed greater closeness with mother.[3] She would not tolerate mother's attention to others; she did not want to play with the other toddlers; she did not like the toddler room. Her tendency to have temper tantrums increased. When her mother was out of the room, she sat, if possible, on the lap of substitute adults. During mother's absences, she showed great interest in the babies at the Center. At such times, she also ate and drank a lot. During these months, Wendy continued to seek very close physical contact with her mother.

Mother attempted to direct her daughter's activities away from herself. Wendy, in turn, seemed to react to attempts at distancing on the part of the mother by becoming low-keyed. But Wendy was always very happy when she was reunited with mother; these were the times when she could—legitimately, as it were—have close physical contact with and cuddle up to mother.

Thus, Wendy ended her second year with the rapprochement crisis quite unresolved and with very little ability either to function separately from mother or to communicate with words instead of gestures and

[3] This seemed to represent a mixture of typical rapprochement behavior and a regression to earlier separation reactions.

actions. Practicing had been delayed and subdued. The usual progression from practicing to rapprochement was not observable in Wendy, since she never reached the point of enjoying the world without close proximity to her mother.

Wendy's Third Year

At the beginning of her third year, Wendy could be characterized as a very feminine, pretty, and appealing little girl, very closely attached to her mother. Her orbit of activity was rather restricted. She tended to stay near her mother, and even if her mother was not present, she tended to remain in one place, often sitting in a chair. When she did move, it was with small, mincing, hesitating steps, and there seemed to be a general inhibition in her motility. Yet at times when her anger, jealousy, or envy were aroused (for example, when another child took something away from her), Wendy would overcome her inhibition and move fast and freely; she got up, ran across the room quickly, and retrieved the object.

An outstanding and enduring characteristic was Wendy's lack of interest in the other children at the Center (except, at times, in babies!). She liked to have as many adults as possible gathered around her; she liked to be the center of attention. It was observed that when everyone's attention happened to be focused on another child, Wendy would look sad.

Wendy continued to look sad when her mother left the room. At such times it was impossible to get her interested in play; instead she would eventually retreat to an observer's lap. A predilection for the two male observers was unmistakably evident. With them, in a one-to-one situation, she seemed quite happy and comfortable until her mother returned.

On the whole, Wendy's relationship to her mother seemed affectionate and close. Even when mother was not willing to give full attention to her, when, for instance, she was reading a book or when she was on the telephone, Wendy seemed satisfied as long as mother remained in her vicinity. Wendy's play, which consisted mainly in playing with dolls and mothering, showed identification with mother; she was also attached to the toy telephone, imitating mother's use of the telephone. The latter play behavior also seemed symbolically to represent Wendy's preference for indirect communication.

In spite of the general affectionate and close nature of Wendy's relationship with her mother, there were times at the beginning of her third year when she was quite determined to do things her own way; at times she would answer "No" to any question she was asked. In such moods she became quite demanding, that is, if she wanted something, she shouted and shrieked and pointed imperiously to the desired object. When she was angry she would hit and bite her mother. One factor contributing to this immediate aggressive drive discharge seemed to be Wendys' delayed language function.

Wendy's mother found her daughter's stubbornness difficult to handle. Her way of coping with the feeling of being overwhelmed by her children's difficulties during the ups and downs of separation-individuation was to run away if possible, to remove herself from the situation. She would become very involved in charitable activities outside of her family. Sometimes she would simply leave the house and let Wendy be cared for by maids or babysitters.

As a response to Mrs. M.'s further retreat from her mothering role, Wendy would react at the Center in the following manner. When mother was out of the room, she would not even look at the mother's chair or at the door (something other children her age would almost automatically do and which, at an earlier phase, Wendy did as well). On the contrary, at such times Wendy looked around as little as possible. (This restriction of perceptual intake served the mechanism of denial.) Wendy's attention seemed inwardly directed, perhaps an indication of imaging. As we have said above, she might attach herself to one adult observer, and only then would she become more animated. The reduction of sensory intake, as well as of activity in general, seemed to be one of Wendy's characteristic defenses. It could be viewed as a persistence of "low-keyedness" beyond its normal place in the practicing subphase.

As the third year progressed, Wendy began at times to protest actively, to cry vociferously, and to resist strongly her mother's departure from the room. She would still not be easily distracted from her sorrow.

When she could be engaged during her mother's absences, Wendy would use the observer as a substitute, either by being passively close to him or her or by allowing *that one person* to help her get on the rocking horse: this was one of the conspicuously autoerotic activities which she liked and to which she regressed. If the contact with the substitute was sustained over a long period of time, Wendy might briefly allow herself to "work" on a puzzle or play ball, but this play would stop as soon as the active participation by the adult was not sustained.

In other words, in mother's absence, Wendy seemed to have an overwhelming need to remain the narcissistic baby. She did not speak much, she did not play much, she did not relate to people much. If she could not find someone to comfort her or care for her, she would eventually comfort herself either by rocking on the rocking horse or by feeding herself, or else she would withdraw and quietly sit on the little chair hugging a doll or a cuddly teddy bear.

At times, when Wendy felt so lonely and lost that she seemed almost paralyzed and out of contact, she appeared to lack the ability to retain an image of the mother, even though mother may have been in the adjoining room. When she was told that mother was in the infant room next door and was asked if she wanted to go and see her, Wendy would not act accordingly and appropriately. She would point to the window and wave "bye-bye," indicating that in her intrapsychic economy, mother was gone as soon as mother was not visibly, tangibly, physically in her vicinity. Thus, it seemed that momentarily she not only lacked emotional object constancy, but also that she lost its cognitive counterpart, Piaget's "mental image of the absent object"; that is to say, she was not able to imagine where mother was when mother was not in her visual field. It seemed, at this time, that when mother was gone, there was no "good mother image" intrapsychically available to Wendy.

There was speculation that this difficulty in object constancy had to do with Wendy's aggression and ambivalence. Mrs. M. described Wendy as a determined child who could, at times, get into battles with her at home and be quite negativistic. At the Center the negativism and determination toward the mother were not expressed; these were entirely displaced to mother or father substitutes. While on the one hand, Wendy was passive and wanted to have things done for her, on the other hand, she would very definitely respond with a "no" to any suggestion that did not quite suit her. The inference about Wendy's ambivalence was drawn from observation of her facial expression, which was often angry and pouting. One observer said that Wendy seemed almost paralyzed by conflictual feelings about her mother when mother was not there, and that this prevented her from seeking comfort in play activity. Even if mother was present, the level of activity did not change very much: it was still centered in the one-to-one relationship and never extended to play with other children or to play with toys on her own.

Subsequent to this state of affairs, Wendy had a very good summer. When she came back to the Center at the age of about 28 months, she had progressed tremendously as far as her treasury of words was concerned and in her ability to express herself in complete sentences. She also began to protest separations much more actively and effectively. She would follow whenever mother went out of the room and would cry vociferously and simply not accept being left. As a result she frequently would have to be taken to her mother or allowed to accompany her to the interview room. Every so often she coerced us into permitting her to spend the entire morning in the infant room with her mother. As a last resort, Wendy would rather abruptly insist on being taken home.

By the end of the thirtieth month, Wendy, while still continuing to protest brief separations, seemed better able to cope with them. For example, at one point Wendy spent much of the morning in the toddler room painting, and when mother came into the room, she did not particularly notice her. Either she was sufficiently absorbed in her activity not to have full awareness of mother's presence, or else she might have tried to ward off such awareness, as if sensing that this would disrupt her autonomous free-play activtiy. She would now quite actively seek a one-to-one relationship, still preferably with a male observer, and try to engage him in play activity. She still would not accept intrusion on the part of another child and would use all her insistence and seductive charms to turn the adult's attention exclusively toward herself. One observer described very vividly how Wendy used more and more impetuous ways if the milder ploys did not succeed.

Though Wendy now at times enjoyed more active play, there were still many times when she preferred babylike activity. For example, when she was in the infant room with her mother, she enjoyed playing baby, going into and staying in the babies' playpen.

In the second half of the third year Wendy's play activities broadened. In addition to baby play and rocking on the rocking horse, she began to enjoy coloring and painting. At home, she was said to enjoy playing with her older sister and did not like to have this relationship intruded upon by any other child who might be visiting the house. With adult observers, Wendy now also enjoyed active games with hoops and balls, rolling them back and forth. As soon as there was even as much as a hint of intrusion by another child, however, the spontaneous joy vanished from her behavior. In short, Wendy seemed to need constant narcissistic supplies to maintain a measure of self-esteem, or, it would be more appropriate to say, delusion of omnipotence.

At around 30 months of age, Mrs. M. reported that Wendy had developed a particular liking for walking. Even when the stroller was available or when father offered to carry her, she preferred to walk and would walk for long distances. Wendy's mother felt that it was the exercise of walking that was so attractive to Wendy, rather than the idea of getting somewhere. This enjoyment of walking was interesting in view of her general passivity and immobility during the chronological age of the practicing and rapprochement periods described earlier, which had rendered her behavior so atypical.

The enjoyment of walking seems to have been one way in which Wendy emerged from her former utter passivity and, at times, angry moods. It toned up her body as if neutralized libidinal and aggressive energies had become available to her, and consequently increased her self-feeling, her sense of identity. The first step toward this developmental progress seems to have been her ability to protest more actively and vigorously when left by mother. This active rebellion then seems to have spread and rendered her generally more active and energetic.

Still, Wendy's mood vacillated, depending on whether mother was absent or present. In mother's absence she still had a tendency to be sad and angry; also she remained negativistic and was especially inclined to reject anything that might bring her close to a female observer. For example, she accepted ice cream from a man but did not want to accept it from a woman. She showed interest in a female observer's pendant, but when the female observer offered it to her, she rejected it.[4] Wendy liked to paint, but one day when her mother said upon leaving: "Paint with your teacher [female] while I'm gone," Wendy did not want to go near the paints.

In the second part of the third year, in spite of all appearances, Wendy's ambivalence conflict with "the mother of separation" bloomed typically and in full force. The belated rapprochement crisis was unmistakeable in Wendy's symbolic play, as was her awareness of the anatomical difference between the sexes.

Wendy's negativism toward the outside world continued until she eventually seemed to have developed something that looked like a phobic reaction to the toddler room and to the people there. It went so far that she would not even take off her coat and boots when she arrived at the Center. The play teacher in charge of the toddler room described how, even when she met Wendy in the hall, the child started to cry and cling to her mother. We thought this phobic reaction to the toddler room, where things at times became noisy and confusing, might also have had something to do with the fact that, as we learned from outside sources, at home in mother's absence, Wendy was subjected to her brother's aggressive play and exciting experimentations with her.

For a short while, with the help of the "toddler-room teacher," Wendy

[4] We could not help but speculate that this peculiar rejection of other-than-mother females was the specifically displaced externalization of the "bad" side of mother, an individual form of splitting in Wendy's case.

had been able to distance herself from mother and play with the other children. She soon must have felt this interaction to be too much of a threat to the exclusive symbiotic-like relationship with mother, and as a result had to ward off relationships with the "other-than-mother" world altogether.

At the age of 32 months, regular individual play sessions with one special observer were instituted for Wendy. She was wary when her "play observer" was first introduced to her and would accept her only after her mother displayed much liking and even admiration for the observer. But even after this acceptance, Wendy needed to be very much in control of the relationship and would not always accept the observer's advances. The observer felt that Wendy's positive mood was easily disrupted by some small distraction and that sometimes it was impossible to figure out what the source of the discomfort had been.

At the first play session, when Wendy's mother left to go to the infant room, Wendy followed her. Eventually she was willing to leave the infant room with the observer, whereupon she went to the cubby room to touch her mother's and her own outer garments that hung there. As described on p. 27, the cubby room in our setting was located between the infant room and the toddler room. It served as a kind of transitional space or room—transitional between the home and the Center, transitional between the toddler room where the children were supposed to be without the mothers and the infant room where the mothers stayed.[5] The touching of the clothes in Wendy's case seemed to reflect some sort of symbolic "refueling". Following this "refueling" episode Wendy was then able to play comparatively independently from her mother for a while. She was even able to join the other children in the toddler room who were playing with play dough. But, in keeping with her characteristic pattern, after a while of playing with the other children, Wendy was again unresponsive to the observer and energetically said "No" when the observer wanted to help her with something.

During one play observation, she took a doll and used play dough to close all of its openings, putting it over the doll's nose, mouth, ears, and belly button, between the doll's legs and on the doll's backside. This seemed symbolic of Wendy's wish to close herself off from the outside world. It was highly suggestive of anatomical concerns as well: she was undoing the fact that she had only openings, instead of a penis like her older brother and her father.

[5] We should mention that Wendy never had a transitional object and also that she never cared, as most of the other infants and toddlers did, for the bottle, not even a nighttime bottle.

In a play session toward the end of the same month, Wendy allowed her mother to be away for an interview for almost an hour, and during this time she played with her play observer. Some of the play was regressive: Wendy played being a baby; she went into the playpen and into the crib, and eventually she even drank from a baby bottle. When the mother returned to the play session, she was displeased to see her child play in a babylike way. To reassure herself and in reaction to the play teacher and the regressive play that the play observer had permitted, the mother emphasized that at home Wendy liked to be Batman or daddy. Mrs. M. then played with Wendy herself, pretending that Wendy was a baby bird and that she, mother, was the North Wind. The observer thought this sequence to be a beautiful symbolization on mother's part of her relationship with her children. From early on, Mrs. M. fostered her children's attachment to their father. This encouragement to turn to father, as well as to play Batman, fostered in Wendy by the age of 3 very early triangulation and perhaps even a spurious oedipal situation.

During one of the play sessions, there was an interesting sequence of events surrounding the cubby room. Wendy took a baby doll and hid it in one of the cubbyholes. When her observer play-acted for Wendy the baby's feelings of loneliness and longing in the cubbyhole and pretended playfully to be the doll's mother, Wendy picked up the doll and very deliberately threw it on the floor. As she did this, she looked at her observer with a smile. It seemed that in this sequence, she enacted something that she was afraid might happen to her. In playing it out, she was able to master her anxiety about being in the way of mother's pursuits and her fear of being discarded by mother.

Wendy then used her play sessions to invent play sequences in which she was the active one in initiating separations and reunions. In various mommy-daddy-baby games, which she liked, she would take the role of the daddy and go out to earn money, which he then brought back. Other times, she would send the observer out to get something, and when the observer came back, Wendy would put her hands over her eyes, thus controlling the moment when she would see, that is, look at, the observer.

From her weekly play sessions, we could also gauge that Wendy was quite concerned with the anatomical difference between the sexes and that she was worried about her body. At one point, she invented a game in which she played doctor to the dolls, which she said were hurt. When asked where the dolls were hurt, she said that they could not make wee-wee. She examined closely a little teddy bear that she said was hurt and sick and to whose "injuries" she applied bandaids. She also said she had been stung by a bee, and shortly afterwards she tried to undo the castration threat by playing games in which she pretended to be daddy or her friend Harry at nursery school. In play with the dolls in the dollhouse, Wendy seemed particularly interested in making all of them make wee-wee and take a bath. When the dolls made wee-wee, Wendy seemed to even out the sexual difference by having all of them sit down on the toilet.

In her play sessions, Wendy also reported some dreams about bugs and bees. Mother reported that Wendy had those dreams on nights when both she and her husband went out. We could not help but feel that Wendy warded off temptations wrought by her own bodily sensations and perhaps also by some disturbing erotized fantasies.

Wendy's play in play sessions was now rich and imaginative. She was able to use play well both to help her cope with her anxieties and to engage other people. She continued to be very appealing to grown-ups, especially to men. However, she still could not use play well socially, in terms of interaction with the other children in the Center when she came to her weekly play sessions.

As to identity formation: during the course of the third year, photographs were shown to all the children, both of themselves and of the other children, as well as of their mothers and of the observers. Wendy had some interesting reactions to these photographs. She identified her mother and her sister by name, but she would call all the other children, inluding herself, either just "boy" or "girl." Eventually, she would say that the photo that depicted herself was "me"; but she would still not use her name. Similarly, when an observer showed her a picture of himself, she became quite confused and could not recognize it as a picture of him. Similarly, in doll play, she would give each doll the name of the corresponding member of her own family, except for the baby, whom she continued to call "Baby" and not "Wendy." (She was, as we stated earlier, the youngest, the baby in her family.) It almost seemed as though there were some fear of letting the "baby" grow up to be a person in her own right, a person with a name, perhaps a fear that she would thereby lose the symbiotic closeness with her mother. Without having any trace of psychosis (this child was fully aware of her separateness!), Wendy seemed actively to refuse to accept and acknowledge the first level of identity, that of being a separate and individual entity and of having her own individuality. She seemed to accept her own identity only as the baby of her mother, in a "pretended" kind of "dual unity."

As we mentioned earlier, Wendy's language development was rather delayed. She never seemed to get much pleasure from talking and communicating with words and seemed to prefer bodily language, which she used very expressively. It was only by the end of the third year that Wendy could freely take advantage of the late spurt in language development. At this time, she first started to use the personal pronoun "I." At the same time, she seemed to have overcome her most acute separation anxiety and she was much better able to manage without her mother's constant presence.

In summary, more than most of the children, Wendy had great difficulty in emerging as a separate little person who could interact with others as a growing toddler. More than the others, she seemed to hold on to the illusion of being a part of her mother and consequently needed her mother's presence. Attainment of the pronoun "I," therefore, seems to have been of special significance in Wendy's development; it occurred simultaneously with a shift in Wendy's anxiety from fear of being left (fear of loss of love, of being unloved) to fear of being hurt (castration anxiety).

CHAPTER 11

Teddy

WE saw in Teddy's case how a child with early traumatization —deprivation of mothering due to adverse family circumstances— seemed to cope with the situation first by staying within the quasi-delusional twilight state of the symbiotic orbit longer than the average child, then by developing a fine instinctive (coenesthetic) sensitivity for knowing when and how to extract every drop of emotional supply from his mother, and finally by finding active ways of attracting her attention by initiating games, showing off, and so forth. Thus, certain behaviors, such as the relative lateness of his specific attachment to mother (compensation by prolonged symbiosis), or later, his excessive clowning, which at superficial observation might have been interpreted as maladaptive, were definitely found to be adaptive for his own particular needs in his particular situation.

Teddy's Mother

Teddy's mother was a person with a diffident, off-hand manner, who always appeared casual, even though she actually was quite thoughtful and introspective. However, when anxiety overwhelmed her, she became less sensitive to her children's needs (while they were preverbal). She was an extraordinarily loyal attendant of our Center for many years. The group was especially important to her during a period when her husband had to be away. The Center's group situation provided intellectual stimulation and emotional support for this intelligent mother.

Mrs. T. was a mother who in general did not take great pleasure in the lap-babyhood of her children. She enjoyed the later periods of her children's growing-up process much more. She had great tolerance for the ups and downs of the separation-individuation subphases and had a particularly outstanding empathy with the primary-process world of the child's second and third years of life.

Teddy's Subphase Development

Teddy, Mrs. T.'s third child, was born at a time of particular difficulty and crisis for his mother. Shortly after Teddy's birth two very traumatic events occurred in the family. Mrs. T.'s father, with whom she had had a very close relationship and to whom she had looked in times of difficulty, died. Less than a month later, Charlie, Teddy's brother, who was older by 14½ months, suffered a serious accident and had to be hospitalized. Mrs. T. spent almost all her time caring for Charlie at the hospital and had to leave Teddy's care to her own mother, who stayed with the family, even though she was understandably upset over the recent loss of her husband.

When Charlie's hospitalization was over and Mrs. T. could return to her task of being mother to Teddy, she was exhausted and depressed. She could give Teddy only minimal care and attention. When feeding him, for example, she held his bottle in such a way that he lay flat on her lap and was turned away from her, so that no eye contact was possible.

Probably as a result of this deficit in mothering, rather than because of any constitutional factor, Teddy was a lethargic baby who did not seem to care to investigate the world around him. His attention cathexis seemed to be turned inward. (He listened more to his insides, to use Spock's phrase.) While he did develop a rather ready *unspecific* social smile, the specific attachment to mother—indicated by the specific smiling response (Spitz, 1946)—and other signs of full-fledged symbiosis and of beginning differentiation were slow in appearing.

From all the landmarks by which we judged, Teddy did not begin to differentiate at the usual time, around 5 to 6 months. His specific attachment to mother, as well as active turning to the outside world, was not clearly evident before he was about 7 to 8 months old. The maturational ascendance of several of the partial motor skills, such as pulling up to a standing posture, sitting, creeping, and so forth, did not give

Teddy the obligatory thrust for individuation. He invested very little energy in practicing these functions.

But Teddy's mother did respond with pride and amusement whenever Teddy acquired a new skill, so that during the early practicing subphase (7 to 8 months) there was some improvement in the mother-child relationship and a corresponding improvement in Teddy's mood and energy level. Compared with other children his age, however, Teddy was still only moderately alert and responsive; he could sustain even that level of alertness only when stimulated by his mother. Mrs. T.'s mood at this time varied from day to day, and Teddy's mood varied accordingly; he was quasi-"infected" (see Freud, A., 1971) by her moods. Much of the interaction with his mother also revolved around imitating, that is, mirroring her. He mirrored her gestures. The mother in turn used her son's predilection for imitating her to teach him games such as "pat-a-cake," "so big," and so on.

When Teddy began to vocalize, his mother imitated the sounds he made, and this led to mutually pleasurable back-and-forth vocalizing. Now Mrs. T. began to hold Teddy *facing her*, and this seemed to make Teddy visually more alert. He appeared more focused, and he gradually showed great interest in looking. He began to make active appeals to his mother by initiating the little games that she had taught him earlier.

Teddy was about 8 months old when he finally developed the obligatory specific smiling response to his mother, though we knew from other signs that the specific attachment to her had begun earlier. When he was 6 to 7 months old, he would respond to his mother when she so much as looked at him with a blank expression, avidly receiving any bit of attention from her. Concomitant with the specific smiling response, he showed signs of stranger anxiety. Interestingly, this happened when he was intently looking at a slightly older boy: he suddenly began to cry. Teddy had shown all along a particular closeness to his older brother, a closeness that had almost a symbiotic tinge. Therefore, one must wonder if this first stranger reaction to an unfamiliar older boy had something to do with his close relationship to his older brother Charlie; stranger anxiety with actual crying occurred when Teddy noticed that this strange older boy was not his brother.

During the next several months (8 to 11 months), during the early practicing subphase, Teddy showed good progress in motor skills: creeping, sitting down from a standing position, and walking while holding on. He was quite active and cheerful, could play away from his mother for long periods of time, and could then return to her and lean on her knee for emotional refueling. He seemed to derive satisfaction from these contacts, even though when she was depressed he received little response from his mother. Teddy at this time was quite friendly and sociable with familiar people, although in the presence of strangers he would stay closer to his mother and would study the stranger from a safe distance.

Head nodding and head shaking, which became a characteristic pattern, was noticed for the first time at this point in Teddy's life. This seemed to be in part an imitation of Charlie's mode of communication with him. Charlie was not only very close to Teddy in age, but the mother fostered a kind of twinship between the brothers from very early on. She often expressed her wish that the boys do everything together. The head shaking and nodding seemed to serve the function of discharging tension, and by its exaggeration it became at times a form of clowning. Subsequently, Teddy used his clownish facial expressions to amuse his mother and other adults.

At 11 months Teddy's good mood, characteristic of the early practicing subphase, was interrupted by a hospitalization of several days' duration for high fever of unknown cause. He had been showing some mild reactions to separation before this, but these were intensified by the hospitalization. He reacted with greater distress to his mother's leaving the room. His need for close physical contact with his mother increased considerably; it was sometimes even expressed in a negative way by slapping and grabbing at her aggressively.[1] At the same time, when Teddy returned from the hospital, he seemed more active, more alert, and also more "vigilant" than he had been prior to his illness. In general he was more assertive in demanding mother's attention.

Later, however, at the chronological age of the practicing period proper (in which subphase we expect the junior toddler's mood to be more or less consistently elated), Teddy's mood remained quite variable. Even when his mother's mood was good, Teddy's mood varied according to his own inner, probably bodily, feelings and pressures. Upright locomotion seemed to make him painfully aware of his separateness, a separateness precipitated by the separation trauma and anxiety-provoking medical procedures of his hospitalization.

It is noteworthy, however, that Teddy still could be brought into a good mood by special attention and stimulation, not only by his mother but by other adults as well (thereby showing how important special attention had become to him). Whereas he enjoyed frequent playful and affectionate interactions with the adults at the Center, he definitely preferred

[1] We could clearly observe in this instance that at the age of 11 months additional frustration and trauma mobilized goal-directed aggression in Teddy.

Charlie, despite his brother's frequent aggression toward him. When distressed over separation, Teddy would be satisfied if he was allowed to go into the toddler room where Charlie was. As early as 12 months and almost continuously thereafter, Teddy was reported as showing considerable interest and pride in his penis and in that of his brother as well. His mother said that he often quietly masturbated at home. This was noticed more in Teddy than in the other boys of his age in our study. (It is reminiscent of other children who made up for lack of adequate stimulation by the mothering person by turning to their own bodies, to autoerotic activities as a way of compensatory self-stimulation.)[2]

Teddy's learning to walk was an interesting process. Although he seemed ready to walk months ahead of time, he did not actually begin independent free walking until he was almost 15 months old. His mother was clearly worried, disappointed, and impatient. She would often say, "Why doesn't he let go when clearly he is able to walk by himself?" We may speculate that the too sudden awareness of separateness brought about by the hospitalization caused an imbalance of libido distribution at the important landmark of free walking. He could walk, but he could not let go. He had to hold on! Mrs. T. was ambitious concerning her children. As we have discussed, the child's ability to walk without holding on has an important signal function for mothers. It proves to them that the child is now growing up successfully, that "he will be able to make it in the big world." Teddy's delay in free walking affected his mother strongly. This in turn seemed to subdue Teddy's pleasure in motor activity and exploration. It seemed as if the important autonomous function of free walking had become enmeshed in conflict, thus depriving both mother and child of the unclouded pleasure and elation which this accomplishment usually brings about. Teddy at this time was low-keyed and lethargic at the Center, and we were told that at home he had begun to have temper tantrums.

As soon as Teddy began to walk freely, however (at 15 months of age), he showed all the signs of the true "love affair with the world." He was more evenly exuberant, active, outgoing, and assertive. His activities were more goal-directed, and the temper tantrums stopped. He was less distressed at separations. His attachment to Charlie continued to be very strong, and he seemed not only to mirror and imitate

[2] Whereas in several of the other infants and toddlers the compensatory self-stimulation had a more or less defensive character and sometimes an autoaggressive admixture to it, in Teddy's early masturbatory activity neither we nor his mother, who was very observant, could detect negative, maladaptive aspects.

Charlie, but truly to identify with him. At this time a particularly strong attachment to certain favorite adults, especially women, was seen, and Teddy's relationship with them in many ways reflected his relationship with mother. It was as if he needed extra supplies to make up for the deficit in mothering during his early life.

By the sixteenth month, Teddy entered the typical rapprochement subphase, indicated by his awareness of his mother's whereabouts. He seemed to need to know where she was and that he would be able to go to her if he wanted. He seemed well-attuned to the degree of her availability and adapted his demands to it. At times he still seemed to have a tendency to drift out of contact with the world, his attention cathexis turning inward.

At 1½ years of age Teddy's rapprochement behavior increased in intensity. He went to his mother more often. Sometimes he would want to share his pleasures and experiences with her, sometimes he just wanted to be near her or to sit on her lap. Even when playing at a distance from her he would often look up at her. Now he avoided contact with those adults who had formerly been his special friends, as if he needed to reinforce the specificity of his relationship to his mother. Separation reactions became more intense, especially on the occasion of two unusual separation experiences observed at the Center when both his mother and Charlie left. Teddy reacted to this double separation with much unprovoked aggression toward the other children. We felt this to be—already at this tender age—an identification with the aggressor: his brother (cf. Freud, A., 1936). Teddy's rapprochement crisis thus seemed to involve not only his mother, but also his older brother Charlie. At the age of 2, Teddy still seemed in the midst of the rapprochement crisis and struggle.

He related more comfortably to adults than to children his own age. He was proud of being a boy, liked to exhibit himself in many ways by clowning, by showing off his motor skills, as well as by exhibiting his body, including his penis. (He liked to run around without pants or diapers.) At the same time, he was quite negativistic and resisted his mother's efforts at toilet training. He seemed torn between a wish for a close exclusive relationship with her and a push toward functioning more independently of her, in identification with his older siblings, both of whom by now went to school. A continuing characteristic after his short period of "shyness" was his striking ability to use substitutes to supply his needs for closeness or stimulation. At the age of 2 he still tended to become lethargic or detached when he was unsuccessful in gaining people's attention or participation. This seldom happened, however, because he had become quite skillful at drawing attention to himself through clever and appealing antics. His aggression seemed often to serve the purpose of getting a response from the other person. In the last months of his second year, Teddy had a tendency to become overstimulated and overexcited in his play,[3] but he could be directed into more structured activity with a little encouragement from an adult.

Summarizing Teddy's Subphase Development

Symbiosis was greatly protracted and differentiation very much delayed, so that this first subphase of separation-individuation overlapped the early practicing period more than usual.

The practicing subphase in its early part was interrupted by Teddy's hospitalization; this seemed to have made him prematurely aware of his separateness, with the result that he had stronger than usual separation reactions at that time.

The practicing subphase proper was delayed because Teddy (due to the recent trauma of hospitalization) was reluctant to embark upon independent upright locomotion. This phase was colored by Teddy's continuous need for maternal stimulation, and it was shortened by the fact that it had started so late and was therefore soon intruded upon by the rapprochement period.

During the rapprochement period, even though Teddy's mother was emotionally fully available to him, she always included his older brother Charlie. Mrs. T., as we said, made a point of identifying the two children with each other, treating them almost as though they were twins. Thus, the rapprochement subphase did not seem to have a distinct beginning or end and lacked full subphase specificity. Still, Teddy entered the third year having attained the expectable degree of object constancy and a high degree of individuality. He had a friendly disposition toward the human environment, although he showed a good deal of aggression directed mostly at children his own age. Teddy sought and enjoyed sensory stimulation through the oral, tactile, and auditory modalities. Chewing, sucking, blowing, and other mouth activities were frequent, and he liked to touch interesting textures. Teddy was stimulated by music, to which he responded with his hands, feet, head, and whole body. His apparently more than average need for stimulation presumably stemmed from the deficit in his early infancy.

[3] This overexcitement was found in many children at the age heralding the ascendancy of the phallic phase.

Teddy's Third Year

At the beginning of the third year, Teddy was still somewhat unfocused in his facial expressions, as well as in his activities. Frequently he would interrupt whatever he was doing and stare into space. This happened especially when his mother was not in the room. (This seemed reminiscent of the imaging behavior of the low-keyed infants, see p. 74). When he was in this unfocused, seemingly unrelated state, Teddy would sometimes strike out at another child, without apparent provocation or reason. An outburst of unprovoked aggression of this kind seemed to help him to snap out of his state of daydreaming and apparent apathy, and he was then quite cheerful, with an impish quality that endeared him to the observers.

Teddy at 21 to 22 months already was strongly affected by the fact that his older brother now went to nursery school and was no longer coming to the Center with him. Teddy seemed lost without his older brother. On days when Charlie was at the Center visiting Teddy, Teddy was in a more consistently alert state.

Teddy was an active boy who liked to experiment with different ways of using his body. He also liked to play with material which gave him sensory stimulation, such as water, paint, and clay; he preferred these to toys.

At the beginning of the fourth subphase (the consolidation of the child's individuality) when Charlie was no longer with Teddy in the toddler room, Teddy, to our surprise, reenacted actively the pattern he passively experienced when his mother used to feed him facing away from her. Teddy was still generally friendly and was interested in people, but he did not like them to come too close to him, and he avoided eye contact.

The vicissitudes of Teddy's subphase development during differentiation and practicing, coupled with the described unusual deficit in eye contact between him and his mother during the symbiotic phase, seem to have been the factors responsible for a peculiar unevenness in Teddy's body-image integration.

We have described Teddy's precocious awareness of certain body parts, particularly his genitals. This was due to his closeness to Charlie, which afforded continuous visual perception of his brother's penis, different but similar in size and other attributes to his own and, therefore, easily assimilated into his own body image schema (cf. also Greenacre, 1959 and 1968). Whereas in his earliest life Teddy was denied the opportunity to face his mother while she fed him, the mother's predilection toward promoting a twinlike relationship between Teddy and Charlie clearly compelled Teddy toward early observation of his brother's body (including the genitals). This opportunity to look at his brother propelled his own body sensations (he detected his penis at 12 months) and reinforced early genital autoerotic activity (quiet and self-soothing masturbation).

Yet a lag of body-image integration made it necessary for Teddy to compensate, in a constructive defensive-adaptive way, for this deficit. His intense peekaboo games and exercise of the visual modality served the same compensatory defensive function.

The following observations of Teddy's behaviors and the understanding of their underlying dynamics bear out these speculations.

Sometime during his third year, when Teddy recognized his mirror image and his photograph as "me," he had an unusual way of pointing at himself. When he was asked, "Where's Teddy?" he would point at his eyes, nose, or mouth, rather than to his whole body, his self. This indicated a lag in age-adequate body-image integration. At the same time, Teddy's great pleasure in sensory and physical activity might have compensated to some extent for this lag of body-image integration. One would be inclined to hypothesize that sensory awareness of his body in motion helped Teddy to feel so very comfortable, because the motion in space made him feel more solidly put together, more of "one piece," as it were.

Teddy's behavior at the beginning of the third year could be understood in relation to two important facts of his life. First, as we mentioned before, Teddy, at the chronological age of rapprochement, seemed always somewhat lost in the absence of his brother Charlie. Teddy had gone through the first three subphases of the separation-individuation process in the presence of, and probably with the help of, a kind of emotional libidinal and aggressive availability of his older brother, compensating, as it were, for the limited availability of his mother. Teddy's mother, who had been so overburdened at the time of Teddy's birth, often said how lucky it was that the two boys were so close in age, because they could do everything together. When Teddy first had to face his growing separateness, he did so in a kind of appersonation of Charlie. At the chronological age of the fourth subphase, he had to separate and individuate all over again, to disengage his body self and his individuality from the former symbiotic-like involvement with Charlie. A play observation afforded opportunity to observe Teddy's strong mirroring identification, possibly even a serious confusion, with Charlie's image. In that play session, Teddy called the bigger boy doll alternately "Teddy" and "Charlie." When the play observer asked him "What is your name?" Teddy replied, "Charlie." When his mother asked the same question, he repeated the same answer. We had the strong feeling that this was not merely a playful wishful fantasy, but that it contained some genuine and strong quasi-delusional identity confusion. In any case, we felt that at least in Teddy's fantasy life, Charlie and he were interchangeable. (Teddy went through a period when he wanted to wear Charlie's clothes and refused to wear his own.)

The second fact of Teddy's early life which seemed to be influencing his behavior at the beginning and throughout the course of the third year was the deficit of mothering that he had experienced during the early months of his life. Teddy was particularly sensitive not only to his mother's physical absence or presence, but also, at the beginning of the third year, to the degree of her availability and to her general mood. This put on him a greater than average burden of having to do everything in his power to engage his mother. This he had done by his clowning, by his cuteness, by his generally appealing antics, and at times by his unpredictably aggressive outbursts.

By the second quarter of the third year, there were indications that Teddy had achieved a greater awareness of himself as a whole person who has ownership and control over his own body and his own body feelings. Teddy expressed this awareness by showing that he regarded his stool as his own possession which he could hold or give. This awareness about the products of his body coincided with Teddy's beginning verbal expressions of ownership. When another boy tried to take a book away from him, Teddy—instead of striking out as he would have done a few weeks earlier—held on to the book and said "Me b.m.," or when another child sat on his mother's lap, he pushed her aside, saying, "No. My mommy." He called the Center "Mine school," indicating that he now had a school of his own, just like Charlie had. This ability to hold onto possessions and to put into words the sense of mine and yours occurred later in Teddy than in the other children and was both indication of, and a spurt toward, a stronger sense of his own individuality (identity). Along with it, Teddy's activities became more purposeful, and he also began to try to control separation experiences more actively. He invented many "peekaboo" and hiding games. He would anticipate mother's leaving and would tell her to leave the room whenever he knew it was time for her to go.

Castration concerns and interest in sex differences were observed in

Teddy after he had developed a stronger sense of individuality and possession. At home, Teddy and his brother were said to talk a lot about taking off the penis and other parts of the body and putting them back on again. At the Center, Teddy became interested in missing pieces of broken things; he needed to have everything in its proper place. He suddenly noticed, and remarked repeatedly about, a doorknob that had been missing for months. He also insisted that coats be zipped up completely and that his mother wear the hood that belonged to her coat. Castration anxiety thus seemed to be expressed indirectly through Teddy's wish that everything be in place, in order, and complete.

Behavior related to castration fears was described when he was 2½ years old. Teddy was very hard to handle in a shoe store; when the clerk tried to remove his shoes, he strongly protested. Haircuts were particularly traumatic experiences for him; he screamed and resisted and his mother had to hold down his arms and legs. On the day following a haircut, Teddy had much greater difficulty separating from his mother; he clearly showed his anger toward her for subjecting him to this experience, and at the same time he was afraid of losing her love.

In his play, as well as in other ways, Teddy demonstrated his continuing castration anxieties, which were augmented by his own greater-than-average aggressive fantasies. In his play with dolls and toy animals, he acted out the wish to cut off parts of their bodies. This was the acme of Teddy's overconcern about things being broken or whole (not broken). He now began to talk more openly about who did or who did not have a penis. Once when looking at a hole between a doll's legs and talking about his awareness of the sexual difference, he started to masturbate and then ran to the bathroom to urinate. It was interesting to follow Teddy's working through his early acute fear of bodily injury in his play. Teddy could always find pleasure in the use of his own body. Once when undressing for toileting, he aimed his penis at his mother with a mischievous and seductive look in his eyes, and followed this with a kind of "peekaboo" game, covering and uncovering his penis with his underpants. Many of Teddy's activities seemed related to awareness of his body and the ways in which he could use it. He clowned or experimented playfully with using things in inappropriate relation to parts of his body. For instance, after playing at shaving his face, he used the shaver on his head and on his mouth. After speaking in the telephone, he held the receiver to his eyes or his tummy and then hung it up in the wrong position. He put bits of play dough in his ears; at the same time he reassured himself by calling attention to how big or how strong or how capable he was. He did this in particular when his mother was absent from the room. He walked with a swaggering gait, sticking his tummy out and stamping his feet. He seemed to be in perpetual motion, wiggling, shrugging his shoulders, or grimacing.

All this behavior demonstrated the connection in Teddy of castration anxiety, separation anxiety, and aggression as a defense. For example, one day after he had been reluctant to let his mother leave the room, Teddy became upset because a cracker fell on the floor and broke. He began to whine and then started immediately to break other crackers, throwing them on the floor. But having done this, he began to smile. It seemed to us that he attempted to cope with his concern over the cracker being broken by actively, and triumphantly, breaking more of them. After this behavior sequence, Teddy went to the infant room where his mother was, played at a distance from her for a few minutes, then went to her, held out his finger to her, and complained, whining, "Bite me." She picked him up and asked, "Who bit you," and Teddy named various people. (The mother was not aware that Teddy wanted punishment and had the need for being bitten because he had just been a bad boy!) Later, back in the toddler room without his mother, he became upset again when some plaything broke. He began breaking it more and more, throwing pieces all over the floor. Then he threw a spoon, which also broke, and he said, "Daddy broke it." Finally, he threw the daddy doll and the mommy doll across the room. All this demonstrates that Teddy had to cope within himself with more than the average amount of not too successfully neutralized, aggressive instinctual energy.

Conflictual feelings, a mixture of yearning for closeness and of aggression, were quite typical of Teddy. He would provoke a quarrel with his teacher and then would burst into tears; but when the teacher picked him up to comfort him, he would kick and hit her and grab her hair, all the while attempting to mold his body tenderly into her body. When she put him down, he again came to her, buried his face in her lap, and flung his arms around her thighs in a gesture that indicated a desire to merge, while at the same time he had to ward off his wish for fusion. This was a remarkable instance of derivatives of the basic (not necessarily ominous) splitting mechanism.

During the third year, it became very important to Teddy to be considered a good boy, to have his mother's approval. This resulted in a tendency to use projection as a defense mechanism. Teddy would quickly blame whoever was around for any hurt he had caused or any injury he had experienced; it also resulted in a tendency toward early formation of superego precursors, which showed in his preoccupation with who was "good" and who was "bad."

Mrs. T. said that Teddy would come to her and say, "Charlie is a bad boy, I am a good boy." Teddy listened one day while his mother told the teacher how he had scratched her nose while she tried to put him to bed. When asked if he had hurt Mommy, Teddy said "Yes, naughty." The teacher interpreted his statement as meaning that he had been naughty to scratch mommy, but Teddy corrected her, "No, Mommy was naughty," looking indignantly at his mother. Teddy also looked for someone to blame when he was hurt physically. Once when the teacher was helping him carry a table, he fell as he was walking backwards. He then hit the playroom teacher sharply several times and said, "You hurt me," and stomped off, clowning and laughing; this was an indication that his reality sense was properly functioning. The teacher felt that Teddy knew that it was not she who caused Teddy's fall, but that he gained satisfaction from blaming her while at the same time making a game of it. Similarly, when he felt hurt or angry because his mother had left, he seemed to blame those who were present for his hurt, and in turn he would try to hurt them. At this time, when Teddy seemed to be so preoccupied with who was good and who was bad, who was to blame and who was hurt, he added two important new words to his vocabulary —"yes" and "I."

These behaviors, which we felt were precursors of precocious superego development, colored the very strong separation reactions he had at that time. At certain times separations were quite intolerable to him. He would cry and beg his mother not to leave. At other times he would let her go, but his behavior showed the strain of having to be without her, and eventually he would have to go and look for her. He became more stubborn, greedy, and aggressive in mother's absence, and he would seek the undivided attention of one of the observers, most often his play teacher. Sometimes he still just looked sad and dejected and sat staring into space, as if he needed to recall the inner image of the good "symbiotic mother." He continued to work hard at mastery of his feelings and initiated many hiding, hello-and-goodbye games with the observers. He liked to take the role of the one who leaves, closing the door behind himself and saying, "I'll be back."

On one occasion it seemed clear that because of his anger with mother for having left, Teddy somehow equated the "bad mother of separation" with feces. He warded off his fear and wish that his mother be flushed down the toilet in a play sequence in which he acted out the following: while he was playing with the doll house family, with the doll house toilet and bathtub, he suddenly became upset because it appeared to him at that moment that the observer was inattentive to him and his play. He poured water over the mother doll and threw the doll into the observer's lap; then he left the room and announced that he wanted his mommy. Instead of going to the interview room or infant room, where mother could have been found, Teddy went to the bathroom, looked into one of the children's toilets, then up at the observer, and asked where his mommy was. The observer took him to the interview room to his mother. A short while later, as they left the interview room, Teddy ran along and said to his mother, "You flush you."

At reunions Teddy often didn't go to his mother directly, his happiness showing only in his improved mood. When he did go to her, he lay his head happily in her lap or tried to squeeze himself into a tight little place beside her chair.

Another interesting feature of Teddy's personality development was that perhaps because he had experienced more than average difficulty in becoming a separate individual, he was more keenly aware of the feelings of others than was the average child in the third year. Sometimes he used this awareness to exert power over them, as he did when he accused his brother or sister of being "bad," whereas he, Teddy, was "good"; he knew full well how badly they felt about his accusations. At other times, however, Teddy could be remarkably considerate and kind. When one of the little girls at the Center appeared particularly restless one day, Teddy shared his favorite toy with her; he very nicely showed her how to use it. Another such instance of empathy occurred on the same day as the incident with the little girl. Teddy had repeatedly pushed another child away from the rocking horse while he was riding it, but after getting off the horse, he very kindly offered the same child the vacated rocking horse before he himself left the room.

After having told his mother or teacher on numerous occasions, "I don't like you," Teddy remembered the slight and did not miss making amends a little while later by reassuring them: "I like you now."

Teddy's psychosexual and ego development progressed quite well in the second half of his third year. He became toilet trained. He was proud that he could do things by himself, such as unzipping his own jacket or pouring juice into his glass.

Mother reported that at home there had been a lot of fighting between Charlie and Teddy, but that now their fighting was no longer due to concern over possessions or competition for attention. Rather, she said, they seemed just to get into one another's way, as individuals asserting their own individual rights. They would fight until one would get hurt enough to come to mother, and she felt that she could not leave them alone together with any potentially dangerous objects within reach. With Teddy's increasing sense of separate existence, and because of his wish for exclusive possession of mother, these battles often took on the flavor of a fight for "survival."

At the Center, Teddy more indirectly gave vent to his feelings that danger was lurking. He expressed fear that a cockroach he saw might bite him and eat him up and Charlie as well. However, his good sense of reality helped him to be able in the next minute to pick up the cockroach, throw it in the toilet, and flush it down.

The relative sizes of things held Teddy's interest, and connected with this was a newly expressed respect for his father's position as the biggest in the family. He painted a little line and a big line, a little circle and a big circle. Whereas previously he had not liked being called the littlest, he no longer seemed to mind as long as others were "littlest" too. In fact, he called everyone except his father "littlest."

During a home visit, Teddy pointed out to the observer several times that daddy was the biggest one in the family. In looking at a book about animal families, Teddy became upset each time one of the girls called the biggest animal the mommy. He would shriek and say, "No, it's a daddy." It was a very important accomplishment that now, in the phallic phase, Teddy was able to achieve true ego identification with his father. He established his individuality in his own right, separating and individuating from Charlie.

Teddy's tendency to become depressed or sad looking, sitting with an unfocused stare while mechanically pouring water or eating, or just doing nothing, was still observed many times during the second half of the third year. This sad mood occurred while his mother was out of the room, and usually when he was reminded of her by the other children who, at this point, often talked about where their mothers were. It seemed that he was thinking off and on, but rather consistently, about his mother. He also showed concern about his own body. The two concerns—as has been noted before—seemed closely related in Teddy's mind.

However, by the end of the third year, despite these occasional periods of sadness, Teddy was accepting separation quite well. He would let his mother leave without protest; although he might look sad or might watch her go longingly, he would play very well for quite a while in her absence. Only after a long time had passed, and when he was reminded of her by the other children talking about their mothers, did he begin to look sad or express his need to go to his mother. When he was taken to her, he was content just to see where she was; he quickly left her, playing his usual hello-goodbye game, and returned to constructive and age-appropriate play in the toddler room. In other words, by the end of the third year, Teddy had reached a reasonable level of object constancy and self constancy, and he had consolidated his individuality.

CHAPTER 12

Sam

IN Sam's case we saw a well-endowed infant striving for independent functioning in regard to both separation and individuation. We saw the resourcefulness with which the baby struggled against engulfment, struggled for his autonomy. Sam was engaged precociously on the track of individuation, far ahead of separation. This discrepancy was due to his partly intrinsically and partly environmentally delayed motor development. Quite early we saw bodily signs of distancing behavior towards his mother. The imbalance between separation and individuation seemed to have had a somewhat disorganizing effect on Sam's play behavior and early language development.

Sam's Mother

Mrs. R. threw herself into her mothering role with great intensity and boundless enthusiasm. Her enthusiasm was greatest when she succeeded in projecting, and thus reinforcing, her "ego ideal": the image of an all-giving mother, who tries to satisfy the infant without waiting for cues of need. This concept was greatly reinforced by her husband.

Sam's Subphase Development

Sam was an easily cared for, placid, soft, cuddly lap-baby. His mother greatly enjoyed his early infancy and especially enjoyed breast feeding him, which she continued until Sam's eighteenth month. Sam was not a "motor-minded" baby, and from the beginning he seemed to prefer small-muscle activity and manipulation of objects to large-muscle activity of the entire body. The early months of Sam's life seemed very pleasurable for both mother and child.

However, even during this early, most blissful symbiotic period, Mrs. R. was intensely overstimulating. She needed Sam to be continuously and exclusively involved in the symbiotic relationship with her. She needed continuous interaction with her baby.

The story of Sam's development from the differentiation subphase (4 to 5 months) on is a saga of his attempts to extricate himself from his overstimulating environment. Beginning as early as 4 to 5 months, we noticed Sam pushing himself away from the mother's tightly enveloping arms by stemming his own arms against his mother's chest and bending his trunk backwards in an almost opisthotonic type of motion.

Sam's very characteristic, peculiar style of separation-individuation behavior resulted, on the one hand, from his probably partly intrinsic slow locomotor development, and on the other hand, from his need to extricate himself from the limiting symbiosis. Because of the slow locomotor development, the separation process did not take place as naturally and harmoniously as it did in other babies who, by the age of 8 or 9 months, would start gradually and actively to distance themselves in space from their mothers.

At the age of 8 to 9 months, when the specific bond with mother is most intense in the average infant, Sam had already begun to prefer strangers to his mother in particular situations. He showed no separation reactions at all. However, even at this very early age, he responded to his mother's disapproval by a lowering of mood.

At 10 months of age Sam continued to turn away from mother and only passively accepted her invitations to roughhousing play. When Sam started to crawl, at about the age of 1 year, he used his skill to distance himself from, and sometimes to avoid, his mother. There still were no separation reactions, and Sam continued to prefer familiar observers to his mother. His mother continued to treat Sam like a lap-baby.

By 11 to 12 months Sam frequently did not listen to his mother even when she spoke to him. To get his attention, Mrs. R. played very roughly with him and began to initiate chasing games in which she would run after him when Sam crawled away. On such occasions Mrs. R. swept him up in her arms, changing the direction of his crawling.

Sam's practicing period was atypical; it started late. He did not reach mastery of upright locomotion at the chronological age of the practicing period proper. The obligatory obliviousness of mother was exaggerated. There was a total absence of separation reactions and of refueling phenomena. He also did not seem to experience a full-fledged elation and love affair with the world.

At the late age of 17 to 18 months, Sam surprised his mother (who by that time was quite worried about him) and other people by free, upright *walking away* from mother at the playground; this was also the time when Sam actively refused the breast. Very soon after he mastered upright locomotion, the first signs of the rapprochement subphase appeared. He no longer ignored mother, and he found pleasure in interaction with her. Indeed, he began to show now that he missed his mother; when she left him, he went to the empty chair in which she had sat. He became hyperactive in her absence, as if he needed self-stimulation to recreate the exciting atmosphere of their interaction. At times Sam would try to run out of the room after his mother and would fret if he could not immediately find her. (All of these behaviors indicate belated separation reactions, telescoped with rapprochement phenomena.)

It was as late as 19 months that Sam showed more typical *early* rapprochement behavior. He showed those signs of rapprochement which in most children heralded the rapprochement subphase. He started to bring toys to his mother and began to experience pleasure in sharing activities and possessions with her. There was an interesting, very individual aspect to Sam's rapprochement behavior: while at times he would climb into mother's lap and sit quietly leaning against her, he would at other times stop in the middle of his approaching her as soon as she herself started to move toward him. If at such a time she would catch him against his will, he would push, kick, and hit her.

At passive separation experiences, separation reactions became quite intense: Sam would cry inconsolably when his mother left the room. Sam's recent mastery of upright free locomotion seemed to have increased his need to be close to mother. It seemed to make him suddenly feel separate—not having the quadruped's feeling of being supported by the extensive horizontal basis of the floor, he suddenly felt very vulnerable. However, after showing this fear of loss and support for a while, Sam went through a period of enjoying explorations at a distance from mother once again and, in general, showed some signs of the elation of a belated practicing subphase. When the rapprochement struggle reoccurred, Sam seemed to go through periods of alternately clinging to mother and then trying to avoid her.

Sam emerged from the period of the rapprochement struggle and crisis a rather somber little boy who could not find much pleasure in relating to the world around him. One aspect of particular interest in Sam's relationship to the other toddlers was that he lost interest in the ones who were approximately his own age and instead attached himself to older boys or to the small babies and their mothers. This brings to mind a character trait seen every so often in people who in later life cannot relate to peers, but for whom only superiors or people in subordinate positions have appeal.

Another characteristic quality in Sam was his tendency to play act, to pretend to be a helpless baby. Interestingly this happened at a time when his mother said that she wished to become pregnant again. Sam thus showed some tendencies to remain involved in the symbiotic relationship, perhaps to please mother or perhaps to recapture an earlier happier time when he was his mother's passive baby.

In the psychosexual sphere, Sam showed signs of sexual overexcitement, as well as greater than average castration anxiety. By the end of the second year he was so afraid of the toilet that his mother gave up attempts at training him. At the same time he became preoccupied with penises, calling a banana a "pee-pee", and calling his friend's penis pretty.

Sam's Third Year

Sam was noisy and frequently uncontrolled and agitated in his play. His mother's erratic attention to him was not in conformity with his needs: sometimes she hovered over him physically, sometimes she dominated him verbally. Sam, in turn, often ignored his mother's instructions and would tell her to sit down when she became too intrusive.

Sam readily went into the toddler room and stayed there without his mother, unlike most of the other children his age who, as we described, needed at first some encouragement to stay in that room without mother. When in the toddler room Sam hardly ever asked for his mother. If he did, he was easily satisfied by being told where she was.

At the beginning of the third year, following summer vacation, Sam's mother reported that Sam had recently decided to do without diapers; he remained dry and, except when he was in his crib with diapers on, he used the potty for his bowel movements. She reported that Sam was proud of his achievement and showed it off to his friends. But then, after a few days, he decided to return to diapers. Toilet training from that time on became a conflictual situation between Sam and his mother, just as autonomous functions like crawling and walking had been drawn into (as yet partly external) conflict during Sam's second year.

Once Mrs. R. could no longer maintain her illusion that Sam was one with her, her symbiotic half, she experienced him as a willful little boy whom she could not control. She said that once Sam made up his mind about what he wanted, nothing could "budge him."

Sam at this age was sexually quite excited. We observed that when Sam's pants were removed for toileting, he masturbated, pushing at the tip of his penis with open pleasure. On one occasion he said, "Nice penis" and then looked at the observer and said, "You nice people."

Sam's pleasure in his body, especially the pleasure with his penis, seemed to spread to the world at large. But certain signs indicated considerably more than the usual amount of bodily fears and castration anxiety. The following sequence occurred one day: he had rocked on the rocking boat in an elated manner, assertively pushing off another boy whenever the latter tried to enter the boat. After rocking, he had linked together the large trains and then put toy animals in them, saying that each animal had a "boo-boo." Thus, it appeared likely that this masturbatory activity was at least in part an effort to reassure himself against castration fears.

In the course of the third year, this castration anxiety intensified. He showed much concern with even minor bumps. When another boy showed him a hurt knee, Sam was very much concerned about it and then said that the teacher had a hurt and that he himself had one also. Throughout this conversation, which took place in the bathroom, Sam, who was without pants, masturbated. At 28 months of age he still did not use the toilet; instead he played in the bathroom, trying out the toilets and pulling the toilets' flushing chains.

By this time, Sam seemed well aware of his mother's pregnancy, although he had not been told about it. He showed his awareness of it by playing baby and also by mothering dolls. He had remarked that his mother looked fat, and Mrs. R. reported that he had said that he himself had a baby inside him.

At 30 months, some important changes seemed to be taking place. Perhaps most important was his increasing need for his mother. This became particularly striking on a day when his mother repeatedly left the room. He did not react to her first departure, but shortly after her return he wanted to be picked up. When Mrs. R. talked about leaving the room again, Sam agitatedly and repeatedly asked her to stay. When she nevertheless started to leave, he detained her. He asked for her shortly after she had slipped away, and it took quite a while before he could become interested in play. In her absence, his play behavior appeared frenzied; he ran from one thing to another. The balance of the relationship seemed to have shifted, with Sam needing much attention from mother and mother paying relatively less attention to him. We must keep in mind that this may have been greatly augmented by the mother's pregnancy—Mrs. R. became increasingly self-absorbed as pregnant women obligatorily do—and Sam reacted to her withdrawal with increased frantic, clinging behavior.

Sam's castration or mutilation anxiety continued. Sam's father liked to take Sam to museums. At the museum Sam asked to see the statue of the "broken lady." He referred to one statue as having a "broken pee-pee." There seemed now to be efforts to master this anxiety through play. Mrs. R. played the game of taking off Sam's nose, and he then took hers off, saying, "I eat it." Playing with an observer, Sam pretended to cut her hair. He thus took the active role, identifying with the aggressor. In playing with play dough, Sam rolled the dough into a long strip, calling it a finger, and then said, "Hurt finger, cut, it's a boo-boo."

Sam continued to attempt to overcome his anxieties through all kinds of defense precursors. One day one of the children's older brothers came dressed up as Superman, and even though Sam was afraid of him and clung to the teacher, later he managed to mirror and playfully identify with the boy. He announced, "I Superman." Sam also tried to put angry feelings into words. Once when he was prevented from taking something away from another child, he said, "I angry."

On the day Sam's baby sister was born, he was brought to the Center by the play teacher. At first, although he needed some reassurance, he did fairly well. He went to the mirror, seemed to get excited at his own antics, and then said, "Sam's all right." The teacher replied, "Sam's an all right boy," and he responded, "Sam's a boy." Later when another boy joined him, Sam said, "only boys." The same day, Sam was repeatedly asked about his mother and baby sister. At first he handled these questions very well. He was engaged in water play and said that the baby was taking a bath; then he said that it was a bunny. But as questions were repeated, Sam began to have more difficulty. First he attempted to avoid the questions, going away from the person who was asking them; then his anger began to well up. He became more driven and fiercely concentrated on his play, hitting and cutting some clay animals, chipping off their limbs and tails, but reassuring himself about his own bodily integrity by saying, "Knife not dangerous for me." He became overly sensitive to aggression directed toward him. When another boy pulled at one of his animals, Sam said, "Charlie hurt me." He had a piece of clay which he stomped on and called a "bunny," the word he earlier used to refer to his baby sister. He put the piece of clay in his pants, saying that he was putting it in his pee-pee (perhaps wanting to send the baby back to the womb?) and insisted that he must take it home; he was upset as it fell out of his pants. Finally he agreed to carry the stepped on "bunny baby" home in a plastic bag.

Sam was in a frenzied, panicky state for most of the month after his baby sister's birth: he was hyperactive, driven, and talked incessantly in a language that was gibberish and which frequently expressed primary-process fantasy material. He did not directly address people when he talked. When he wanted something he simply named it over and over again, seeming to expect that it would magically appear. While much aggression was expressed in both the manner and content of his activity, it was rarely directed externally at people. He made monsters out of play dough, labeling them Mommy Monster, Daddy Monster, and Baby Monster. He said that he was patting the baby monster, but actually he was pounding it. There was a suggestion that Sam was concerned with primal-scene observations when he took the daddy and mommy monsters he had made out of play dough and rolled them together.

Castration concerns continued. When the play teacher had a minor accident, Sam said, "Teacher all broken." He wanted to fix a scar his mother had by putting band-aids on it. An immediate association demonstrating how defenses are structured *in statu nascendi*—in this case against looking and voyeurism—was suggested by his fear that the sun might hurt his eyes: he covered the eyes of the toy animals to protect them. Looking at a picture of a bright sun and clouds, he was pleased by the clouds and wanted to make some more to cover the sun. It seemed that the fear of the sun and its blinding quality had to do with seeing his baby sister, and also his mother and father, in the nude.

Strikingly, Sam never referred to what one may assume had been his central concerns at this time, namely his mother's absence from the Center and the new baby. The extent of his avoidance and denial could be seen in his reaction to the principal investigator. A number of times she tried to talk to him about his mother and the baby. He would either run away or act as if he heard nothing. Then he took to running from her or telling her to go away as soon as he saw her. Thus he reacted to the investigator's "intrusiveness" much as he had reacted to his mother's from early on; and at the same time, this behavior expressed his need to ward off the memory of his mother, whom he missed and perhaps also resented for abandoning and betraying him. In his play there were occasional references to babies. In addition to the baby monster, he also bathed and flooded the baby in his water play.

That the mental representation of the mother was particularly dissociated from the "mother in the flesh" was confirmed by the following behavior: When Mrs. R. was in the hospital, she called Sam every morning. According to Mrs. R., at the beginning of these telephone conversations, Sam insisted that it was not she, his mother, to whom he talked on the phone, but simply a "nice lady"; on the other hand, he could not tear himself away from this "nice lady," and proceeded to talk to her for some 45 minutes, not letting mother hang up the receiver. We can only speculate on the meaning of Sam's behavior, which seemed to reflect different levels of emotional object constancy, if not outright defensive splitting. He may have had a need to protect the good image of the mother from his own anger, to separate it from the image of the bad mother who had left him for "another baby"; he may have had to deny the existence of that bad mother image, at the price of a temporary perceptual dedifferentiation.

How unsteady and confused Sam's inner representation and outer perception of the libidinal object had become at this juncture could be inferred from the above description of his telephone behavior, and also by a very instructive episode at the Center. On one of the first days his mother and the baby were home from the hospital, Sam refused to leave the Center, insisting that his mother was at the Center and that *she would take him home*. He could not understand that his mother was home and that *he* must go home *to her*.

His mother said that Sam was proud of and protective toward his baby sister. She backed up this statement with a description of what happened when she took the baby out for a walk. Sam repeatedly told people not to look into the carriage because they would make the baby cry (fear of the evil eye? see Petö, 1969). We felt that Sam did not want people to see the baby, thus acting out his wish that the baby should be invisible, that is, nonexistent, but perhaps also trying to ward off his own wish that the baby be afflicted by the "evil eye."

From 30 to 36 months, we observed in Sam a sound tendency toward libidinal object constancy and internalization of the object and self-representations.

As was frequently seen with Sam, he responded well to any situation in which any adult could give his ego quiet support and attention. Even in a frenzied state, he would readily calm down and function more constructively as soon as an observer could give him individual attention and work adequately with him. This became particularly striking on a day he happened to be the only toddler present in the toddler room at the Center. Not only was he much calmer and more able to take pleasure in play, throughout the rest of the month he remained relatively calm and more constructive in his play activity. He became more able to focus on things in the outer world, instead of so often being tuned in to what appeared to be his inner sensations. Instead of flitting disconnectedly from one activity to another, he became interested in the activities of other children. When told that he must wait for his turn for a special set of blocks another child was using, he managed to join the other child in his play. It was quite instructive to observe, however, that after a longer absence from the Center, his mood regressed; he appeared less calm, and his play again seemed less well organized.

On his third birthday, Sam enjoyed the activities in the room, was calm and well integrated, and engaged in structured play. He made a tall structure with blocks. He sat quietly at the birthday table. His speech was more related to reality situations. Again we could see how well he responded to any person or situation which furthered age-adequate functioning.

Sam's mother saw Sam as not only a good and competent, but indeed as an almost invulnerable little boy who could take everything in his stride. She felt that he was not affected at all by the fact that she had to give so much attention to the new baby. She reported that Sam, at this point, was attached mainly to his father. When she expressed a wish to join them on an outing, he told her to stay home with the baby.

In summary, we have seen that Sam was able quite early actively to seek out and use people other than mother as a refuge from the symbiotic demand and overstimulation which emanated from her. From early on, he often preferred to be held by a person other than his mother; later, he could use the toddler room teacher to help him overcome disturbing feelings after the birth of his baby sister. Even though his subphase development was so atypical (delayed motor development and prolonged nursing), he eventually did experience the elation of the practicing period to some degree. Maybe it was fortunate in his case that the mother became preoccupied with a new baby; experiences such as the physical separation during mother's hospital stay made him more aware of his separateness, with the resultant obligatory realization of missing—and hence longing for—the erstwhile symbiotic mother.

We saw early avoidance behavior (looking and pushing away from mother) develop later into the defenses of denial and disavowal *in statu nascendi*. Although during his third year Sam resorted to regression and splitting in stressful situations, he was also able optimally to use the resources of his autonomous ego.

Part IV

Summary and Reflections

CHAPTER 13

Variations Within the Subphases with Special Reference to Differentiation

IN this concluding part the senior author will summarize the results of this observational study conducted with her co-workers, past and present, for more than a decade and a half. These studies provided a glimpse into that bedrock of mental life that does not divulge its content and nature by verbal means—the "unrememberable and the unforgettable" (A. Frank, 1969).

The senior author (Mahler) expressed in 1963 the following:

> At an advanced stage in their lifework some psychoanalysts seek to come closer to the actual fountainhead of their reconstructive efforts. Some, like myself, seek verbal and preverbal observational data—*in statu nascendi*—such as will confirm, refute, modify, or elaborate psychoanalytic hypotheses. Through a study of normal infants and their mothers, I have been trying, not only to complement my psychoanalytic work with neurotic adults and children, but also to gain additional perspective and to validate previous studies in the area of infantile psychosis. I have maintained a rather personal interest in one specific aspect of the rich heritage that Freud bestowed upon us, namely, his emphasis on the fact that a lifelong, albeit diminishing, emotional dependence on the mother is a universal truth of human existence. The biological unpreparedness of the human infant to maintain his life separately conditions that species-specific prolonged phase which has been designated "the mother-infant symbiosis." I believe it is from the symbiotic phase of the mother-infant dual unity that those experiential precursors of individual beginnings are derived, which, together with inborn constitutional factors, determine every human individual's unique somatic and psychological make-up (p. 307).

She went on to say:

> I feel that our study has proven, clinically, clearly enough, that the libidinal availability of the mother, because of the emotional dependence of the child, facilitates the optimal unfolding of innate potentialities. . . . I have tried to demonstrate by specific instances how this factor contributes to, or subtracts from, harmonious synthesis of the autonomous functions in the service of the ego, the neutralization of drives, and sublimation, by activating or *temporarily* hindering the flux of developmental energy, a process which Ernst Kris (1955) has so beautifully described [italics added]. The rich abundance of the developmental energy at the period of individuation accounts for the regeneration of developmental potentialities to an extent never seen in any other period of life, except perhaps in adolescence. It illustrates the sturdiness and potential adaptive capacity of the human species and demonstrates the importance of the catalyzing influence of the love object.
>
> I wished to indicate in particular the extent to which the normal infant-toddler is intent upon, and usually is also able to extract, contact supplies and participation from the mother, sometimes against considerable odds; how he tries to incorporate every bit of these supplies into libidinal channels for progressive personality organization. On the other hand, I also want to point out in what predicament mothers in our culture find themselves; in spite of their own unconscious conflicts about their maternal role, and while struggling with their fantasies about the growing infant, they must nevertheless respond to the rapidly changing, primary process dominated cues of their infant's hatching from the symbiotic membrane to become an individuated toddler (p. 322).

The present volume offers an account of how much we have learned since the time when the above was written. But it also serves to emphasize what the reader must feel by now—something of which the authors are keenly aware—namely, that there are many more questions that we were forced to leave unanswered, or only partially answered, than there are questions to which we have been able to furnish substantial clarification.

The hypothesis of the symbiotic origin of the human condition triggered our first informal pilot study, a study that set itself the limited task of trying to find out in what way the child who attains an average normal or neurotic structure succeeds in the process of attaining his individual entity and identity—something that the symbiotic psychotic child is unable to achieve.[1] The first part of this parallel project yielded a much more specific hypothesis, complementing our previously formu-

[1] This study was undertaken in 1959 by M. Furer, M.D., and Ann Haeberle Reiss, Ph.D., with the assistance of the junior author of the present volume, Anni Bergman. It was continued by the senior author of this volume and by Dr. Furer, as co-principal investigators, with several other participant observers, most of whom were engaged also in the parallel study of "Symbiotic Child Psychosis" (see also the Acknowledgments and the Preface to this volume).

lated theory of the symbiotic origin of the human condition, namely, that of the subphases of the separation-individuation process.

This second hypothesis evolved as a consequence of the fact that during the course of our naturalistic pilot study, we could not help but take note of the clustering of variables at certain crossroads of the individuation process, in that they tended to occur repetitively. This strongly suggested that it would be advantageous to order the data that we were collecting on the intrapsychic separation and individuation process in accordance with the repeatedly observable behavioral and other surface referents of that process. We subdivided the process into four subphases: differentiation, practicing, rapprochement, and "on the way to object constancy" and the consolidation of individuality. The timing of these subphases cannot be determined with precision: they overlap as much as the zonal libidinal phases do.

As described in detail by Dr. Pine in Appendix B, it is natural that what began as an unsystematic naturalistic study grew into a systematic, predominantly cross-sectional research project—a kind of normative study—in which we sought insights and conclusions by way of comparing and contrasting the infants and toddlers at the same age level, from the point of view of their stage of differentiation from their mothers (object representations) and the integration of their individuating self representations.

As Part III illustrates, however, this study further evolved into an longitudinal, albeit limited, study. In following the development of the individual children intensively and uninterruptedly, we naturally observed the unfolding of their symbiotic and separation-individuation processes.

Translation of the observable phenomena of early noncohesive ego states (in our terms, the "autistic" and "early symbiotic" periods) into psychological terms is exceedingly difficult. Extrapolations drawn from behavioral data from the preverbal phase are even more precarious than those from later periods of life. To understand *preverbal* phenomena, as Augusta Bonnard (1958) succinctly stated, "We are compelled to seek out to a great extent their connotations through their continuance into later stages, or through appraisal of regressive manifestations." This second kind of approach (to seek understanding of development through appraisal of regressive manifestations) was adopted by the senior author in collaboration with Dr. Furer in the 1950s up to 1963. It came to fruition in several articles of the early 1960s, and particularly in the book, *On Human Symbiosis and the Vicissitudes of Individuation: Infantile Psychosis* (Mahler, 1968*b*).

In the study presented in this volume, however, we were trying to validate our conception of the ubiquity of human symbiosis by following its continuation into later stages of development, that is, into the second half of the first year and into the second and third years of life. Study of the second part of the third year also served as the platform from which we, as psychoanalysts, would both look back upon the individual children's separation-individuation processes and ahead, in order to try to prognosticate in our own minds the future course of individual personality development.[2,3]

Thus, our modest pilot project grew into a normative study that may potentially enrich psychoanalytic developmental theory by virtue of its consensually verifiable propositions.

What we started out with was, of course, whatever general psychoanalytic tenets, propositions, and assumptions about the individual's quasi-"prehistoric" past we had at our disposal. We tried to employ certain important, hitherto generally accepted and guiding psychoanalytic propositions about the preverbal phase in order to make sense out of our detailed observational findings within the psychoanalytic frame of reference.

In what follows we shall try to point out, both in summary and in amplification, how our data seemed not only to verify but, more importantly, to some degree to modify, these accepted ideas concerning early extrauterine life. In some instances, our data seemed to refute some

[2] Follow-up glimpses have shown us that the consolidation of the individual child's ego and drive constellation in the second part of the third year remains in many respects characteristic of his subsequent development; that is to say, it has a kind of historic continuity from that point on.

Later examinations, especially psychological tests, show that whereas, of course, the phallic-oedipal phase and its resolution may substantially alter the vicissitudes of the 3-year-old's basic personality characteristic in their adaptive and defensive aspects, the 3-year-old as we knew him at that stage would shine through the subsequent layers of development.

[3] Psychoanalyst observers, particularly those involved in observational research of the preverbal phase, were always preoccupied and even haunted by the ambition to find early detectable variables (beyond the cognitive factors) that would be helpful in prediction of later development; and even though we knew that we had to be very modest and humble, such a limited longitudinal study as ours made us even more aware of it. We had to remind ourselves again and again that human development is not linear; it is characterized by shifts in the fields of experience; we have repeatedly emphasized massive shifts of cathexis. Those characteristics of the child that are innate and near-biological—which we loosely subsume as his inborn endowment—seem to endure, that is to say, they remain relatively stable and immutable through ongoing development. Those other characteristics, however, which are the result of transactions and interactions with the object world (e.g., early defensive patterns, early identifications) are extraordinarily variable, and so is their outcome; there are ever-ongoing changes which yield to massive shifts of cathexis at crossroads of development (cf. E. Kris, 1950 and 1962; M. Kris, 1957; A. Freud, 1958; Ritvo and Solnit, 1958).

"rules" previously taken for granted about the human being's individual beginnings; in many instances, the rules had to be singled out as particularly in need of further clarifying research.

As the study of the mother-infant pairs has taught us, and as the foregoing sample section illustrated, there are both universal trends in the separation-individuation process and an infinite combination of individual factors and early environmental influences. This great array of individual differences creates a kaleidoscopic interplay of variables, augmented by the rapidly proceeding psychosexual and aggressive drive development, as well as ego development, in the course of the separation-individuation process in interaction with "the average expectable environment" (Hartmann, 1939). It is the combination of these variables that accounts for the uniqueness of each individual child's life style and personality (Mahler, 1963; Mahler, 1967*b*; Pine, 1971).

As psychoanalyst clinicians, we wanted to find out which course the "normal" separation-individuation process takes. But we also expected to find out what sort of variations, minor middle-range deviations, these normal infants of average "ordinary devoted mothers" would display in their earliest development. We wanted to discover how observation of these deviations would further our understanding and assessment of the variations of normality or, possibly, the depth and breadth of middle-range or minor pathology.[4]

Mental health, as well as pathology, is determined, as we see it, by (1) the individual child's endowment, (2) the early mother-child interaction and relationship, and (3) crucial events in the child's growing-up process—in other words, by positive and negative experiential factors, which impinge upon the equisitely pliable makeup of the child's individuating psyche (Mahler, 1963; Weil, 1956, 1970). We paid particular attention to those data that may indicate phase-specific points of vulnerabilities of the intrapsychic separation-individuation process. We cannot define these points precisely; yet in this study we came nearer than ever before to being able to determine where they are located in the developmental process. We came to regard certain constellations of variables as danger signals (cf. Settlage, 1974).

In addition to the determination of points of vulnerability, it was necessary to try to define crucial adaptive or maladaptive mechanisms that promote or hinder the developmental process in the course of the early phases and also to determine the subphase specificity of potential stress

[4] We have not lost sight of the fact that valid assessment of outcome is impossible before the oedipal and post-oedipal, that is to say, latency periods, as well as adolescence, have been traversed.

traumata (see E. Kris, 1956). (The important questions of timing and of mechanisms will require additional systematic research of our data.)

As the first precondition for mental health, all our children, with individual variations, were in the range of normal endowment; it was this criterion, among others, that made them eligible to be subjects of our investigations. (We aimed to exclude less than normally endowed infants.)[5]

Through our special interest in the second determinant of later health or pathology (the early mother-child interaction and relationship), we learned how much we had to expand and broaden the category of Winnicott's "ordinary devoted mother" (1957*a*). We experienced also how unspecifiable—in terms of cause and effect—the influence of middle-range variations of "ordinary devoted mothering" is in creating minor pathology in the child.[6] In other words, the concept of "good enough" mothering (Winnicott, 1962) came under scrutiny.

Three variables involving the mother are of particular importance in shaping, promoting, or hindering the individual child's adaptability, drive, and ego development, and the beginning structuralization of precursors of his sugerego:

1. The mother's personality structure.
2. The developmental process of her parental function (Benedek, 1959).
3. The mother's conscious, but particularly unconscious, fantasy regarding the individual child.

These three variables, together with the child's potentialities, determine the degree to which the child is able to fulfill the mother's specific fantasies and expectations. These variables are, of course, interdependent.

In reference to the third basic ingredient of individual growth and personality formation of the child, we endeavored to determine in particular those experiential factors that either may have impinged on the child's personality at those points on the developmental curve that represent general vulnerabilities or may have acted upon the individual child's specific sensitivities.

Taking our five children as examples, we rather frequently came to points at which our psychoanalytic metapsychology required certain

[5] From our point of view, the infant's "sending power," his innate ability to evoke the kind of mothering he needs, should be particularly emphasized as an important attribute of his endowment; this aspect of his innate endowment has constituted an implied assumption throughout this volume.

[6] It became amply evident that a randomly selected sample of "average mothers" does not necessarily constitute a group of the category of mothers whom Winnicott designated as "ordinary devoted mothers."

shifts in emphasis; we also arrived at points at which our data lent different meanings to some hitherto accepted assumptions.[7]

Psychologists and psychiatrists, whether psychoanalytically oriented or not, routinely expect, for example, that the earlier the occurrence of traumata and the more unfavorable the earliest phases of extrauterine existence—the symbiotic phase, the differentiation subphase and the practicing subphase, that is, the first 14 to 15 months of life—the greater the proclivity to later, severe personality difficulties, borderline pathology, or even psychosis. This appears to be true only if (1) the infant's innate endowment is greatly abnormal, and/or if (2) the experiential circumstances are stressful and consistently counteract subphase-specific progress far beyond the "average expectable." That is to say, if developmental conditions from the beginning are so greatly deviant that the effect of stress traumata is ongoing and cumulative, then those structuralization processes that development from about 15 months on is expected to achieve will be disturbed. Such extreme circumstances seemed to have prevailed only in two or three of our sample of 38 children.[8]

Of the five children described in Part III, Sam and Teddy were the ones whose development seriously concerned us. Sam's differentiation in terms of self-boundary formation seemed to lag far beyond his individuation, and Teddy's outward-directed attention cathexis beyond the symbiotic orbit did not take place before the chronological age of the early practicing period. Yet as far as we know from our assessment of him at the end of the third year, Sam did emerge without failing in his cognitive functioning. Furthermore, in spite of his hyperactivity and overexcitability, given a fair chance in a structured environment, the failing impulse control of his ego was easily restored. Teddy, in particular, and quite unexpectedly, also seemed to remain very much in the middle range of adjustment and "mental health."

Among the hitherto widely accepted psychoanalytic "rules" for the evaluation of average development is the theory that predictably alternating gratification-frustration experiences are necessary for the structuralization of the ego and for facilitation of the replacement of the pleasure principle by the reality principle. Even though this universal

[7] In processing our data, we arrived every so often at points at which we had to face squarely the problem that even in the earliest phases of infant and toddler development, genetic and dynamic overdetermination played a role in creating developmental conflicts and crises in which the hierarchy of contributing factors could be only tentatively determined, but by no means resolved (cf. Waelder, 1960).

[8] These two or three children have not been dealt with individually in this book.

proposition could be verified in a very broad sense, we found that, as far as the infinite developmental details are concerned, this verification was far from unequivocal and, in fact, was subject to unbelievably complex variability.

Also, we had accepted the idea that, for normal development, the gratification-frustration sequences must be such that the younger the infant, the more prominent must be the gratification elements as compared with those of frustration. In our frame of reference, then, we would have expected that if, in the earliest phase of extrauterine life—that is, in the normal autistic phase—undisturbed homeostasis had taken place, and if, in the symbiotic phase, optimal attunement between infant and mother—that is, optimal mutual cueing, a perfect fit of the dual unity—had occurred, and consequently a blissful state of well-being had prevailed, such children would tend to remain merged in their state of symbiosis; their primitive ego would not be called upon to differentiate before what we believed was the optimal duration of symbiosis. This, we thought, would give them the best head start toward future development and the greatest resiliency against the onslaught of later traumata.

Since we were not able simply to verify the hitherto accepted rule, we felt obliged to examine our data in detail in order to find out which innate and/or nurturing variables are responsible for belated or late differentiation and which are responsible for the opposite: precocious differentiation.

Reconsideration of Early Versus Late Hatching

As limited as our data on the earliest phases may have been (see Chapters 3 and 4), they seemed to necessitate qualifications of the concept of "precocious ego development" and the concept of differentiation. These modifications became necessary because of the fact that individual evolution of "ego" appears a most variable process, particularly in its first stages. We found that there is no clear distinction in the literature of the innumerable integral, but not yet cohesive, elements of the evolving ego. What we wish to emphasize is that the differentiation process in some infants seems to be precipitated by precocious activation of fragments of the pre-ego, or of ego nuclei,[9] beginning in the symbiotic phase.

[9] We borrowed the term "ego-nucleus" from Glover (1956), without full utilization of the classical conceptualization he has attributed to it.

This nuclear pre-ego precocity may manifest itself in hypersensitivity in a certain limited area of a sensoriperceptive modality. It may create hyperacusis, startling at noises, or visual hyperalertness, as well as very early gustatory hypersensitivity or oversensitivity to touch.

This wild shoot, this premature differentiation of a fragment, creates an unevenness that hinders, rather than promotes, structuralization and integration of the ego as a cohesive structure. This may be unfavorable for the smooth evolution in the earliest subphases of the separation-individuation process.

The more abruptly, suddenly, and prematurely the infant becomes aware of the external world beyond the symbiotic orbit, through such a fragment of pre-ego precocity, the more difficult it seems to become for him to ward off fear of early symbiotic object loss. While the specific smiling response may appear very early in such cases, indicating the early establishment of the specific bond, so may strangeness reactions and stranger anxiety.

In such instances, in order that the awareness of separateness not be too traumatic, there is a great need for the mother to be endowed with a particularly sensitive "coenesthetic empathy." It is important that the mother furnish a particularly well-attuned external or auxiliary ego, a particularly sensitive protective shield. (It is also important that the mother as protective shield gradually recede, as it were, so as not to hinder the individuating ego's gradual exercise of autonomy.)

In the course of the symbiotic phase, the mother's ministrations libidinize the infant's body (Hoffer, 1950*a*). In the differentiation subphase, behaviors indicating an active process of bodily self-libidinization are observable. These behaviors occur with particular intensity when the admiring onlooking adult (especially the mother) mirrors the infant, and the infant in turn responds to and mirrors the onlooker. It seemed that this libidinization through looking on, as well as talking to, elicited an intensification of the infant's activity in a way that suggested triggering of a kind of affectomotor self-libidinization; in fact, some infants behaved as if they wanted to arrive at a kind of climax of experiencing their bodily sensations!

To repeat: as far as the separation-individuation of the individual infants was concerned, the traditional assumptions, the questions of satisfactory versus strenuous symbiotic states and precocious versus delayed differentiation (pertaining to structuralization of the ego), tended to appear rather complex, and no regular proportionate relations among the various factors could be discerned in the middle range of normalcy with our present research tools.

Bruce's symbiotic phase was precarious in contrast to that of both Donna and Wendy, which seemed to be ideal. Yet all three of these infants seemed to differentiate early, in terms of becoming aware of the world beyond the symbiotic orbit. Bruce's early differentiation and early specific attachment were triggered by his hyperalertness to sound [startle]; Wendy's early differentiation was attributable to mainly visual and gestalt-perceptive oversensitivity and precocity.

In contrast, Teddy, who had experienced a great deficit during his symbiotic phase, differentiated very late. Sam, whose early development occurred in an overwhelmingly symbiotic-parasitic atmosphere extending far beyond the chronological symbiotic phase, seemed to differentiate very late as well. To our surprise, however, he resorted to quite precociously developed quasi-physical precursors of the defense mechanism of disavowal—namely, behaviors of avoidance and body distancing. Sam's case, in particular, drew our attention to the great difference between the two tracks of the separation-individuation process (see Chapter 12).

It bears special emphasis in this concluding section that our study convinced us that the maturational pressure, *the drive for and toward individuation* in the normal human infant, *is an innate*, powerful *given*, which, although it may be muted by protracted interference, does manifest itself all along the separation-individuation process.

If the timetable of these two lines or tracks of the developmental process is substantially divergent, then overlapping of subphases becomes a problem, as we described by comparing the early development of the precociously walking little boy (see Chapter 4, pp. 61–63) with that of Sam. We were impressed by Sam's early and active defense of his individuation. We were also impressed by the alert contemplativeness with which he seemed, from his position in the playpen, visually to take in movements and goings-on in the nursery—a cognitive-affective individuating aspect of his development. He was like a strategist contemplating his next "moves." We saw in him an early onset of individuation, with separation lagging behind.

Sam had a kind of double life from his tenth to seventeenth month, suckling at his mother's breast at night and even at naptime, but distancing and warding off intrusion and interference with his individuation on any other occasion. For a long time it appeared dubious to us whether Sam could overcome the prolonged appersonation (Sperling, 1944) that he suffered far beyond the symbiotic phase and, to a great extent, beyond the end of his second year. We doubted whether he would progress sufficiently in his autonomous individuation,[10] particularly in his self-boundary formation.

In Wendy's case, her mother thoroughly enjoyed her, and therefore there were certainly no early *experiential* factors (at least none that we observed) that would have accounted for signs that heralded early differentiation of a sensory-perceptual nature—startling at sudden movements of people and overreacting or becoming anxious at strangeness as early as her fourth month. Wendy became quasi-addicted to contact-sensual handling by her mother, and well into her third year she sought self-stimulation by rocking on the rocking horse as much and as often as possible. She remained consistently uninterested in the "widening world of the toddler" (see Murphy, 1962).

From the above, it follows that our observations did not bear out the English school's contention. According to the latter, precocious differentiation of the ego (as a structure) occurs if the burden of adapting to external reality is left too early and to too great a degree to the infant. As Wendy's case illustrates, early differentiation may be brought about by *intrinsic* precocity of a sensory-perceptive ego nucleus and not through any inadequacy of the mother-infant mutual attunement. In her case this was due to her innate, albeit moderate, degree of oversensitivity.

Neither did our data bear out *our* expectation that substantially delayed differentiation is necessarily a danger signal per se—that is, unfavorable for ongoing development. This assumption seemed to be contradicted by Teddy's case, among others. As we have said, among the five representative children, only Teddy and Sam, who were at the two extremes of the gratification-frustration series, differentiated late. (Teddy experienced mainly frustration. Only in the routine, oversimplified sense was Sam on the side of overgratification, as set forth above; this later became the equivalent of frustration, by interfering with his subphase-specific needs.)

By contrast, the two children who had been very well gratified during the symbiotic phase, Wendy and Donna, as well as the unpredictably frustrated Bruce, showed signs of differentiation very early.

Of the early differentiating children, some had very early stranger reactions. Others, for example Wendy, who had a very early exclusive

[10] It is of some significance that these warding-off patterns seemed to give way to introjective identification with mother at the actual stage of the rapprochement subphase, which occurred very late in Sam's case. For distinction between introjection and identification, we refer the reader to Heimann (1966) and Loewald (1962).

attachment to her mother because of her aforementioned perceptual oversensitivity, rather early perceived and over-reacted to any "strangeness" in her environment. Wendy could not use her early maturational differentiation in the service of normal curiosity vis-à-vis the strange person. She did not develop the kind of stranger reactions we saw in the other children. Rather she seemed to reject all aspects of the environment at the Center. This we would call *strangeness* reaction. Wendy's early attachment, her longing for exclusive symbiosis, seemed so deeply rooted and pervasive that there was hardly any area that was not drawn into her quest for symbiosis. She showed every sign of wanting desperately to maintain it, even to the extent of disregarding, discarding, as it were, her predominantly maturational sensory-perceptual precociousness. The too-early maturational pressure toward individuation that this precociousness fostered and with which, according to developmental tests, her overall endowment did not harmonize, seemed to predispose Wendy to early vehement separation reactions and to approach behaviors that practically canceled out any distancing behavior. She reacted consistently and stubbornly against distancing attempts by her mother.

In Teddy and Sam, examples of late-differentiating infants, there was a substantial delay of stranger reactions as well as of separation reactions. Neither child had shown the subphase-specific expectable stranger or separation reactions during the chronological age of either the differentiating subphase or the early practicing period.

Within the complexities of the above described structuralization processes in their adaptive and defensive aspects, we were most impressed by the tenacity of the pressure that the thrust of the individuation process exerts from the differentiation subphase onward. This finding caused us to regard *individuation* as an innate given, which reveals itself with particular force in the beginning of life and which seems to continue during the entire life cycle (Erickson, 1959). In Sam, we saw a child who, amidst a smothering envelopment in symbiosis as early as 3 to 4 months of age, developed quasi-physical precursors of defense mechanisms. Even though this child seemed unusually radiant and expressed with his whole body his pleasure in his symbiotic sense of well-being long past the chronological age of symbiosis, those simultaneous behaviors aimed at distancing appeared to us to be potential precursors of disavowal or even of isolation. They contaminated the obligatory attachment behavior as well as his separation reactions at an age when these reactions are subphase-specific. Separation reactions at a higher level did not occur in Sam until very late (at the height of his delayed practicing period proper, at 17 months of age). His early stranger reactions were quite abortive and also occurred very late in his life.

In Teddy, differentiation also came late. Symbiosis lasted for a long time with him. Hatching—that is to say, cathectic investment of the outside world—occurred very late, not before his eighth month, and it had, even at that late age, a waxing and waning quality.

Stranger Reactions and Separation Anxiety

A positive finding of our study was that *stranger reactions* at perception of the other-than-mother are dependent on broad sensorimotor, quasi-cognitive functions of the ego that go far beyond the affect of anxiety. In addition to anxiety, the stranger evokes mild or even compellingly strong curiosity. That is why we have emphasized throughout this book that *curiosity* and *interest* in the new and the unfamiliar are as much a part of stranger reactions as are anxiety and wariness. Even in children with strong stranger reactions, such as Bruce, curiosity and wonderment about new people and new sensory experiences competed with wariness, sobriety, and anxiety reactions. Another important finding of our study, we believe, is that in normal development, stranger reactions of a different structure from those of the 7- to 9-month-old recur at the beginning of the rapprochement subphase, that is, at 15 months or later.

We have discussed the fact that in the rapprochement subphase, the normal child gradually becomes fully aware of his separateness. As his sensorimotor intelligence is being replaced by representational intelligence, he seems to realize more and more clearly his relative smallness and his helplessness. This experience renders the senior toddler much more vulnerable to events in the outside world, for example, to the absence of his parents, to illness, to the birth of a sibling, and so forth. Severe separation reactions can be the consequence of even minor traumata, and more than the expectable degree of ambivalence may ensue. In less favorable cases, regression to the stage in which the symbiotic matrix was first differentiated into either all "good" or all "bad" may occur. This splitting of the object world may become a proclivity that may interfere with expectable normal repression (Kernberg, 1974). Whether and how far this split of object representations will spill over to affect the self representation as well will depend on the degree to which self-object differentiation has progressed.

CHAPTER 14

The Epigenesis of Separation Anxiety, Basic Mood, and Primitive Identity

WE feel that we have refined our knowledge of separation reactions as far as both their structure and their epigenesis are concerned. We learned that separation reactions change during the course of the subphases; they are subphase-specific, as we have described in Part II. They are also, however, individually variable, as amply demonstrated in Part III of this volume.

The differentiating child (5 to 10 months old) usually reacts to mother's absence not with open distress or crying, but rather with what we have come to call "low-keyedness." In the five representative children, low-keyedness was greatest in Wendy, mild in Donna, variable and unpredictable in Bruce, absent in Sam, and very late in Teddy.

In the practicing subphase, the thrust in autonomous ego development, along with interest and pleasure in functioning and exploration, helps the child to overcome the lowering of mood, the low-keyedness, in mother's absence. In other words, the delight in motility and in discovery makes low-keyedness an episodic occurrence, counteracted by the joy of practicing, and it is easily overcome by short "refueling" experiences. This was so in all our children except Wendy, who continually resisted using her maturationally ascending and expanding functions. Normally, these functions are used automatically by the ego in the service of separation from mother and exploration of a wider segment of reality. Early self-reliance, even though not consistently progressive, was definitely greatest in Bruce. His excellent endowment helped him to adapt, albeit defensively, without becoming totally emmeshed in conflict with his mother. Bruce's successful disidentification from his mother, his turning to his own autonomous functions and to his father, saved him, we felt, from serious developmental disturbances and from gender identity failure.

Separation reactions occurred with varying intensity in all children during the *rapprochement* struggle. These seperation reactions were of a different quality and order from the earlier ones; they had to be described for each child individually, since they were quite specific in each child. They were, in fact, the most important indicators of the individuating toddler's conflicts on the way to internalization. These separation reactions depend on a host of variations in the mother-child relationship as well as on the vicissitudes of the earlier subphase characteristics.

Of the five representative children, Bruce, Wendy, and Donna had the most severe separation reactions in the course of the subphase of rapprochement. Bruce's reactions were rendered more poignant and complicated by the birth of his sister when he was 16 months old. Yet his separation reactions, though they were very intense, seemed "self-limiting" as it were, as least as far as his manifest behavior was concerned. A number of data seem to point to the probability that repression in the service of adaptation set in very early in Bruce. This was coupled with very early reaction formation (see Mahler and McDevitt, 1968) [1] The separation reactions ended abruptly when Bruce turned to his father and to other substitute adults in addition to making the utmost use of his own autonomous resources. Donna and Wendy, on the other hand, were not capable of overcoming their separation crises quite so successfully. Wendy could not really become involved in anything unless her mother was close by or another adult interacted with her. This seemed to be the result of the aforementioned characteristics of her pre-rapprochement development, augmented by her mother's tendency to detach herself from her children as soon as they became differentiated. Donna,

[1] From 14 to 16 months on, one can and should look for behavioral and also symbolic signs of whether repression will succeed in staving off a proclivity toward more permanent and ominous splitting. We feel that it is the capacity of the primitive, yet already somewhat structured, ego to *repress*, that, along with many other factors, *ensures* an outcome more benign than borderline pathology (see Kernberg, 1974).

for her part, could not become involved when her mother *was* present.[2]

Teddy's separation reactions were, on the one hand, delayed; but on the other, they were also complicated by his very strong "identification with the aggressor" (A. Freud, 1936)—his older brother, his twinlike alter ego—a kind of kinship that his mother very actively fostered. Teddy detected his penis very early, and he found pleasure in it, seemingly for a comparatively long-lasting, conflict-free period. In fact, he showed sensual, tactile pleasure and interest in his own penis and that of his older brother. His mother approved of these activities and seemed to foster them, which may have helped him develop a self-confident masculine gender identification. This was coupled with a somewhat greater than optimal (possibly innate or possibly early acquired) component of aggression in the absence of provocation, probably a belated reaction to his very early severe frustrations. During the rapprochement period, he seemed to react to separations with anger rather than with anxiety. He also developed a quite conspicuous early "empathy" with mother and peers—a most interesting trait, and difficult to understand. We feel that it may have had to do with his partial identification on a rather high ego level with his mother and also with his older brother. Both identifications were at first of the mirroring type, but gradually they seemed to become true ego identifications.

In Sam, separation anxiety was larval up to the second half of the second year. It reached its acme in his third year, triggered by the birth of his sister. It was markedly interwoven and confused with his body multilation and castration anxieties.

[2] We regarded Donna's potential for ego development based on endowment and early experiential factors as one of the greatest of all our children. Hence, one of the biggest surprises in our study was her developmental disturbance in the rapprochement subphase. This seemed to be the outcome of several unexpected, partly unrecognized, factors of Donna's separation-individuation process in the first two subphases. Her protracted difficulty in the rapprochement subphase and beyond was adumbrated as early as the early practicing subphase, during which her conspicuous cautiousness was not sufficiently taken into account by the observers. Neither did we take Donna's early finicky eating habits and marked fears seriously enough. Her mother's intolerance of aggression and very subtle reluctance vis-à-vis her baby's individuation, we also took into account in retrospect only. We overemphasized perhaps the pathogenicity of the "shock traumata" that befell Donna from 19 to 28 months.

Assumptions about Basic Mood and Its Relation to Gender Identity

Another question on which we believe our study has thrown some light is the development of basic moods.[3] We found that in the practicing subphase a mood of elation seemed subphase-specific, obligatory, and dominant (Mahler, 1966*a* and *b*). In addition, this mood often manifested itself in a quasi-delusional but age-adequate sense of grandeur, omnipotence, and conquest. This mood of the junior toddler—at the crest of mastery of many of his autonomous functions, the paradigm of which is locomotion—necessarily had to give way to a more realistic appraisal of his smallness in relation to the outside world. A gradual recognition of the disproportion of his illusion of grandeur and the obstacles in the way of successful adaptation to the exigencies of reality has to take place from the fifteenth to eighteenth month onward.

In boys and girls alike, the repeated experience of relative helplessness punctures the toddler's inflated sense of omnipotence. The child recognizes for the first time his separateness from his mother. This is an achievement of representational intelligence that makes possible the internal capacity to differentiate self representations from object representations. This brings in its wake (in normal development) the gradual realization on the part of the child that he is relatively small and helpless and has to cope with overwhelming odds as a relatively weak and lonely (because separate) individual. Hence, the dominant subphase-specific normal mood of the rapprochement subphase becomes one of relative soberness or even temporary depression.

Our data indicate that the boy's active, aggressive strivings, his gender-determined motor-mindedness, seem to help him to maintain (with many ups and downs, to be sure) the bouyancy of his body-ego feelings, his belief in his body strength, and his pleasure in functioning. In other words, the momentum of the boy's motor function seems to counteract the too abrupt deflation of the "practicing grandeur" and omnipotence. Even though the boy in the rapprochement subphase also shows soberness and increased hypersensitivity about his separateness from mother, as well as about impingements upon his autonomy, and even though in the beginning of rapprochement he shows increased dependence on his

[3] Definition of mood, as distinguished from the concept of affects, has occupied the minds of many investigators. We feel that the discussion of this issue by Edith Jacobson (1953) is, for our purposes, the most relevant and acceptable one. In our instance, we refer to mood as the habitual mode of response to inner and outer stimulations with positive or negative affects.

mother's participation, on the whole, he pursues his own motor and perceptual-cognitive activities with more or less confident tenacity. Under favorable conditions, the boy actively exercises his separation from and reunion with mother. The active darting-away behavior described earlier (p. 77), which seemed more prominent in boys than in girls, is but one example of this.

Our data indicate that the girl is more prone to depressed mood than the boy (see Gero, 1936). The realization of separateness is compounded in the case of the girl by a lesser degree of motor-mindedness and by her awareness (which occurs much *earlier* than we had previously believed [Greenacre, 1948; Mahler, 1963]) of her anatomical "shortcoming" (see Roiphe and Galenson, 1971).

Despite the gender difference, both boys and girls come to recognize, sooner or later, gradually or abruptly, the limitations of their magic omnipotence, but they still seem to maintain the illusion of the parents' omnipotence (see Jacobson, 1964).

As the rapprochement subphase evolves, it is most interesting to observe the different flavor of the girl's reinvolvement with mother as compared to the boy's. Every so often, the girl expresses symbolically in her play and in her verbalizations her dissatisfaction at being shortchanged or outrightly hurt (that is to say, castrated) by the all-powerful mother, whom she overtly blames for her fantasied shortcoming. Often an overt struggle with mother ensues, in which an ambitendent clinging-dependent and coercively demanding behavior is the rule.[4] Characteristics of the girl's behavior in the third year indicate that penis envy may have become repressed and the claim for the penis displaced to the mother as a person. The ambitendent rapprochement struggle which represents the externally acted-out rapprochement crisis is internalized later on. However, every so often, it is perpetuated in the symptomatic and symbolic difficulty in leave-taking from mother.

In favorable cases, successful repression and transient solution of this very early penis envy occurs in the latter part of the third year. At that time, true ego identifications with mother, especially with her mothering function, in terms of transmuting internalization, may take place (Tolpin, 1972). This identification with mother forms a basis for feminine gender identity, but often a typical early tomboy behavior, or anal and phallic

[4] Ambitendency is conceptualized as alternating action in opposite directions. The alternation occurs with greater or lesser rapidity; it connotes doing and undoing. In later development, the conflictual opposing impulses, which had been acted out in the ambitendent behavior, become internalized as *ambivalence* conflict (see Mahler and McDevitt, 1968, p. 11).

aggressive acquisitiveness, betrays continuation of the wish for a penis and reaction-formation against dependent feminine wishes.[5]

In boys, the rapprochement struggle seemed generally less stormy. Its gender quality is much more covert. It asserts itself, we think, with less conflict if the mother respects and enjoys the boy's phallicity all along, especially in the second half of the third year. Furthermore, we have the impression that identification with the father or possibly with an older brother facilitates a rather early beginning of the boy's gender identity. In some cases in which the mother has been interfering with the boy's autonomy, establishment of his early gender identity is threatened and disturbed, particularly if she is unable to relinquish her son's body and the ownership of his penis to him. Some mothers foster—in fact, force—passivity in the boy. In this case, the rapprochement struggle might take on the character of a more or less desperate biphasic struggle on the part of the boy to ward off the dangerous "mother after separation." We cannot help but speculate that the fear of reengulfment by the dangerous "mother after separation," the fear of merging that we sometimes see as a central resistance in our adult male patients, has its inception at this very early period of life.

Given favorable mothering, the boy seems better able to cope with the anxiety that Stoller (1973) termed "symbiosis anxiety," and to disidentify from mother (Greenson, 1968), to avoid her or at least to resist her in a more covert way. Furthermore, we found in the play of the normal 2- to 3-year-old boy, many indications of his turning to his father, whom he aggrandized, that is to say, overidealized. We found that material representing the mother as castrator appeared more sparsely in the boy's play and verbalization than in those of the girl. The fear of mother as the reengulfing, infantilizing agent appeared more often in the boy. If, however, the mother is too intrusive and consistently interferes directly or indirectly with the boy's phallic strivings, the ambitendent struggle described in the case of girls may ensue in the boy as well and may even give way to passive surrender. The latter is particularly harmful if the father image does not lend itself to idealization and to true ego-identification.

[5] We know of at least two children in whom the overinflation of their feeling of omnipotence and grandeur, the plethora of their early narcissism, augmented by the mirroring admiration by mother and the surrounding adult world, proved definitely unfavorable to their ability to replace the belief in magical omnipotence by sound secondary narcissism and enduring confidence in a "good" object world. On the other hand, we also know of several cases of boys and girls whose adaptive and defense organization later in life—possibly in their resolution of the oedipal phase—amply corrected an apparently frustrating (less than optimal) early subphase development.

In summary, whereas the girl's penis envy appears very early, during rapprochement, and her lack of a penis is blamed on the mother, the little boy's conflictual attitude about his penis seems to occur later: in the phallic phase. That which corresponds to penis envy in the girl is in the boy of that age a vague fear of reengulfment by the mother (see Harrison, I., in press). Therefore, the boy's main concern is to find other-than-mother ego ideals with which to identify. In normal development the threatening castrator in the boy's case appears to be the father, not the mother. (Because of our research design we unfortunately could only guess at this latter hypothesis rather than ascertain it through direct material from our study.)

Because of the described differences in the gender-specific vicissitudes of the separation-individuation process, it seems quite plausible that the proclivity to a basic depressive mood is greater in girls than in boys. But in both boys and girls the carrying power of the self-confident subphase-specific mood of the practicing period, the reestablishment and regeneration of self-esteem and confidence in the world, will generally depend on the *pace and the timing* of the replacement of the feeling of *omnipotence* by sound secondary narcissism. The building of a realistic self-esteem in the course of the rapprochement subphase is very much dependent on the active *aggressive* momentum of the individuation thrust, which, however, must be neutralized.

As we discussed in detail in Chapter 6, the facilitating role of the environment has added importance in the rapprochement subphase. Also important are the mechanisms by which identificatory and disidentificatory mechanisms and internalization and externalization processes are brought into action. To be optimal they must be gender-adequate; that is, different in boys and girls.

Of the children we discussed in some detail, Bruce was one who was most able to approach new situations with enthusiasm, against great environmental odds. Bruce had a good early practicing period, briefly upset by his mother's depression. However, he rallied his forces and after many reverses learned to walk around 1 year of age. He used this newly acquired function to explore the world with great elation and confidence. This quality of enthusiasm in his learning and exploration remained with Bruce. It seemed to help him to disidentify from his mother, turn to his father, and find comfort in the world around him. Yet, his basic mood during and after the rapprochement phase vacillated between enthusiasm and pensive soberness. In addition to Bruce and Teddy, we had many other cases of boys in whom the preoedipal basic mood, by the end of the rapprochement subphase, tended to be a positive, optimistic one.

On the other hand, Donna, the child with the best overall innate endowment, was already subdued at the time of the early practicing period. She was happy only if her mother was in sight. She could invest neither the other-than-mother world nor her own self with confidence. She seemed, at times, overcautious in her motility. Though Donna crawled and walked at the same age as Bruce and later on, during her practicing period proper, displayed a typical "love affair with the world," she seemed to find separating from her mother forever painful and conflictual. Her basic mood during the third year was one of anxious indecisiveness. To our great surprise, in spite of her superior individuation (due to superior endowment and apparent "optimal mothering"), her elated mood of practicing yielded (in her twentieth and twenty-first month) to greater than average mood swings.

A major contributing factor to Donna's developmental disturbances was probably the accumulation of shock traumata at the end of her second and in her third year. On account of her above average aggressive endowment this augmented her predisposition to a later neurosis. Manifestations of her greater than average aggressivity were discernible in her earliest subphase (in her homelife, in particular). Later these disappeared and seemed to become repressed in the course of the rapprochement subphase. They were replaced by early fears, by anxious overcautiousness and greater than average ambivalence. It is noteworthy in this connection that Donna's mother was particularly intolerant of her own aggressive strivings and, consequently, of the aggressivity of others as well.

Sam, whose symbiotic phase was artificially prolonged, started the practicing subphase late. He crawled late, and he did not achieve and then master upright locomotion until the ages of 17 and 18 months, respectively, the chronological height of rapprochement. At that time, his mood became elated for a short period only and soon gave way to restless anxiousness and excitability.

From our small sample of 38 children, we have the impression that the self-confident and enthusiastic mood of the practicing period seemed to extend beyond the rapprochement subphase more readily in those children in whom early practicing—the first moving away from mother—was pleasurable. This was the case with Bruce and with Teddy. It seems that the pleasure in the early forays into the other-than-mother world, more than any other variable, carried the child through later difficulties, helping him to approach new situations in a positive and confident mood.

Teddy, adaptively but also defensively, we felt, (see Mahler & McDevitt, 1968) delayed hatching. Yet after hatching he used every possible means to interest and occupy his mother's attention, as well as to elicit attention from others (by clowning, exhibiting his penis, mirroring his older brother, teasingly threatening his mother with directing his penis toward her, and so on). His early aggression, which went beyond the momentum of his ascending locomotor activity pressure, may have been a belated reaction to frustration, on the one hand, and, on the other, a mirroring "identification with the aggressor"—his brother who was older by 14½ months (A. Freud, 1936). His early phallic prowess seemed at first rather unencumbered by reactive defensiveness. Only later, at the height of the phallic phase and the adumbration of the phallic-oedipal period, did Teddy seem to have to cope with castration anxiety. With him as with several other boys, this seemed to go underground and become internalized. There was coy seductiveness and simultaneously some defensiveness, and occasionally anger, but never open hostility toward mother. (The study of a possible struggle with father was not at our disposal with our methodology.)

Teddy's case and that of his brother (not discussed here in detail) would, along with the history of many other of our boys, indicate that the active, aggressive carrying power of the motor function in boys helped them not to succumb as readily as the girls to a basic depressive mood in the preoedipal period. But as we elaborated earlier, there were some exceptions to this rule: those were cases of boys in whom stress traumata inflicted by gross interference on the part of the mother set developmental obstacles and in whose cases the father was concomitantly an inadequate object for identification.

Wendy was different from all the other children in that she never seemed to defend herself against symbiotic engulfment. In fact, it seemed as if she worked against the maturational growth process, which increasingly prompts the toddler to separate, to "board off" the self representation from the object representation. As we have already described, Wendy was intent for a very long time—way into the chronological age of the fourth subphase—on having an exclusive relationship with mother or with substitutes for mother, male and female alike. She insisted on a one-to-one relationship with adults, alternating between seductive, appealing behaviors and morose fretfulness. We believe that she was the most narcissistic of the five representative children and that she remained fixated far too long at the stage of mirroring identification with her mother. Regression was her main defense mechanism. She was also the least social of the five children. Her basic mood for a long time—well into the third year—depended almost entirely on mother's mood or on her mother's attitude toward her and toward people with whom Wendy came into contact. Her overall development, though by no means severely disturbed, was substantially delayed.

CHAPTER 15

Reflections on Core Identity and Self-Boundary Formation

THE steps of building, the self representation from the self-object representations of the symbiotic phase are rather elusive.

We followed children from the twilight state of symbiosis to a point where they emerged as individuals in their own right, with a definite sense of "I," "me," and "mine," with a sense of who and where they are, even if this sense was still to an extent dependent on a syncretic context and subject to many distortions. We soon were apprehensive about the difficulties inherent in tracing the steps of body-image formation, as well as differentiation of bodily and mental self representation in an observational study. We felt from the beginning that finding behavioral referents pertinent to this eminently internal process would be very difficult.

What the infant feels subjectively, inside his own body, especially in the beginning of extrauterine life, eludes the observing eye. That is to say, behavioral referents are barely existent. We may assume, however, that the earliest perceptions are of the order of bodily sensations such as we expounded in Chapter 4. It is in keeping with this view that Freud (1923) described the ego as first and foremost a "body ego."

Quite aside from the inherent difficulty of determining which behavioral and affectomotor surface referents may be regarded as integral steps of building bodily feelings, body-image, and eventual self representations, we experienced additional difficulties in this respect due to the nature and method of our study. Our particular setting was not geared to observation of the intimate and quiet reflective situations of home life: the baby in the crib by himself, cooing quietly, touching his body, playing with his feet, looking at his hand movements in a way that at first leaves doubt in the observer's mind as to whether the infant has any awareness that the spectacle he is watching occurs by his own volition, with his own body parts, or whether he "thinks" that they move by themselves.

Our research design deprived us of the opportunity to observe the infant's detection of parts of his body—his toes, his feet, the important "belly button," and especially his penis. Some situations at the Center, however, seemed to substitute in part for the serious handicap of our methodology, our not being a witness to consistent and continuous intimate home situations. By carefully observing the behaviors as well as by viewing our films, we could sometimes observe *in statu nascendi* affectomotor self-libidinization, which may be a forerunner of integration of body-self feelings.

We noticed *in vivo*, and this was borne out in our analysis of the films, episodes in which the 5- to 8-month-old, surrounded by the admiring and libidinally mirroring friendly adults, seemed electrified and stimulated by this mirroring admiration. This was evident by his excited wiggling of his body, bending his back to reach his feet or his legs, kicking and flailing with the extremities, and stretching with an exaltedly pleasurable affect. This obvious tactile kinesthetic stimulation of his body-self, we believe, may promote differentiation and integration of his body image.

From about 7 months on, babies start to play games with their mothers that we surmise (ever since Anna Freud taught us that it was not altruism that dictated this behavior) serve to delineate the infant's own body-image from that of the object. The baby takes bits of food and puts them alternately into mother's mouth and into his own; he grabs mother's pendant and puts it into his mouth, and so on. Mothers in turn respond to the baby's emerging playful experimentations with body feelings by playing games of comparing the baby's body parts with their own ("This is my nose, where is your nose?" "pat-a-cake," "so big," and so on). Comparative scanning, checking back to mother, especially to her face, is at its peak. Passive and later active peekaboo is a game with a double purpose—to find mother, but also to be found by her. To be found by mother, to be seen by her (that is to say, mirrored by her) seems to build body-self awareness, which we must surmise from observation of the endless pleasure in this repetitive game. These are some observations about the emerging of the body self representation in the differentiation subphase.

At the stage of the beginning practicing subphase, our task becomes a bit easier. At this point, the infant starts to move by his own steam; he propels himself in space and seems at long last to have learned that not only are the arms and legs his own, belonging to his body, but that he can coordinate them and ready them to go. We have repeatedly talked about the relative obliviousness of the practicing infant and toddler to minor bumps and hurts during this period. As the infant crawls and later walks on his own, the frequent falling and knocking against unyielding objects in the environment seems to augment his feeling (the cathexis) of his body-self boundaries. These encounters with the unyielding inanimate surroundings seem to serve as a kind of aggressivization, a firming up and delineation as it were, of his body-self boundaries. These obligatory experiences help him to integrate his body image in conjunction with the firming effect of the kinesthetic sensations that the "performance motor function" of his musculature conveys. Thus, the relative obliviousness to minor pains during the period of practicing might serve the purpose of making it possible for the child to have repeated, alternating experiences of pleasure and minor pain as the outside world is actively touched, felt, and explored, or passively experienced as hard, unyielding, and at times hurtful, while the body-self representations are in the process of being formed. In contrast is the libidinization of body boundaries by the mother's handling of the baby's body, as well as by tactile contact with the cuddly, soft, and otherwise soothing "transitional object."

By the end of the practicing period and during the rapprochement subphase, we begin to see (as we have described in Chapters 5 and 6) the baby's taking possession of his own body and protecting it against being handled as a passive object by the mother; for example, he struggles against being put into the reclining position.

Here is the conflict: On the one hand is the toddler's feeling of helplessness in his realization of separateness, and on the other hand is his valiant defense of what he cherishes as the emerging autonomy of his body. In this struggle for individuation, and the concomitant anger about his helplessness, the toddler tries to reinflate his sense of self, to approximate the forever lost illusion of omnipotence of the practicing period. This is the time of the rapprochement struggle, from which the toddler may emerge through transmuting internalization (Tolpin, 1972) and other identificatory mechanisms with a measure of integration of his self representation, or he may get caught up in an uncertainty about his own identity as a viable separate being. Such uncertainty may be the effect of insufficient separation of his self representation, particularly in terms of differentiation of self-boundaries.[1] As a result, fusion, or reengulfment, remains a threat against which the child must continue to defend himself beyond the third year. The outcome of this conflict may not be decided even by the vicissitudes of oedipal and postoedipal development.

As far as "core identity" formation is concerned, even if we had the opportunity to observe intimate moments in the baby's life, we feel that we nevertheless would not have been able to see the infant building the *core* of his self representation. We are reminded of Winnicott (1963), who said:

> *In health* there is a core of the personality that corresponds to the true self. I suggest that this core never communicates with the world of perceived objects and that the individual person knows that it must never be communicated with or be influenced by external reality. Although healthy persons communicate and enjoy communicating, the other fact is equally true, that each individual is an isolate, permanently non-communicating, permanently unknown, in fact, unfound. (p. 187)

Winnicott goes on to say:

> The traumatic experiences that lead to the organization of primitive defenses belong to the threat to the isolated core, the threat of its being found, altered, communicated with. The defense consists in a further hiding of the secret self. . . . The question is: how to be isolated without having to be insulated? (p. 187)

The task to be achieved by development in the course of the normal separation-individuation process is the establishment of both a measure of object constancy and a measure of self constancy, an enduring individuality as it were. The latter achievement consists of the attainment of

[1] Mirror reactions are most relevant for following the process of building self representations and differentiating these from object representations. Put on the mattress before the floor-length mirror, when the baby first shows an interest in the image, he becomes excited and flails his arms in discharge movement. Later, at 6 to 8 months, his movements slow down and he appears to become thoughtful as he seems to relate his own body movements to the movement of the image in the mirror. (The children who did not respond motorically at this age would look at the image with some perplexity.) At a still later age, 9 or 10 months, the child makes deliberate movements while observing his image, seemingly experimenting with, sorting out, and clarifying for himself the relationship between himself and "the image." (The infant's and toddler's behavior vis-à-vis his mirror image represented a specific research project conducted by Dr. John B. McDevitt. It awaits publication by him.)

the two levels of the sense of identity: (1) the awareness of being a separate and individual entity, and (2) a beginning awareness of a gender-defined self-identity.

By the end of the second year we found striking consolidation of constitutionally predestined gender-defined differences in the behavior of boys and girls. The boy's pride in his penis and the girl's body narcissism seem to have had their inception during the anal phase. The full attainment of the second level of identity must await, however, the phallic phase of psychosexual development. In other words, the phallic phase has to be reached in order for the toddler to receive the decisive impetus for integration of the gender-determined body-self image. This development is dependent on differentiation and integration of a cohesive gender-determined ego structure, which in turn is dependent on stratification and hierarchic organization of libidinal zonal cathexis and synthesis into a whole of the representations of parts of the mental images of the body-self (see also Loewenstein, 1950).

We must emphasize again that the development of the sense of self is the prototype of an eminently personal, internal experience that is difficult, if not impossible, to trace in observational studies, as well as in the reconstructive psychoanalytic situation. It reveals itself by its failures much more readily than by its normal variations, to which this book has deliberately confined itself.

CHAPTER 16

Some Concluding Remarks about the Significance of the Rapprochement Crisis

GIVEN our special task and special setting and method, the third year, particularly its second half, became empirically our platform for assessing retrospectively the degree of structuralization of the ego, and for making educated guesses about relative future normalcy as well as minor or middle-range pathology in our subjects. We tried to evaluate in the phallic phase (and in a few cases, via the material of play sesions, in the fourth year as well), the outcome of the first three subphases of the separation-individuation process.

We came to the realization that we have to be extremely cautious and tentative in making even short-term predictions, for even these appear to be rather precarious. Our study unequivocally indicated, however, (at least in our by no means representative sample) that there were certain crossroads of the separation-individuation process, nodal points in structuralization, maturation, and development, at which certain events are particularly traumatic. These are, for example, the precocious differentiation of ego-nuclei, lack of environmental encouragement, and increased unneutralized aggression in the early practicing period; the mother's failing to release the infant's body in the beginning phase of the rapprochement crisis; and so on. We also found constellations in which traumatic situations remained dormant until the growth process reached those nodal points or crossroads at which stress traumata surfaced and caused disturbances (probable primal scene observations accentuating castration anxieties, surgical intervention in the family at an early age giving accretion to ambivalence, and so on).

Throughout the whole course of separation-individuation, one of the most important developmental tasks of the evolving ego is that of coping with the aggressive drive in the face of the gradually increasing awareness of separateness. The success with which this is achieved depends on the strength of the primitive ego, that is, the evenness of its structuralization (see Weil, 1973). This enables the child to use neutral or neutralized aggression in the service of the ego and helps him to accept separateness without being overwhelmed by the age-specific anxieties: fear of object loss, fear of loss of love, separation anxiety and/or castration anxiety.

We learned that the gradualness of the replacement of the pleasure principle by the reality principle—the gradualness of the awareness of the intrapsychic process of differentiation of the self representations from the object representations through identificatory processes—is a tortuous route. The two main tracks, individuation versus separation, the ego's structuralization and the awareness of separateness, are parallel developments. The infant's primary narcissism, the belief in his own and in his parent's omnipotence, must gradually recede, that is to say, it must be replaced by autonomous functioning. The active aggressive momentum of the innate given—the individuation thrust—must be invested with neutralized energy without undue impingement by ambivalence.

This would ensure the beginning of investment of the self with sound secondary narcissism, allow the apparatuses of the ego to attain secondary autonomy, and last but not least, allow for cathexis of the object world with a measure of neutralized libido, thus promoting sublimation (E. Kris, 1955).

Our limited study gave us an inkling as to why even the preliminary development toward the Oedipus complex and the infantile neurosis is so unpredictable. But it also gave us a kind of mandate to build with unrelenting, cautious optimism better instruments, more sophisticated psychoanalytic developmental theories for understanding the "unrememberable" and the "unforgettable" realm of the mind, which we believe holds the key for prevention.

Up to this point in the psychoanalytic situation we have been trying to understand that realm of the mind more or less by coenesthetic empathy. At some future time we should be able to come to a more well rounded empathetic-intellectual understanding of screen sensations and other derivatives of the preverbal phase (cf. Anthony, 1961).

We learned a great deal in this study about why smooth and consistently progressive personality development, even under ordinary favorable circumstances, is difficult, if not impossible. This, we found, was due precisely to the fact that separation and individuation derive from and are dependent upon the symbiotic origin of the human condition, upon that very symbiosis with another human being, the mother. This creates an everlasting longing for the actual or coenesthetically fantasized, wish-fulfilled, and absolutely protected state of primal identification (Ferenczi's absolute primal omnipotence, 1913), for which deep down in the original primal unconscious, in the so-called primarily repressed realm, every human being strives.

In addition, smooth and consistently progressive personality development is rendered exceedingly difficult by the exquisite complexity of the human being's task to adapt as a separate individual to the ever-increasing dangers of living in a contaminated and essentially hostile world.

It seems to be inherent in the human condition that not even the most normally endowed child, with the most optimally available mother, is able to weather the separation-individuation process without crises, come out unscathed by the rapprochement struggle, and enter the oedipal phase without developmental difficulty (Mahler, 1971). In fact, as we have discussed in Chapter 7, the fourth subphase of the separation-individuation process has no single definite permanent terminal point.

One of the main yields of our study was the finding that the infantile neurosis may have its obligatory precursor, if not its first manifestation, in the rapprochement crisis, which we have therefore made a particular focus in our book. It often continues far into the third year and may overlap the phallic-oedipal phase, in which case it interferes with repression and with the successful passing of the Oedipus complex (see A. Freud, 1965*b*; Nagera, 1966).

As we see it, much of our understanding of health and pathology may depend on developmental aspects, the most important of which, from our point of view, is the qualitative assessment of residues of the symbiotic as well as of the separation-individuation periods.

Through cross-fertilization of the structural and refined psychoanalytic developmental theories, we already possess *instruments* which, if used to amplify the libido theory, might bring us further in our understanding of the widening scope of neurotic symptoms in childhood as well as during the entire life cycle.

We easily forget the fact that the apex of the libido theory that holds the key to neurosis, the Oedipus complex itself, is not only a drive theory, but equally importantly an object-relations theory. There is a tendency to underestimate the potentiality of the ego and of the precursors of the superego to create intrapsychic conflicts at early levels of development.

We feel that our understanding of infantile neurosis might profit by integration of data gained by observation and reconstruction of the very first phases of the child's extrauterine existence. This, we believe, may be greatly enhanced by observing the path of the infant's differentiation and disengagement from the symbiotic matrix, and by tracing the first steps of internalized conflict.

In our clinical work as well as in our observations of mother-child pairs, we came across—to our own surprise—*developmental conflicts* that are *phase-specific*, even though individually variable. These occurred with amazing regularity from the second half of the second year on.

As the senior author described in a paper in the festschrift for Heinz Hartmann (Mahler, 1966*b*), it is precisely at the point at which the child is at the peak of his delusion of omnipotence—at the height of the practicing period—that his narcissism is particularly vulnerable to the danger of deflation.

At that time, from about the fifteenth to sixteenth month, there develops in the toddler the definite awareness of his own separateness. As a result of the maturational achievement of the ego, culminating in free upright locomotion and advanced cognitive development, the toddler is confronted with a new and disturbing reality, in the face of which he is no longer able to maintain the delusion of his omnipotent grandeur.

In the third subphase of the separation-individuation process, the rapprochement period, while individuation proceeds rapidly and the child exercises it to the limit, he becomes more and more aware of his separateness and begins to employ all kinds of partly internalized and partly still acted-out coping mechanisms in order to deny the separateness. One of the frequently observed coping behaviors is the toddler's insistent claim for the mother's attention and participation. But, as we said before, internalization processes go on at this point with rapid speed, building structures that contribute to the autonomy of the ego independent of the outside world.

The junior toddler gradually realizes that his love objects, his parents, are separate individuals with their own interests. He must gradually and painfully give up both the delusion of his own grandeur and his belief in the omnipotence of his parents. The result is heightened separation anxiety and disidentification from, as well as coercive dramatic fights with, mother (less so, it seemed to us, with father). This is the crossroads that we have termed the *rapprochement crisis.*

The rapprochement struggle has its origin in the *species-specific* human dilemma that arises out of the fact that, on the one hand, the toddler is obliged, by the rapid maturation of his ego, to recognize his separateness, while, on the other hand, he is as yet unable to stand alone and will continue to need his parents for many years to come.

Three paramount, anxiety-generating conditions of childhood, which may continue far beyond the second year of life, converge in the rapprochement period: (1) The fear of object loss is partly relieved by internalization, but it is also complicated by the introjection of parental demands; this not only indicates the beginning of superego development, but it also expresses itself in the fear of losing the object's love. This fear in turn manifests itself in a highly sensitive reaction to approval and disapproval by the parent. (2) There is a greater awareness of bodily feelings and pressures, augmented by awareness of bowel and urinary sensations during the toilet-training period. (3) In most instances, there is a reaction to the discovery—rather earlier than we thought—of the anatomical difference between the sexes, which prematurely precipitates castration anxiety or penis envy.

Developmental forces enabled many of our children to resolve the rapprochement conflict and to proceed to higher and broadened levels of object relationship and ego functioning, even though some developed transient developmental disturbances. In 1963, the senior author made an observation that our research has further borne out, that "the normal infant-toddler is intent upon and is usually able to extract emotional supplies and participation from his mother, sometimes against considerable odds." We have learned more details about the adaptive and defense mechanisms (precursors of later defenses) with which the child succeeds in warding off those still partly environmental influences that stand in the way of his establishing the secondary autonomy of his increasingly cohesive ego structure.

In some children, however, the rapprochement crisis leads to great ambivalence and even to splitting of the object world into "good" and "bad," the consequences of which may later become organized into neurotic symptoms of the narcissistic variety. In still other children, islands of developmental failures might lead to borderline symptomatology in latency and adolescence.[1]

[1] We deliberately have not dealt with these vicissitudes in detail in this book.

Fixation at the level of rapprochement may be seen every so often in the widening range of child and adult patients who nowadays seek our help. Their most pervasive anxiety is separation anxiety; their affects may be dominated by narcissistic rage with temper tantrums, which may subside and give way to altruistic surrender (A. Freud, 1936). Their basic conflict is to be sought and found, we believe, in the primitive narcissistic struggle that was acted out in the rapprochement crisis, but that may have become a central internal conflict pertaining mainly to their uncertain *sense of identity* (Erickson, 1959).

In closing, we wish to indicate the connection between the rapprochement crisis and the infantile neurosis as it has been classically conceived. An understanding of fixation at the rapprochement crisis throws some light, we believe, on the genesis of neurosis in those patients, in particular, whose main problem is that which the late Maurice Bouvet (1958) described as one of finding the "optimal distance" between the self and the object world. There is an oscillation between the longing to merge blissfully with the good object representation, with the erstwhile (in one's fantasy, at least) "all good" symbiotic mother, and the defense against reengulfment by her, which could cause loss of autonomous self-identity.

These mechanisms are the outcome of the basic conflict that arises in a fundamental and primitive form in the rapprochement subphase. The complex developmental processes of the rapprochement subphase and its successful or unsuccessful resolution undoubtedly affect the manner in which the child will subsequently negotiate the oedipal crisis.

The tendency toward splitting of the object world, which may ensue as the child's solution to the pain of longings and losses of the rapprochement crisis, must make for greater difficulty in the resolution of the complex object-related conflicts of the oedipal period, promoting ambivalence and throwing an ominous cast on the oedipal and postoedipal personality development.

In these, and perhaps in other diverse ways, we believe, the infantile neurosis becomes manifestly visible at the oedipal period; but it may be shaped by the fate of the rapprochement crisis *that precedes it.*

Appendices

The Data Analysis and Its Rationale: A Case Study in Systematic Clinical Research

APPENDIX A

The Available Data

The Mothers and the Children

DURING the pilot study (1959–62) and the more formal research years (1962–68), we studied 38 children and their 22 mothers. We have, increasingly over the years, focused on more intensive study of the children we worked with after 1962. Our intensive work with these latter children gained from a cumulative enrichment of concepts from our first pilot observations through the later, more formal studies of additional mother-infant pairs. Periodic contacts with many of the second group of children continued subsequent to the main periods of intensive study. A summary of characteristics of these children and their parents appears in Table 1.

TABLE 1

Summary of Selected Characteristics of Research Subjects
Group I: Sept. 1959–Jan. 1962. N = 17 children of 16 mothers
Group II: Jan. 1962–June 1968. N = 21 children of 13 mothers

CHARACTERISTIC	GROUP I	GROUP II
A. Age		
1. Average age at entry into study	13 months	2½ months
2. Range of ages at entry	1–27 months	1 week–10 months
3. Average age at termination of regular attendence	31 months	31 months
4. Range of ages at termination[1]	20–40 months	7–48 months
5. Average duration of participation	18 months	28½ months

[1] Some children remained with us until after 36 months for various reasons. Nonetheless, they were only studied until the 36th month.

CHARACTERISTIC	GROUP I	GROUP II
B. Sex		
6. Number of boys	8	12
7. Number of girls	9	9
C. Parity[2]		
8. Firstborn	11	3
9 Second born	3	12
10. Later than second born	1	6
D. Number of Siblings in Study[3]		
11. Number of families with one child in study	12	
12. Number of families with two children in study	8	
13. Number of families with three children in study	2	
14. Number of families with four children in study	1	
E. Parental Age[4]		
15. Average age of mothers at entry into study	Data incomplete	31 years
16. Range of ages of mothers at entry	Data incomplete	25–43 years
17. Average age of fathers at entry into study	Data incomplete	36 years
18. Range of ages of fathers at entry	Data incomplete	26–65 years
F. Parental Education[4]		
19. Average education of mothers (in years)	Data incomplete	15.3 years
20. Range of education of mothers (in years)	Data incomplete	12–18 years (high school to master's degree)
21. Average education of fathers (in years)	Data incomplete	16.7 years
22. Range of education of fathers (in years)	Data incomplete	12–20 years (high school to Ph.D.)
G. Religion of Families (and Children)[5]		
23. Protestant	7 (8)	5 (10)
24. Jewish	3 (3)	4 (5)
25. Catholic	4 (4)	2 (4)
26. Mixed	3 (3)	2 (2)

[2] We do not have this information on two of the children from Group I; here the numbers total 15 instead of 17.

[3] It makes no sense to divide this by subgroup. However, we should note that the large number of second- and later-born children in Group II is due to the fact that many are siblings of our earlier children.

[4] These data are incomplete for Group I parents. On the whole, however, they are much like Group II.

[5] Figures are given for the number of families of each religion and (in parentheses) for the number of children in the study as well.

The Raw Data

Our orientation throughout was bifocal, the subject always being the mother-child dual unit. The most valuable sources of data were the observations of mother-baby pairs by participant and nonparticipant observers (the latter behind a one-way screen). In addition, we filmed the children individually and in interaction with their mothers. Later on, especially in the third year of life, observations of the toddlers as a group were added. We also found that for the understanding of the senior toddlers (third year) individual play sessions were of great importance. Testing, interviews with fathers, home visits, were also instituted.[1] A full summary of the kinds of data available is given in Table 2. In the following discussion, we shall comment on each part of the data collection process. The numbering in the following section corresponds to the numbered items in Table 2.

1. In the setting up and scheduling of our *participant observations*, we developed two aims: (1) to get consistent, if brief, coverage of each mother-infant visit (daily log) and (2) to get detailed, selected observations of areas that we felt were of special importance to us. The latter observations were coordinated, as often as feasible, with a running account by a nonparticipant observer (see below) covering the same period of time. (We made our peace with the fact that having flexible attendance—as far as possible and compatible with the study—to meet the mothers' convenience and preference, would often create scheduling problems.)

The participant observers functioned in the room with the mothers and their children. Eventually, we became realistic about the fact that a portion of the participant observer's time and attention had to be absorbed by "participating," rather than observing. The maintenance of the atmosphere, "running things," and the interaction with the mothers to "keep things going" required effort and time and had to be kept in mind continually along with the necessity of gathering observational data. We fulfilled this double requirement by assigning one participant observer to be responsible during each session for the running of things: she greeted the mothers, assisted them with removing the babies' coats if necessary, provided refreshments, kept an eye on an infant left in the room when the mother was out for an interview, tried to keep conversa-

[1] Unfortunately not enough manpower, time, or money was available to realize this important facet of our work to a sufficient degree.

TABLE 2

Data Collection

TYPE OF DATA	FREQUENCY	WHEN DONE	METHOD	RECORDER
1) Participant observations	One or two per week for each mother-child pair; approximately 40 dictated observations per month	Throughout	2–4-page dictated report describing child's behavior, mother-child interaction, mother's behavior in the group and her comments about child and herself, and mother's personality	Research psychiatrists, senior participant observers in charge of infant and toddler rooms
2) Coordinated observations by participant and nonparticipant observers	Weekly up to 9 months Biweekly 9–18 months Monthly over 18 months Approximately 25 dictated observations per month	Last five years of data collection	30–50 minutes' observation of mother-child pairs. 2–5 page running account	3 participant observers and nonparticipant observers
3) Area observations	Approximately 20 per month	Last four years of data collection	Inferential formulations and judgments (with examples) recorded in eight areas selected for their bearing on the separation-individuation process. 2–3 pages	Nonparticipant observers

4) Interview with mother	Weekly	Throughout	3–5-page dictated report on child's development, parent-sibling-child relationship and family events	Research psychiatrists, senior participant observers
5) Interview with father	Once or twice yearly	Throughout (but less regularly at first)	4-page dictated report on child's development and father-child relationship	Research psychiatrist
6) Filming Films of mother-child pairs recording selected sequences of behavior	According to a chronological guideline pertinent to each subphase	Throughout (but more systematically later on)	Filming of mother and child from inside the room. Dictated film observations describe behavior of mother-child pair. Film notes are prepared to describe film sequences	Research photographer
7) Home visits	Approximately one 2–3-hour informal visit bimonthly	Throughout, but irregularly at first and systematically later on	4–5-page dictated report of behavior of mother (occasionally father) and child in home setting especially as contrasted to behavior in the group setting at the Center	Senior participant observers and participant observers

TYPE OF DATA	FREQUENCY	WHEN DONE	METHOD	RECORDER
8) Developmental tests of children	Testing of each child at least four times at approximately 5, 10, 18 and 30 months	Throughout	Administration of standardized developmental tests and preparation of developmental profiles	Infant tester (not member of research team)
9) Personality tests of mothers	Initial psychological evaluation of all mothers	Once for each mother	Projective test battery	Clinical psychologist (not member of research team)
10) Observations of senior toddler group	Each toddler group session	From start of toddler group	2–4-page dictated reports	Participant observers
11) Individual play sessions with senior toddlers	Weekly while in the toddler group and for a year afterwards	Last 2 years of group plus follow-up year	One staff member worked with each child in a playroom	Senior participant observers and psychiatrists

tion going if silences seemed awkward. In short, she addressed herself primarily to the exigencies of the moment. She also prepared the daily log of each mother-child pair's visit, which included the highlights only: time of arrival and departure, special events, prevalent mood. In addition, afterwards she wrote an extensive observational record on those mother-child pairs with whom she had had particular contact or whom she had been able to observe in some detail.

The other participant observer or observers (usually at least one, but at times two or more) could devote full attention to a particular mother-child pair. They could make coordinated, timed, detailed observations (simultaneously with a nonparticipant observation from the booth), and could leave the room in order to dictate such observations with a minimum of delay and attrition of recall.

We developed guidelines for the participant write-ups, indicating that the observer's attention was always to be bifocal, that is, on the mother-child pair rather than on one or the other alone; that they should feel free to rely upon their empathic sense in understanding what was going on in the child, in the mother, and between the two of them, and that they should think and observe in behavioral and motivational sequences. Thus, we wanted the observers to think in terms of large and meaningful units of behavior and to use their own thoughts and general experience to organize the phenomena; at the same time, we asked them to support their statements with detailed evidence of particular observed behaviors. This sounds like a large order, and it is at first; however, we found that with practice the participant observers' observational and retentive powers increased. Their knowledge, over time, of the observed mother-child unit, and of other mother-child units which provided comparison and contrast, helped them considerably.

It should be clear here, that the observers functioned more as sensitive clinicians than as cameras: we relied upon their experience to understand phenomena in spite of the potential subjectivity in this. We tried to lessen the effects of this potential subjectivity through multiple observers, through observations repeated over time, and especially through discussion in our weekly clinical conferences.

2. The *coordinated observations* of the mother-child pairs were made by the nonparticipant observers from a one-way mirror booth for periods of approximately 30 minutes or more at a time. Time limits were not rigidly adhered to. The account of an interesting sequence, for example, would not be interrupted because the time had elapsed; rather, the nonparticipant observer was instructed to stay until the particular sequence (say, a mother's return from an interview and her child's reac-

tion to this) was completed. Early on, we gave up the idea of continuous coverage from the booth as unfeasible in our particular study, primarily because our subjects came frequently and for long periods of time.

Later on, for at least 2 to 3 years, we consistently arranged that the nonparticipant observers coordinate their running account of a mother-child pair with the participant observer, so that there would be at least two accounts of the half-hour under detailed observation. In this double observation, we relied upon the nonparticipant observations for correct sequence and accuracy of behavioral-descriptive detail. Nevertheless, we also encouraged the nonparticipant observers to make certain summary statements rather than to limit themselves to mechanical description of events. Instructions to nonparticipant observers again stressed the fact that they were to observe the mother-child interaction rather than one or the other partner of the unit.

These coordinated observations had an interesting earlier history, reflecting a gradual coordination of some of the more formal and some of the more clinical aspects of the research. At first, the nonparticipant observers only made ratings of various behaviors from behind the one-way mirror (see the "behavior ratings" in Appendix C). The senior author found that without accompanying clinical description, without the spelling out of the clinical rationale of the rated phenomena, and particularly comparison of lap-babies with toddlers using the same rating criteria, the ratings were misleading and could be integrated neither into the rest of the research, nor in her hypothesis development. In other words, these rating scales were unusable as such by the predominantly clinically oriented research staff, who were involved in day-by-day study of the data. They, therefore, asked the raters to write up their observations in addition to giving the rating itself and to give the detailed reasons for the specific rating in each instance. For the principal investigator this led to a significant period of discovery of the opportunities for, and value in, accommodation and coming together of systematic clinical and methodologically more formal approaches—and also of the opportunities for cooperation between the psychoanalyst as researcher and the researcher trained in psychoanalysis. Ultimately (in our later, upstairs setting), after the ratings themselves were dropped, we reached the arrangement just described (coordinated participant and nonparticipant observations)—a procedure that we found to be very fruitful.

3. In addition to the running account, there were specific *area observations*, which for the clinician observer were most valuable substitutes for the previous ratings. The observers were instructed to define and comment on the area observations. (This was introduced and worked

out carefully by Dr. Kitty La Perriere during her participation as the psychologist participant observer in the years 1963–66.) The areas were selected for their relevance to the subphases of the separation-individuation process that was spelled out as early as 1962. They were: locomotor activity, sensorimotor activity, object relations (mother and others), relationship to inanimate objects, reactions to pain and frustration, aggression and ambivalence, vocalizations, as well as affect and mood and body and self.

In order to foster a relatively independent observational set on the part of the nonparticipant observers, especially after the senior author had developed the subphase hypothesis, we attempted to keep their interaction with the rest of the staff limited. As a rule, they did not participate in our staff conferences; they were not acquainted with the subphase theory and the hypothesized subphase characteristics of behavior; nor were they acquainted in depth with material other than their own about the mother-child pairs. Not infrequently, this relative isolation presented us with personnel problems because the work of the nonparticipant observer required a person of many talents (ease and facility in writing and a good clinical sensitivity to the transactions between mother, child and other people), yet the job was on the research assistant level (since we tried to keep these observers separate from much of our formulative work) and it therefore offered little interaction and relatively little feedback. There was considerable staff turnover in this job, and we were able to maintain effective distance between these observers and the rest of the staff only for one year.

4. *Interviews with mothers* were conducted weekly, at times in the infant room, at times in a separate room with or without the child present. In the original setup, partly because of our cramped quarters, we more often than not had the infant with the mother during our interview. Also, our interest at that time did not preclude the child's being present, and the child's presence or absence was determined by his tolerance for being away from mother. Our aim in these interviews was at first to observe mother-child interaction in this more intimate setting, isolated from the rest of the group, and to obtain information from the mother on the child's development and on home life and family events. Each mother had a regular interviewer with whom a consistent relationship was developed over time. Later on, especially when Dr. McDevitt joined the project in 1965, the emphasis shifted to investigation and minute and careful study of the separation reactions themselves.

5. In our endeavor to gain a comprehensive picture of our subjects' developmental course, we felt *interviews with fathers* to be indispensable.

We were long aware that we needed additional information about the father's personality, his role in the family, his attitude toward his child and their interaction, and especially the child's specific relationship to the father. From the start of the research we had placed observers in the room. Soon we noticed that many of the children seemed to respond positively to one of the research psychiatrists, the principal male member of the research team, Dr. M. Furer, who was frequently in the infant room at that particular time. We assumed that this reaction was related to the children's relationship with their fathers, most of which, according to the mothers' reports, were of a similar favorable nature.[2]

After Dr. John B. McDevitt joined the project, he introduced more systematic and definitive contacts with fathers. In order to gain information and to form some impression of the fathers, and especially of the child's interaction with his father, a series of occasional interviews with the fathers was set up by the research psychiatrist. The fathers responded with interest and enthusiasm. They tended to interpret the interviews first as calling for information about their child, which they were willing and felt competent to provide (at times with greater objectivity than the mothers). Most of them also felt free to talk about their relationship with their child, some connecting it with their past history or experiences in psychotherapy.

In addition to these interviews, we also had Father's Days in the infant room, days when the fathers brought their children if possible. This enabled us to observe interaction in the setting most familiar to us, one where we had standards for comparison to the mother-child interaction.

6. We continued to regard our *film records* as documentation rather than raw data. Our aim was to have available on many of our mother-child pairs a longitudinal record of subphase-relevant behavior. Our filming schedule followed chronological age as well as the subphases of the separation-individuation process, since we intended to make available cross-sectional comparisons of our children at different age levels. And finally, the filming was selective rather than exhaustive. We took samples of behavior that we considered relevant, and as a rule, we did not film the same behavior twice in close succession just because it happened to occur.

The filming was done from inside the infant and toddler rooms rather than from a fixed position in a booth. And, just as location was not fixed, so too the filmed moments were not fixed time samples. Thus, especially

[2] But later on, Drs. David Mayer, Herman Roiphe, William Greenspon, Robert Holter, John McDevitt and Ernest Abelin (in this order) served as participant observers as well.

at the start, considerable selection was left to the judgment of the photographer, who therefore had to be an active member of the research team rather than an ancillary technician. The flexibility of location of the camera as well as of timing had been of great benefit to the study. When we saw, however, that a certain amount of direction was needed to ensure comparability of the film records of the different mother-child pairs, we drew up guidelines pertaining to the frequency and duration of filming as well as general directives about the content to be filmed. When we formulated the subphases, we initiated filming at about 5 months of age and then at stated intervals in each subphase. We also added systematic filming of the child when mother was out of the room and upon her return.[3]

A complete longitudinal record of a mother-child pair runs approximately 4,000 feet, with periods of more or less frequent coverage depending upon the child's rate of development in the separation-individuation process. Most important for our study was the use of these films for cross-sectional comparison of child to child. To date, eight or nine issue-oriented films have been put together from our records of individual mother-child pairs to illustrate (1) the subphases of the separation-individuation process, (2) a preliminary study of basic moods, (3) highlights of mother-child interaction, comparing two children of the same mother, (4) object constancy, (5) adaptation and defense *in statu nascendi*, (6) aspects of the separation-individuation process as related to reconstruction, (7) separation reactions, and (8) developmental aspects of libidinal object constancy. In addition, the senior author has put together numerous reels for teaching purposes for lectures to students of the New York and Philadelphia Psychoanalytic Institutes, and elsewhere. We have started to organize a film library with both longitudinal and cross-sectional filing of the film records. All of our films have accompanying film notes (typed and filed in notebooks).

7. The pattern of *home visits* underwent a gradual change. Originally they were fairly rare occurrences and tended to take on the quality of a formal visit, thus altering the quality of the events observed. As home visits became more frequent and were assigned to specific workers who could arrive at the home with some regularity and whom the mothers grew to know, we became more successful, to varying degrees to be sure, in witnessing parts of fairly representative days in the lives of the families

[3] Up to 5 months of age we took 100 to 150 feet of film per month per child. From 5 to about 17 months we filmed weekly, totaling 300 feet per month. From about 17 to 24 months we filmed biweekly (about 150 to 200 feet per month), and then monthly (about 100 feet per month) in the third year.

seen, and particularly the routine care (feeding, toileting) of the child who participated in the study. The mothers came to accept to a great extent our suggestion that they go on with their day as usual, affording us some measure of knowledge of the climate and activities that seemed characteristic for a given family. By and large, visits took place during the day and in the course of the working week. In most instances, this made it impossible to observe the father's (and at times the older siblings') interaction with the mother and the child, though once in a while fathers were also home.

We were interested in possible differences in the child's or the pair's functioning at home and at the Center, and over time we came to be impressed with such differences in at least one important area: vocalization, and later, verbalization. These seemed to occur markedly less at the Center than at home, and this was borne out both by the mothers' reports and by our own comparative observations. Various factors probably contribute to this difference of which an important one is, we believe, related to the fact that verbal communication has its roots in the intimate one-to-one relationship between mother and infant—an intimacy found much more in the home than in even a familiar setting like ours.

8. The *testing of the children* was done regularly, as indicated in Table 2. The experienced child tester (from the Child Study Center, New Haven) wrote up a full and detailed description of observations and formulations in addition to preparing developmental profiles for the child.

9. A standard psychological test battery (Wechsler Adult Intelligence Scale, Rorschach, Thematic Apperception Test) was used in the *testing of the mothers,* and a full test report was prepared.

10. *Observations of the senior toddlers* were handled as were the participant observations in the infant room. These were added, of course, only when we began to have a senior toddler room, but this was rather early on in the study. The child's behavior, peer interaction, relationship to the observer-teacher, and use of play materials were at the center of observation. Mother-child interaction was kept to a minimum (the mothers were generally not present), but our interest continued to be on the child's handling of this absence itself and of the reunion.

11. Finally, *individual play sessions* supplemented our observations of the older children. One of the major reasons for these was to get closer to the (by now) richer fantasy and play of these children. In individual sessions, the elaboration of fantasy could be observed with less interruption. With three children they were continued weekly well into their nursery age (fourth year).

Staff Conferences: Efforts at Synthesis

Throughout the years of the study we had two regular kinds of conference. These conferences dealt with the raw data (the reported observations) and the data produced by our various attempts at organization of the material (to be described later in this section).

1. The semiweekly *clinical staff conference*, attended by most of the staff with the exception of the nonparticipant observers, was the focal point of immediate data utilization. The fact that several people observed the same situations was utilized in a freewheeling, spontaneous discussion that helped in the recollection of observations and allowed for comparison of impressions and the formulation of a total picture as it emerged from the mosaic of individual observations.

At times a particular mother-child pair was scheduled for review. Observational notes and personal recollections found valuable supplementation and stimulation in the viewing of the longitudinal film record of the mother-child pair under discussion. At other times, two mother-child pairs were selected for a comparative discussion, for example, contemporaries with differing developmental patterns, or perhaps successive children of the same mother. Then the cross-sectional films were used.

The staff conferences proved to be extremely useful in sharpening our observational powers, in improving observational and recording techniques, and most importantly, in furthering our understanding of the subject matter—the separation-individuation process. The material arising in these discussions was recorded in the form of minutes of the meetings. These informal periodic summaries themselves became part of the regular record of available data.

2. The authors of this volume and other senior members of the research group had frequent *research conferences* of approximately three hours duration. At these times, among other things, problems of methodology and research strategy were discussed. Many of the procedural and substantive formulations that appear in this volume had their birth in those meetings—in discussions, in progress reports to funding agencies, and in papers prepared and read in the group.

This completes our description of the data we collected. Let us now turn to our attempts to work with these data.

APPENDIX B

A Research Rationale

NOT surprisingly, the observational setting (the nursery and toddler rooms, and other data-collection situations) and the multiple modes of recording described in Appendix A produced voluminous data. These data comprised a set of observations of infant development and infant-mother interaction of the first two to three years of life that is not excelled by any other that we know of. However, the very richness of the data threatened to overwhelm the research process and to drown the researcher in a flood of fascinating but discrete and unsystematic clinical vignettes and the theoretical bits that can be created around them. We combatted this in two ways: first, by always anchoring our formulations in our central organizing ideas about the separation-individuation process, an approach that lent order to the many discrete observations; and second, by developing an array of approaches to data collection and data analysis that included more systematic, as well as more clinical and individualized, procedures.

It was never our belief that we could, and never our intention that we should, codify all of our observations in a standardized, let alone quantifiable, form. But one early attempt to do this with a segment of our observations (see the behavior ratings described in Appendix C) can be used as a counterpoint to make clear our eventual approach to data analysis and the process of arriving at formulations. In the behavior ratings, two nonparticipant observers simultaneously but independently made ratings on pre-set numerical scales and pre-set variables for each of the mother-child pairs. These ratings could then be assessed for inter-rater agreement and be subjected to correlational analyses producing clusters of variables—from which, loosely speaking, inferences about "types" or "factors" could be made. This is essentially a *static* view of the process of discovery of "results." That is, a data analysis is carried out and the results are "read off."

This mode of approach is seen in clearest form in the traditional model of experimental or correlational quantitative research, with carefully designed small-scale studies directed to specific issues. And yet, in surveying the experimental literature on almost any subject, in seeing the ebb and flow of supposedly "established" findings, and in watching how the ingenious experimenter criticizing the work of his colleagues is so often able to come up with ideas that alter the explanation offered for a particular phenomenon or set of findings, one becomes aware that such research, while objective in its conduct, is subjective in its implications. That is, it is the rare study—at least on problems that are likely to be relevant to the kinds of issues which psychoanalysis confronts—in which results are not ultimately filtered through the mind of the experimenter in his attempts to make sense of an essentially open-ended set of findings. In this way, some of the unsophisticated illusions about the reading off of "results" from experimental work are not unlike some of the illusions regarding the work of the psychologist as tester—that is, the idea that the results of the research or the diagnostic examination, as the case may be, are simply read off from the materials provided by the particular technique utilized, rather than being the result of a complex inferential process whose rules are not clearly set.

Thus, although, even the more classical process of experimental research often does not produce results that can simply be read off in a static way, our approach to arriving at formulations from data involved a still more "active" process. Our modes of study at different phases of the work were both *the result of*, and *a contribution to*, our formulations in a snowballing process of the development of ideas. We did not develop a method and then "find" results through it. Rather, we had inklings, or sometimes even moderately strong convictions, or sometimes internally contradictory uncertainties, about a particular phenomenon or about an area of mother-infant functioning and the like. These then were built into modes of organizing, of pulling together, of looking at, relevant *segments* of the data that could then be used to expand, confirm, clarify, or alter our initial conceptions.

For example, the data analysis in terms of "orienting questions" (see Appendix C, p. 260)—questions about phenomena presumed to be relevant to all subphases of the separation-individuation process—itself represents an achievement of the research and not simply the formulation of a method that might have produced results. The orienting questions represent intermediary formulations en route to subsequent clarification.

They represent our understanding (at the time) of a wide variety of phenomena whose relation to the separation-individuation process we could not even have begun to think about before the research began. That, to date, some but not all of these questions have received extensive study and considerable clarification is testament both to the seminal nature of our ideas at that point and to the still incomplete nature of our work now. Or similarly consider the "areas" and the earlier "categories" (see Appendix C. p. 266): the selection of many of these for data analysis represents our growing awareness that a number of important phenomena of early childhood development (for example, language, toilet training) can be considered from the point of view of their relevance to, impact upon, and influence by the course of the separation-individuation process, especially in the later subphases.

A good example of a research process akin to this one is the productive effort at systematic study of detailed psychoanalytic data that has been pursued under the leadership of Dr. Joseph Sandler at the Hampstead Clinic over the last several years in the "Indexing Project." In the indexing process (as in our work) one does not worry about mastering all of the data; one cannot worry that somewhere else in the data there lies something that will present a further complication; rather, one simply does what one can. And what one can do turns out to be a great deal when the approach involves the regular checking of specific clinical bits from the therapeutic hours (or infant observations) against the concepts that the theory offers to deal with these bits. Through the mutual back-and-forth movement between the clinical data and psychoanalytic theory, Sandler and his associates have been able to clarify, sometimes reconceptualize, and add considerable elaboration to central psychoanalytic theoretical concepts (Sandler, 1960; Sandler, Holder, and Meers, 1963). Here, the encounter between clinical phenomena and organizing ideas is in its most immediate relationship—other than in the analyst's own mind in the course of the analytic session itself. The aim of the indexing is not simply to produce a set of items in categories that will only *then* be studied. Rather, the major discoveries take place in the process of trying to deal with the mal-fit between clinical data and theoretical categories, that is, in the process of indexing itself. So, too, with our process of formulating questions intended to guide the scrutiny of the raw data; these questions and the selection of areas for study are already formulations resulting from past work, and their statement in explicit form permits us to investigate them further.

In addition to illustrating our research process *in process* and providing examples of the approach to data analysis that we found necessary (or, perhaps, most comfortable for us) to take in this study, the approaches that we shall describe in Appendix C can also be used to show the task we sought to confront in getting into the systematic study of the data. What was that task? To find base lines, standards, and criteria for the assessment of the significance (both in the sense of the meaning and the importance) of the phenomena to which we were witness.

What does this mean? The psychoanalyst follows certain ground rules in his practice. The couch, the analyst sitting outside of the patient's visual field, the regularity and near-inviolability of sessions, the basic rule, are not only the conditions for the optimal working of the analytic process but they, in their regularity and degree of standardization, also provide the very basis for understanding the phenomena of analysis—for enabling us, for example, to interpret the patient's view of the analyst as (in large part) transference, or for enabling us to consider lateness, absences, or interruptions to the flow of association as (again in large part) resistances. Beyond this, the analyst can look to certain, often only implicit, guideposts to take stock of what is going on—be this the transference, the patient's current functioning, aspects of his dream life, the general idea (in the background of the analyst's mind) of all other patients previously seen, or the countertransference. Regularities, rules of the road, standards, and base lines, make the work possible.

This, too, is very much the way the psychologist's thinking works in the encounter with the data of psychological tests. The advantage that the tests offer in the assessment of a particular patient's functioning is not in the absolute constraints offered by the rules of testing—for in this there is always individual variation in the tester—but rather in the relative regularities in the procedure and in the array of ideas for organizing the phenomena that permit the tester to build up an *internal* set of norms and expectations that permit him to inquire intelligently about particular idiosyncratic variations in response, and which enable him to assess the significance of specific responses in the context of different age levels, different environmental circumstances, or different pathological syndromes.

So too, our attempts to categorize data were meant to give us a sufficient number of repeated encounters with particular varieties of phenomena so that we could develop a set of internal comparative standards, bases for knowing what was going on. This is not at all rare in clinical research.

Take the following example: "Why do clouds move?" Piaget asked many children (Piaget, 1930). And when they answered, he felt free to ask many further questions, thereby following the ins and outs of their thinking and early reasoning processes. He did not constrain himself with a standard set of questions in the interest of maximizing objectivity. But, on the other hand, he did not freely follow the child in every direction in which the child's mind went. If the child took off from the question to discuss something quite irrelevant, Piaget would note this process itself, but that is not the same as following the child down the pathways indicated by these ideas—as is done in analytic work where the child is free associating. Free and unconstrained exploration within a moderately constrained phenomenal realm is what characterizes Piaget's "clinical method" (Piaget, 1929*a*).

The advantage of this approach to phenomena is this: The clinical researcher, through his repeated observations, develops an internalized set of standards against which he can measure the responses of any particular individual. He develops a conception of the range and varieties, sometimes with developmental sequences or the conditions for certain individual idiosyncratic responses, in the realm of the particular phenomena.

Provence and Lipton (1962), in their work on institutionalized infants, provide a second example of this kind of work. These authors studied the development of infants in a "sterile" (in both senses of the word—clean and sanitary, but dehumanized) environment and recorded the aberrations of development that occurred and the partial recovery of these children when placed in homes. Their procedure provided them with repeated contact with the phenomena seen in individual infants developing at each stage in this particular context. Their observations were, on the one hand, entirely open, picking up whatever their eyes would see or ears would hear, and on the other hand, partially guided and carried out through semistructured testing and observational procedures. But it was the fact of repeated encounter by the researchers that permitted them to formulate such things as the remarkable regularity in the nature of the defects in development in these infants; to learn that particular apparatuses develop (in the sense that they are physically available to the child), but that they do not become functional for the child's adaptation when there is no mother to help organize and elicit them; to note and to be able to describe in a quite differentiated way the specific impacts on particular ego functions of this overall experience for the infants, and the like. Similarly, the aim of our methods of data collection and data analysis was to give us an opportunity for repeated encounters—in a rich yet to some extent constrained way—within a particular phenomenal domain.

Let us give yet another example, this time from work one of us has reported elsewhere (Pine, 1970). In the course of a longitudinal study of the development of "average" (or actually, unselected) children, there was an opportunity to study the small-scale and frequently unnoticed bits of behavior in the child when confronted with stimuli likely to arouse, on the one hand, scopophilic and on the other hand, anal impulses. The situations, in brief, were these: a puzzle-like set of procedures that included certain arousing stimuli as part of the materials that the child had to work with, and talks with the mothers about the child's behavior at home when confronted with relatively natural situations that arise in dressing or undressing, or in toileting. Given the opportunity to observe or hear about this in some 30 children, a number of regularities began to stand out—although these were quite to the side of the initial intentions of these particular procedures in the research. But again, the researcher's repeated encounter with the phenomena led to the discovery of regularities and variations on the theme that might not otherwise have come into view. These regularities could be understood in terms of multi-functional aspects of the behavior with which the child encountered these stimuli. The child developed, that is, he slowly and automatically "constructed," behaviors wherein gratification was retained while anxiety was minimized all in accord with the proscriptions and opportunities of his particular familial surroundings. These formulations, and others similarly obtained regarding separation situations, have been recorded in detail elsewhere (Pine, 1970, 1971). The senior author's work on problems of symbiosis and separateness over the years has also provided just such an experience of repeated, yet seemingly infinitely variable, encounters with a particular kind of human phenomena—encounters that have culminated in the present work.

Given the complexity of our research and the subtlety of the clinical phenomena under study, combined with our wish for some degree of consensual validation of the phenomena, all of the work was carried out by us and a group of our co-workers who were not only well trained, but were particularly well versed in the clinical phenomena and clinical theory of the separation-individuation process. Our decision, some years ago, to work with such a close-knit and experienced staff—even at the risk of researcher bias—has seemed to us appropriate to the complexity of the phenomena under study (and to the need to maintain appropriate and empathic relationships to the mothers and children) and has not seemed to prevent us from enlarging and altering our concepts at many points along the way.

APPENDIX C

Some Research Strategies

JUST as our observational setting underwent an evolutionary change during the more than 10 years of the study (for example, the addition of the room for the older toddlers, the move to a new setting), so too did our efforts to organize the collected data. But the sequence of changes cannot be described in linear fashion. The whole process involved an organic development, with old approaches appearing in transformed ways later on, yet with many constants persisting throughout the entire process. Thus, there was a dominant open-ended clinical orientation throughout, with the observer conceived of as the integrative organ for the flow of phenomena observed. Additionally, at all stages of the work we made attempts to classify the observations into one or another set of areas that, for one reason or another (dependent upon the stage of the research), we felt at the time to be centrally relevant.

What *did* develop in a linear fashion over time were the following: (a) the progressive establishment and clarification of the research rationale (see Appendix B); (b) the steady refinement of the rationale for our selection of classification categories (this rationale was increasingly geared to our growing formulation about the separation-individuation process); (c) an increasing tendency to organize the data in terms of time sequences to make possible comparative studies of all children at a given month of their development and comparison of each child with himself over time; and (d) with the development after 1963 of a clearer and fuller statement regarding the subphases of the separation-individuation process (see Mahler, 1965*b*), the possibility of gearing data analyses specifically to those subphases (see The Orienting Questions, p. 260). In regard to this last point, a 7-year study was begun in 1963 (following several earlier years of work on the separation-individuation process) with the aim of verifying, modifying, and refining the subphase hypothesis. At this point in the work, Dr. Manuel Furer took over the direction of the clinic for symbiotic psychotic children, with the present senior author remaining as principal investigator for the study of the normal separation-individuation phase.

Original Approaches

As already noted, a dominant open-ended clinical orientation, with efforts at classification of observations into categories, was present from the beginning. In addition, at the outset we had plans for assessing a variety of variables (pain and sensory thresholds, relatedness, frustration tolerance, means of communication, consistency of behavior, expression of emotions, activity/passivity trend, autonomy/independence, discrimination and selectiveness, and so forth) that were partially drawn from our interest in symbiotic psychosis, partially from our understanding of what was central to normal child development, and partially from a kind of catch-all approach to data collection. Some of these variables are still central to our thinking; some not.

Behavior Ratings[1]

Beginning in about the third year of the study (1961), we developed some approaches involving standardized, quantified ratings of a variety of sorts. These grew out of earlier clinical observations, and the variables rated were formulated through study of notes in the observational records. In the end, these procedures did not seem to us to be too fruitful for the production of specific "findings"; their lasting value to us has been rather in their very formulation: they required us to link our concepts to observations; they helped us develop a more precise language in tune with the phenomena under study; and at a personal level, they were the initial vehicle through which a path was opened for the clinically sophisticated senior author and staff to move to more systematic modes of data collection and analysis in ways that still seemed clinically viable—a path that led to the present collaboration.

Our first attempt was in a set of what we called "behavior ratings."

[1] The following discussion (pp. 253–259) has appeared in slightly different form in a paper by F. Pine and M. Furer entitled "Studies of the Separation-Individuation Phase: A Methodological Overview," in *The Psychoanalytic Study of the Child*, Vol. 18. New York: International Universities Press, 1963, pp. 325–341.

In our initial broad approach, all of the normal toddlers and their mothers were observed and rated according to a set of 58 variables by nonparticipant observers working together in pairs. The variables were culled from earlier clinical notes. A series of three half-hour observations of each child was made by a pair of raters before they made a final rating of the child on each variable. The series of three observations was repeated at a later point when the child was several months older to make possible the assessment of developmental changes. Preliminary scanning of these ratings had shown excellent interrater reliability, and the preliminary analyses of the data suggested that the ratings picked up significant aspects of the individual mother-child interaction.

What were the variables? One set had bearing on the development of object relationship: the child's reaction to his mother, to other adults, to other children, and to inanimate objects. This included the amount of time the child spent with the mother, spatial position in relation to her, and preferred sensory modalities of communication between mother and child. We also studied the amount and the quality of the mother's comforting and the child's receptiveness to it, the range of comforting behaviors available to the mother in her contacts with the child, and the degree of manipulativeness in her comforting. We also studied the nature of the child's appeal to the mother for comforting and the degree to which he could sustain this appeal in the face of mother's delay in providing it. In general, we studied a variety of modes of approach and contact between mother and child for their bearing on the separation-individuation process.

A second set of variables culled from our participant and nonparticipant observational notes and impressions related to the development of those ego functions that had some potential indicator value about the course of the separation-individuation process. This included signaling communication and motor functions. The first of these bears on the communication processes necessary for maintaining contact between mother and child even as the child becomes increasingly separate from the mother. Our interest in the second (motor development) stemmed initially from the senior author's hypothesis (Mahler, 1958*b*) about the rapid development of locomotion, which, outpacing the child's emotional readiness for separation, may be the trigger that sets off the symbiotic psychotic fragmentation of the ego. Variables related to communicative activity included the development from autoerotic to communicative use of the mouth, as well as and some developments in language. In the latter, we examined, for example, the specificity of the child's communications and the ways in which such communication was used to appeal to the mother. Motor behavior, too, was studied, and patterns of motility (in relation to separation from the mother, to mastery of the environment, and to motor grace) were assessed (cf. Homburger, 1923).

All of these issues—in mother-child interaction and in the child's development—were translated into specific descriptive categories that were rated. For example, one item was entitled "focus in motor behavior." The rater was asked to decide whether a child's motor behavior was (1) typically wandering and rarely goal directed, (2) slightly more wandering than goal directed, (3) slightly more goal directed than wandering, or (4) typically goal directed and rarely wandering. In another category, entitled "success in evoking maternal response,"—when the child wants or needs some response or satisfactory substitute from the mother, and when the mother does not seem instantly aware of the need—the rater was asked to decide whether the child (1) ably evokes a response every time, (2) can generally, though not always, evoke a response, (3) can rarely evoke a response, or (4) is unable to evoke a response and seems at a loss. The general plan in the analyses of these data was to assess individual patterns of mother-child relationships and to correlate these with particular patterns of the emergence of ego functions and of their integration in the child.

Some suggestive early findings from quantitative analyses of these ratings are given in Pine and Furer (1963) and Pine (1964). However, a variety of complications developed that require consideration. This research strategy suffered from providing both too much and too little of the very specification and concreteness that the rating categories were designed to provide, as will become evident in the following discussion.

When we were initially faced with the problem of deciding how to collect comparable observations and descriptions on all of the children, we considered recording descriptions of certain kinds of behavior as they occurred and then quantifying them in some way for comparative purposes. But it quickly became apparent that we needed more concrete specification of the "certain kinds" of behavior to be observed. And we ran into the problem of defining what were the units of a behavior sequence—when did it begin and end? Practically, collecting extensive descriptions that would later have to be codified and rated would have resulted in time and financial demands not easily met. Hence we decided on the system described above—with a priori descriptions of behavior possibilities (drawn from our past observations and clinical experiences) and with direct rating of a child by a rater (by having the rater simply check off one of the a priori descriptions rather than record the observed behavior in detail). We planned that the more descriptive material, lacking here, would come from the clinical work. But such a priori descriptions as were used in the categories at times did not quite fit any one child in the groups studied later. Raters would then force their ratings, often into the more innocuous categories, with the result that the categories did not always differentiate adequately among the children. In addition, some ratings within categories were simply too broad and included all of the cases, allowing no ratings of the other three positions in the scales.

On the other hand, the category descriptions were often not specific enough so that each rater would consider slightly different behaviors in making his ratings of a particular child. It has certainly become clear that, the more the rating categories are spelled out in terms of observable behaviors, the more rater consensus is likely. Thus, we found it considerably easier to work with descriptions of motor patterns than with inferences about the child's reaction to internal bodily processes or with the development of body image. Other more subtle and more tentative research approaches have to be developed for the study of the latter.

Midway through the collection of data we eliminated those categories that did not permit the raters to differentiate among the children and in which interrater reliability was low (when raters could not agree on what a child was like). Eliminating the poorest categories on these counts meant dropping out about one-fourth of the original 58 categories. We continued work with the remainder.

The elimination of the poorer categories by no means solved all of our problems; the rapid developmental changes taking place in the normal toddlers created other ones. We cannot take a picture of a child if he won't hold still. And hold still he won't. New developments are constantly taking place, and the variations from moment to moment even within the course of a day (say, with fatigue or hunger) are great. Moving pictures, yes; but a photograph, no. And yet the rating procedure was relatively static. It could not show all of these moment-to-moment variations or the dynamics of change. We initiated more frequent observations and ratings (bimonthly, within the limits of our staff capabilities), but even these gave no more than a series of relatively static descriptions of the child, and we gradually replaced them with observations of specific areas of interest to us and with the coordinated participant and nonparticipant observations already described.

While, in the clinical work, the processes of information gathering and of discovery are temporally closely linked, in these behavior ratings and subsequent correlational analyses the two are far apart. When ratings are collected for even a dozen children over a year or two, there is a long delay between any specific rating and the final correlational analyses carried out when all of the data are in. While, in some research settings, this delay need not be a problem, we found it to be a major problem because it made it difficult to compare the quantitative findings with the clinical events at any specific moment. Our research, based we had hoped on a cross-fertilization between more clinical and more quantitative procedures, had not always had such cross-fertilization precisely because of the delay required to carry through the formal research design. It was true that the clinical and quantitative data may have mutually enriched each other at a later date, when all analyses were completed; but instead of waiting we tried to bring the clinical and quantitative work closer together—through written descriptions of the observed phenomena on which ratings were based—with greater degrees of success; but ultimately we shifted to still systematic but nonquantitative approaches.

One aside is worth noting, however, for its historical interest. These behavior ratings, which foundered in large part because they did not keep pace with the infant-toddler's growth, were in fact formulated before we had developed a conception of the subphases. Indeed, as at other points in the research where apparent methodological problems led us to new insights, the mal-fit of these behavior ratings to the developmental process may have been a contributing factor in the formulation of the subphases at that particular point in time.

Comparative Observations of the Individuating Children in the Mothers' Presence and Absence

Another avenue of study using fixed ratings involved an experimental and observational procedure. The level of functioning of the children from toddler age on was observed and evaluated when their mothers were present and when they were absent. We were interested in the extent to which certain achievements were maintained by the child in the mother's absence. In which children was ego functioning not impaired in the mother's absence, and in which areas? Here, by means of brief separations of the child from the mother, we hoped to study the dependence of the child's functioning on the physical presence of the mother.

We assessed six areas: play, attention span, understanding and use of language, and gross and fine motor skills. Raters were asked to judge whether the level of functioning in each of these areas was higher or lower in the mother's presence than in her absence, according to criteria that were spelled out in a rating manual. If such changes in functioning were found in the mother's absence, it still remained for us to draw on our clinical material to explain them. Developmental tests of the children in the infant and toddler group were matched with these six areas so that we could explore the question whether those functions that the toddler had developed to a higher level are retained better in the mother's absence than were less fully mastered ego functions.

This work was initially set up in an attempt to create a relatively compact, and yet meaningful, experimental situation—varying only the presence of the mother and gauging changes in the toddler's reaction (presumably referable to the mother's presence or absence). The problem with the infants and young toddlers, however, was that no sooner was the mother out of the room than the mothers of other children and the infants' participant observers often markedly changed in their handling of the child. They became more watchful and nurturant; in short, they assumed the maternal function. Thus, more than the mother's presence varied, and it was difficult to refer specific changes in the toddler solely to the presence or absence of the mother. But in spite of this, the method gave some interesting observations that were relatively comparable for all of the children.

In the normal toddlers, for example, the children not only worsened but also improved in certain kinds of functioning in the mother's absence, and they also changed in the quality of their functioning. All this depended on the subphase position of the child—it was related to the mother-child relationship—and to the child's innate predisposition. In any of these cases there was a suggestion that the child's functioning was not yet autonomous but drew in some way upon the mother for its enhancement or impairment. Thus, one child—a child whose gross motor (locomotor) behavior was highly developed for his age, and whose mother had always nurtured and valued that behavior—fell off in the level of his gross motor behavior when the mother was absent. This child had always obliged the mother by performing well, in the way that she wanted, but such performance still seemed dependent on the mother's presence to some extent. At what point did motor excellence become autonomous in the sense that it was maintained even in the mother's absence?

Another child, in sharp contrast, had a motor pattern that was typically aimless and wandering; he fell often, and hard, without a whimper. His mother had a hands-off policy in many aspects of her son's care, refusing to frustrate him, neglecting at the start to support bowel and bladder control, ignoring his many hard falls. His aimless motor behavior seemed to lack in internal direction what he lacked in direction from his mother. But this behavior, too, seemed to be associated with the physical presence of his mother; in her absence he improved in his gross motor behavior—falling less, for example, and becoming somewhat more goal-directed. This close link between his motor functioning and his relationship to his mother perhaps foreshadowed the later improvement in motor functioning that came when the mother-child relationship changed. When verbalization developed in the child, and when the mother was able to use this medium of communication to provide a more focused and organizing care, the child showed a developmental gain not only in the verbal area but also in the motor area.

Ratings of Mothers

In addition to these two fairly elaborate research plans, we also formulated a fairly simply procedure for rating each mother on variables that more or less reflected her tendency (both with regard to her child and to herself) to foster or display (1) infantile, (2) age-appropriate, independent, or (3) precocious pseudo-independent behaviors.

In spite of the degree of planning and effort that went into these formal rating schemes, in actual operation they ran into many of the methodological difficulties already noted and were often out of tune with the broad clinical process of the research. They made a distinct contribution to our work but, as noted in our discussion of the research rationale, this contribution was principally in the process of specification, of linking concepts to observation, of clarification of variables, a contribution that was intrinsic to the very formulation of these research strategies. Following these efforts, and while the clinical-observational approach continued to be followed, we turned to quite different modes of data systematization, which we shall now describe.

From 1963 on (after the senior author had tentatively formulated the subphase theory)—when reasonably clear and elaborated formulations of a series of subphases of the separation individuation process (see Mahler, 1963) had been made on the basis of the observational work and the clinical and research meetings—we began to formulate a procedure for organizing systematic clinical data analysis coordinated with the subphases.

What emerged after a period of conferences, soul searching, and studying of accumulated data and actual observations was the formulation in 1964 and 1965 of "orienting questions."

The Orienting Questions

The orienting questions were intended to orient our experienced clinical staff in their reexamination of old observational notes. While our observations were not made initially with these questions in mind(indeed they could not have been, since the questions grew out of these observations themselves), the fullness of our various observational notes made it possible for us to go back to these notes with new questions in mind—asking of our old observations, in effect, what they could tell us in relation to these newly formulated organizing questions.

In order to facilitate a discussion of these questions, we shall restate briefly the subphases of the separation-individuation process (see Part II). Briefly, then, we find four subphases of the separation-individuation process, as follows:

1. The *differentiation* subphase from 5 months on (with dawning awareness of separateness);
2. The major spurt in autonomy called the *practicing* subphase from 10 to 15 months (with attention directed to new motor achievements, seemingly to the near exclusion of mother at times);
3. The *rapprochement* subphase from 15 to 22 months (with renewed demand upon the mother, who is increasingly experienced as separate, and with continued growth of the autonomous ego apparatuses);
4. Progress toward the gradual attainment of libidinal *object constancy* (from 22 to 36 months).

In our research meetings, as we worked over potential questions with which we could approach the observational data collected earlier with the study of the subphases in mind, we found ourselves using four criteria to guide us in framing and selecting questions. These were: (1) that they be relevant to all four subphases of the separation-individuation process (rather than, say, being focused on a specific event of a single subphase); (2) that each question steer us to data capable of contradicting or altering as well as confirming our current view of the subphases (for example, we sought phenomena at a previous or subsequent subphase that we believed particularly characterized a different one); (3) that each question have multiple theoretical implications (so that, following the immense task of data analysis we were about to undertake, we would be more likely to have some theoretical yield); and (4) that each question be phrased in such a way that it required minimal inference on the part of the persons who were going to go back to the data to pull out and summarize events under the heading of each of the questions. We formulated nine orienting questions.

Our method of data organization was as follows: Each worker went back to the notes, from the earliest to the latest months available for a particular child, with the nine orienting questions in mind and with instructions to draw out and summarize the data relevant to each question. We felt it would have been highly desirable to have had each worker focus on only one question, applying it to the data for all children at all ages; this worker would have become an "expert" in that single question and could therefore apply more or less common standards to the data of all children. But lack of time made this impossibile. It would have required *each* worker to go through *all* of the old notes on *all* children (in order to rate each child on any one orienting question). So instead we assigned each child's record to a single worker who then abstracted for *all nine* questions for that *one* child. This produced data on any *one* question that was contributed to by several different workers, each working from the notes on his or her particular child-mother pair. Proceeding in this way, it took workers approximately one year to carry out the process of data abstraction for children from age 5 to 24 months.

The abstraction of data was done on the basis of each month's material. In the end, therefore, we had notes on each question for each child for each month and were able to make cross-child comparisons for any question at any age or sequential comparisons for a particular child over time. The workers were asked to cull the major relevant material in summary form (one or two pages at most per month) and to give a brief "key statement" summarizing the central features of the data on that question for each child-mother pair at that time.[2] These key statements were all charted for ease of visual comparison among children.

The aim of this procedure was to reduce our voluminous data to workable form, but to reduce it according to theoretical guidelines that would give us a repeated encounter with a certain portion of the data so that we could develop a clearer set of expectations, comparative standards, and clinical familiarity with particular phenomena. The results of this work are reflected in our discussions of the subphases in Part II. There were nine orienting questions:

1. *Approach-Distancing.* What are the characteristic approach-distancing patterns in the mother-child pair and the preferred "average distance" during this time period? Note the "fit" of the two members of the pair in this. Consider behavioral indices, such as body and eye movements, the smiling response and the mother's response, speech and other vocalization.

[2] Dr. John McDevitt was particularly active in formulating this mode of abstracting from the old data.

Consider also intrapsychic approach-distancing, such as sleep and the mother's emotional availability.

This question, phrased largely in behavioral and bodily terms, forms the counterpart to the whole process of the intrapsychic attainment of awareness of separateness. In terms of observable behavior, it is clearly linked to the child's incessant wandering away ("toddling"—which gives its name to this period) from mother in the second subphase (practicing) and his more prominent shadowing of her in the third (rapprochement), but it also is specially suited to the assessment of distancing phenomena in the first subphase (differentiation).

For example, we were interested in the infant's melting into his mother's body and the changes in this as the differentiating infant drew back from the holding mother's body, feeling the separateness of his own body, and scanning the "other-than-mother" world; the spontaneous peekaboo games of this period and the infant's exploration of his mother's face also bear on approach and distancing behavior. The question also focused our attention, for particular children, on the mother or the child as initiator of greater or lesser distancing and the relation of this to the stage and success of the child's individuation. The "fit" of mother and child in this altered us to possible intradyad conflict, pathological accommodation, or age-appropriate reciprocity. The behavioral indices we list in the question make clear our broad view of the range of behaviors through which distancing can be accomplished or overcome at different subphases; in this regard only, these are seen as potentially functionally equivalent behaviors.

2. *Newly emerging ego functions.* What is the child's attitude toward, and his use of, newly emerging capacities: locomotion, manual skills, speech, sensory functioning, scanning (of mother and "other," visually and with contact perceptual modalities), and other cognitive capacities (such as anticipation, judgment, and so forth)? Note the evenness of the new functioning (maintenance, regression), the accompanying affect, and mother's attitude toward it.

This question grew from our interest in the child's seemingly full absorption in his own motor functioning when he first learns to walk, an absorption which, for a few months, even overshadows his interest in his mother much of the time. The question was worded to permit us to learn about the child's relation to newly emerging functions at other stages (when they do not seem to us to preclude interest in mother—for example, developing speech is most often in close relation to her), as well as to permit us to study the natural growth of those capacities that comprise the building blocks from which any individuated personality must grow. The reference to the evenness of the new functioning (and its susceptibility to regression), the child's affect, and the mother's attitude toward it gave recognition to our expectation that these capacities grew in the soil of the mother-child relationship and were highly responsive to maternal attitudes and dependent upon appropriate maternal interest and noninterference for their relatively conflict-free development. This reflected a continuation of our interest in what we described in the previous section (ratings of children in mother's presence and absence)—with a revised mode of study.

3. *Preferred modalities.* What are the child's preferred, avoided, and other idiosyncratic (even if rare) sensory, motor, vocal, or other behavioral modalities during this period? Describe these with reference to expressive, exploratory, tension-regulating and discharging, and coping behaviors. Note similarities and differences in the preferred modalities in these several areas. Note also its fit with the mother's modalities (compare question 8) and with her expressed or implicit encouragement or discouragement of particular modalities.

Our initial interest in this question stemmed from an interest in the child's individuation. The degree to which his preferred modalities differed from his mother's, or were used in different ways, we felt, might give some clues to the start of an individuated personality. Beyond this, however, the question was intended to focus also on the development of preferential modalities *in relation to* the mother's preferred modalities and their application in a network of functional interconnected mother-child behaviors (identifications and internalizations).

Our interest in this question grew also, by contrast, from the study of deviate development of various modalities (with atrophy, stylized or bizarre use, or hyperreliance) in the symbiotic psychotic children (cf. Bergman and Escalona, 1949).

4. *Distressing and pleasurable experiences.* What are the more distressing and the pleasurable experiences for the child at this time? Describe the situations in which the distressing or pleasurable experience is seen and with which it is usually associated, and describe the specific affective accompaniments of it. For each age, note also the degree of distress associated with passive separation experiences (even if these are not the major sources of distress).

This question was aimed at providing us with material for assessing the degree to which experiences of separation and/or the awareness of separateness were relatively more distressing experiences at one or another subphase and, conversely, the degree to which contact with mother or (contrariwise) active distancing from mother was a central source of pleasure (as opposed to exercise of attained functions, play with toys, interaction with others, with the nonmother). Our expectations of the relatively greater significance of awareness of separateness as a distressing experience in the first and third subphases (see Part II) were already developed when we formulated this question, but we did not (and do not now) assume that these experiences are more than "averagely expectably" distressing except in pathological situations. (We later developed an interest in the child's capacity for pleasure, but this was not yet articulated when we formulated this question.)

5. *Alertness.* What is the characteristic state of the child's alertness: its level, maintenance, lability, intensity, and its exaggerations in either a positive or a negative direction (for example, withdrawal into sleep, hyperalert and overexcited states)? Consider also the principle foci of investment and the direction of attention inward or outward, and toward body or body parts, mother or others, inanimate objects, and ego functions or specific action patterns.

The degree of focus on inanimate objects, self, and nonmother in contrast to mother, and the capacity to retain a state of alertness even in the mother's absence vary, we believe, in the different subphases—they are, in fact, some of the defining attributes of those subphases. This question reflects, in particular, our interest in the criteria for saying when the infant has "hatched" from the mother-infant dual unity, when psychological birth has taken place—as represented in his "listening" only to his insides, or, later, turning his attention to mother, to others, to the inanimate world of things.

6. *Basic mood.* What is the child's characteristic mood, considering the varying affects in terms of their position on a dimension from depressed to exuberant? Note any characteristic variants from this, the steadiness and maintenance of the mood, and the rapidity of mood swings. Watch for indicators of mood in facial expression, gestures, vocalization tone and content, and body tonus and activity level.

When we first formulated this question we had a sense that mood would somehow be an indicator of the child's awareness of separateness, as well as his pleasure or unpleasure in it. Mood also is the most general indicator of the state of the child's relationship to himself and the world. In addition, we felt that mood—the likeness or unlikeness to mother's mood—would give an indication of the child's individuation and of the autonomy of his functioning. (At the present time, as we described in detail earlier, we can add that it is an important sign of deviant development if the child's mood is contrary to what is expectable for particular subphases.)

7. *Tolerance of disruption.* What is the child's characteristic tolerance of disruption or potential disruption from within or without, including such sources as external stimuli, externally imposed pain and frustration, impulse pressure, and anxiety? Where appropriate, note startle, distractability, attention span, modulation of impulse, extent of loss of homeostasis, and the rate of return to base line.

This question focuses more on problems of individuation than separation. It referred us to the intrapsychic modulations developed by the child, as indicated by his capacity to delay, displace, control, or re-equilibrate. In contrast, we wanted to learn about the stages in the child's reliance on the mother as auxiliary ego for retaining homeostasis, and about pathological extensions of this reliance into later age periods. This question has links to earlier work on tics and other patterns of discharge and mastery or lack of mastery of the instinctual drives (see Mahler, 1944, 1949*a*).

8. *Mother-child similarities and differences.* What are the outstanding similarities and differences in the mother's and the child's behavior in this period? Note, in particular, matching of moods, of tempo and temperament, style of reliance on particular ego functions (locomotion, sensory modalities, verbalization), and social attitudes (relationships to other persons). Note any information on the mechanisms of how these (similarities or differences) come about (for example, maternal encouragement, child's negativistic refusals).

This question approaches in a more broadly defined way the issue approached in question 3 with respect to preferred modalities; that is, the development of particular individuated styles of functioning in the child in relation to the styles of the mother. Individuation need not refer simply to being different from mother. The child becomes himself in large part through identification with mother and other major persons in his life. Individuation is reflected not in differentness per se, but in the stability of function within the child and in the interlocking features of those functions that, however like those of another child, are always distinctively patterned in relation to drives, fantasies, modes of interaction, and the expression and control of both positive and negative affect.

The question of what happens with mothers who have infants that are very different from themselves (for example, active infants of placid mothers) was also in our minds when we formulated this question.

9. *Body and self.*[3] What are the behavioral indicators of the child's developing awareness of body boundaries, differentiation, separateness, object

[3] John B. McDevitt's mirror experiments during several years of the research are of particular interest here.

constancy, sense of self and "I-ness," or sexual identification during this period?

Note that this question was defined at a much more abstract level than the others, requiring higher levels of inference from the abstractors. There was sufficient theoretical interest in the question to warrant our attempting to answer it. It was precisely our wish to find a wide range of possible indicators of these intrapsychic phenomena that led us to tap, through this orienting question, the kinds of inferences that our staff could make. Observations of mirror behavior, of the child's response to life-sized dolls, of the child's play with moving, mechanical toys were all part of our recorded data. These, as well as any other chance or unanticipated indicators, were listed under this question.

These then, were the nine orienting questions. Parallel with these questions, we developed another approach to the systematic classification of segments of the large body of available data. We turn now to that.

The Categories

From the start of the study we attempted to record, to organize previous recordings, or to discuss observations, in a series of categories—our aim always being to bring together related material on a single child over time or on different children. This choice of procedure reflected our intention *not* to focus on individual case studies as our primary unit for data synthesis but rather to focus on phenomena of a specific developmental phase of presumably universal import. We sought to abstract general phenomena from the observations made concerning specific persons.

Some of the categories changed over time, dependent upon our interests at that time, while others remained fairly constant. Since the categories were never seen as attempts to lead to quantification or rigorous experimental study, it never seemed amiss to change them as our judgment changed regarding their potential usefulness to us. Instead, we conceived of them as ways to help us focus our thinking and our discussion on specific substantive areas at given moments in time. It was always of great value that we managed to retain considerable continuity of staff over the many years of the study, staff that could go back to old observations and draw out of them material now reflecting this interest, now reflecting that one.

As indicated earlier, our use of many of the categories had considerable continuity over time even though we changed them in some ways at times or dropped some for a while. This continuity is not surprising; though our understanding of the separation-individuation process changed and grew over the years, our basic conceptions about child development remained fairly constant. The categories, in general, read like a "what's what" of child development—reflecting our understanding of which of many diverse areas were important to know about and describe. At one point, for example, we were working with the following 17 categories: (1) feeding and oral behavior, (2) toileting, bathing, and routine bodily care, (3) motor and cognitive behavior, (4) sleep and fatigue phenomena, (5), individuation, (6) reaction to people other than mother and father, (7) separation reactions, (8) imitation, play, fantasy, relationships to inanimate objects, (9) communication, (10) aggression, ambivalence, and autoaggression, (11), reaction to pain and frustration, (12) mother's personality and behavior, (13) mother-child interaction, (14) differences between behavior at home and the Center, (15) important events in the family, (16) father's personality and that of other family members, and (17) the child's prevalent characteristics. These 17 categories had been applied to the data at an early phase of the work. At that time, all of the observations for a particular month were redistributed into these categories for purposes of study. (The "area" observations, by contrast and as described earlier when we spoke of one of the tasks of the nonparticipant observers, were based on single observations of selected areas. The 17 categories were used to organize multiple observations gathered in varying ways.)

What changed as the study progressed was not our basic approach in terms of sectioning the data into more digestible categories, but (1) the explicitness of our rationale regarding our aims in the study of the categories and (2) the degree of systematization and follow-through in our categorizations themselves.

With regard to the first of these, our rationale was as follows: Initially, our categories reflected our feeling that this was an area that we ought to know about, or that this area might help us better to understand the separation-individuation process. As our clinical observations and discussions proceeded, we began to form much clearer notions of the separation-individuation process and its subphases. At this point, for purposes of further study, we were able to keep a sharper conceptual distinction between the categories (which we felt reflected important areas of child development) and the separation-individuation process itself (which we now felt we understood in some detail as a normal epigenetic process). At this point we approached the categories with one or both of two questions: How does our current understanding of the separation-individuation process shed light on this general area of child development? and How does our understanding of this area further enlighten us in respect to the separation-individuation process? We pursued the study of categories where we felt we had reason to expect suggestive hypotheses in response to these questions.

With regard to the second change referred to above, the increased systematization and follow-through in the task of categorization itself, we proceeded thus: Starting in 1967 we selected a set of categories to be applied systematically in a manner similar to the application of the orienting questions described earlier. The work was done as follows: The data to be used were the key statements and notes abstracted monthly for each child under the nine orienting questions. The data abstraction based on orienting questions had been completed, and we now, without going back again to all of the raw data, sought to bring together some of the data in a set of four categories that were of particular interest to us. They were: (1) object relations, (2) mood, (3) libidinal and aggressive drive development, and (4) cognitive development. We felt that these categories gave us a basis for beginning to tie together some major areas of psychoanalytic interest with the separation-individuation process as we were coming to understand it.

This time, since the data were not as voluminous (based on already accomplished data abstractions rather than the total raw data pool), we were able to assign one category to each of four workers. Each worker then became a specialist in that category and reviewed all of the data for all children from the point of view of that category. Data were summarized on a monthly basis for each child (in a brief one- or two-page note), and then an essay was written comparing all of the children for that category for any particular month.

The work with the categories has become intermeshed with all of our thinking about the separation-individuation process. They were, as were the orienting questions, a tool for our thinking, a framework within which to organize our thinking at particular points in the study. They are represented implicitly in our discussions in Part II.

Reconstructive and Synthesizing Aspects

Working individually with the observational data on the children, we found no difficulty in placing the behaviors of the children in a number of discrete categories as we proceeded with the analyses from the earliest months of the first year into the second year of life.

Two chance observations, concurred in by the several clinical investigators in the study, were made during analyses of the data of the second half of the second year of life, which led to the formulation of new aims for the work on the third year. While these observations were not expected by us as we proceeded in the work of data analysis, once encountered and put into words they immediately made sense and made us realize that we were then moving into the study of a new stage in the child's life that needed new approaches.

First, we noticed that the data would no longer comfortably "fit" into discrete categories. It began to seem increasingly arbitrary to describe an item of behavior without reference to more and more of the total array of behaviors seen in the child at a particular period of time. It seemed that the behavior of the child was becoming increasingly integrated or, put otherwise, was increasingly expressive of some central themes of the child's life, a fact that had to be borne in mind when describing or explaining discrete items of behavior.

The second observation had to do with sex differences. Until this point, the children had often seemed to us to fit into various subgroups—from the separation-individuation point of view—subgroups containing both boys and girls. But now, while on the one hand, the complexity of the children made it difficult to group them, on the other hand, those common traits that existed were suggestive of a growing trend towards sexual differentiation and gender identity formation.

In other words, the data of the third year of life required a different approach not only because emotional, cognitive, and verbal development had reached new levels but also because the children's personalities had by this time become more solidified and integrated in many respects. In the third year the children were quite verbal, and they engaged in a great deal of fantasy play (which required us to have individual play sessions with the children in order to begin to understand them). The senior toddlers in general seemed much less involved with their mothers (who were not in the room) and much more involved with their "nursery-school teacher" and in their peer interactions. Thus, in our mind, the material of the third year was of quite a different sort.

We developed three new aims in our study: (1) to study the fourth subphase of the separation-individuation process, the gradual attainment of libidinal object constancy, in relation to the child's individual development through the previous subphases. (2) to study early phases in the formation of character (or the consolidation of the personality) in the third year of life. (3) to study the beginning formation of gender identity in the third year.

In stating these aims we intend to indicate that we were interested in the third year of life not only because it was the fourth subphase of the separation-individuation process (the achievement of libidinal object constancy), but also because it represents the end product of the first three subphases and should bear the stamp of specific experiences and modes of resolution of developmental or other difficulties as they appeared in those previous subphases. Thus, our analyses were no longer a category-by-category description, but an attempt to conceptualize clinically each child's attained relationship to his mother, his sense of separateness and identity, and the relationship to his own autonomous apparatuses as they appeared in the third year of life—and then to retrace the earlier steps in the separation-individuation process to see how they were represented, reconciled, integrated, omitted, or in conflict in this third year resolution.

The observation reported earlier, that it became impossible late in the second year of life arbitrarily to separate out specific aspects of a child's functioning without regard to the whole, can also be stated in terms of the beginning development of character or the consolidation of the personality. To the degree that this is organized around maleness or femaleness, gender identity becomes a central focus. That is, what we believe we see is the coming together of those complex behaviors that characterize each individual child's previous subphase development (as well as his psychosexual stages and the development of aggression) as these bear on individuation, on the one hand, and sexual identity, on the other; and, furthermore, that this coming together around central themes and modes of functioning is the beginning of a more consolidated personality structure.

Here again, our mode of approach was to formulate what we could of the character and personality of each child in this third year of life and then to retrace, from our earlier category analyses of that child's first two years of life, the representation, reconciliation, conflict, new meanings, or omission of significant aspects of early development as they appeared in his personality in his third year.

The third year is of considerable theoretical significance. Some of the themes to be borne in mind as we discuss this period in the future are: self-constancy and object constancy, the sense of identity, the internalization process and the nature and outcome of internalized conflicts involving libidinal and aggressive drives, other aspects of ego development and learning (such as the shift from the primary to the secondary process as well as the shift from the pleasure principle to the reality principle), the nature of the child's play and fantasy, and the child's interaction with his peers. But what ties this together is our focus on the antecedents of current subphase phenomena and personality.

In summary, this last approach varied radically from what we did at earlier stages of the child's life. Rather than to continue a month-by-month analysis of specific categories of the data for all children, we turned to a child-by-child analysis in which we made an assessment, first, of the outcome of the first three subphases of the separation-individuation process, and second, of personality development as it appeared in the third year of life. Some of the results of this work are reflected in our case studies Part III, which followed the children's development through the third year of life.

REFERENCES

Abelin, E. L. (1971). "The Role of the Father in the Separation-Individuation Process," in *Separation-Individuation: Essays in Honor of Margaret S. Mahler*, edited by J. B. McDevitt and C. F. Settlage. New York: International Universities Press, pp. 229–253.

———. (1972). "Some Further Observations and Comments on the Earliest Role of the Father." Paper read at the Margaret S. Mahler Symposium on Child Development. Philadelphia, May 1972. Unpublished.

Abraham, K. (1921). "Contributions to the Theory of the Anal Character," in *Selected Papers of Karl Abraham*, translated by D. Bryan and A. Strachey. New York: Basic Books, 1953, pp. 370–392.

———. (1924). "The Influence of Oral Erotism on Character Formation," in *Selected Papers of Karl Abraham*, translated by D. Bryan and A. Strachey. New York: Basic Books, 1953, pp. 393–406.

Alpert, A. (1959). "Reversibility of Pathological Fixations Associated with Maternal Deprivation in Infancy," in *The Psychoanalytic Study of the Child*, Vol. 14. New York: International Universities Press, pp. 169–185.

Angel, K. (1967). "On Symbiosis and Pseudosymbiosis," *J. Am. Psychoanal. Assoc.*, 15:294–316.

Anthony, E. J. (1961). "A Study of 'Screen Sensations,'" in *The Psychoanalytic Study of the Child*, Vol. 16. New York: International Universities Press, pp. 211–246.

———. (1971). "Folie à Deux: A Developmental Failure in the Process of Separation-Individuation," in *Separation-Individuation: Essays in Honor of Margaret S. Mahler*, edited by J. B. McDevitt and C. F. Settlage. New York: International Universities Press, pp. 253–273.

———. (1972). "Parenthood: Some Aspects of Its Psychology and Psychopathology." Paper read at the Margaret S. Mahler Symposium on Child Development. Philadelphia, May 1972. Unpublished.

Anthony, E. J. and Benedek, T. (1970). *Parenthood: Its Psychology and Psychopathology*. Boston: Little, Brown.

Arlow, J. A. (1959). "The Structure of the Déja Vu Experience," *J. Am. Psychoanal. Assoc.*, 7:611–631.

Bak, R. C. (1941). "Temperature-Orientation and the Overflowing of Ego Boundaries in Schizophrenia," in *Schweizer Archiv. Neurol. Psychiatr.*, 46:158–177.

———. (1971). "Object Relationship in Schizophrenia and Perversion," *Int. J. Psycho-Anal.*, 52:235–242.

———. (1974). "Distortions of the Concept of Fetishism," in *The Psychoanalytic Study of the Child*, Vol. 29. New Haven: Yale University Press, pp. 191–214.

Bakwin, H. (1942). "Loneliness in Infants," *Am. J. Dis. Child.*, 63:30–40.

Barglow, P., and Sadlow, L. (1971). "Visual Perception: Its Development and Maturation from Birth to Adulthood," *J. Am. Psychoanal. Assoc.*, 19:433–450.

Bell, S. (1970). "The Development of a Concept of Object as Related to Infant-Mother Attachment," *Child Dev.*, 41:291–311.

Benedek, T. (1938). "Adaptation to Reality in Early Infancy," *Psychoanal. Q.*, 7:200–214.

———. (1949). "The Psychosomatic Implications of the Primary Unit: Mother-Child," *Am. J. Orthopsychiatry*, 19:642–654.

———. (1959). "Parenthood as a Developmental Phase: A Contribution to the Libido Theory," *J. Am. Psychoanal. Assoc.*, 7:389–417.

———. (1960). "The Organization of the Reproductive Drive," *Int. J. Psycho-Anal.*, 41:1–15.

Benjamin, J. D. (1950). "Methodological Considerations in the Validation and Elaboration of Psychoanalytical Personality Theory," *Am. J. Orthopsychiatry*, 20:139–156.

———. (1961). "The Innate and the Experiential in Child Development," in *Lectures on Experimental Psychiatry*, edited by H. Brosin. Pittsburgh: University of Pittsburgh Press, pp. 19–42.

Bergman, A. (1971). " 'I and You': The Separation-Individuation Process in the Treatment of a Symbiotic Child," in *Separation-Individuation: Essays in Honor of Margaret S. Mahler*, edited by J. B. McDevitt and C. F. Settlage. New York: International Universities Press, pp. 325–355.

Bergman, P. and Escalona, S. K. (1949). "Unusual Sensitivities in Very Young Children," in *The Psychoanalytic Study of the Child*, Vol. 3/4. New York: International Universities Press, pp. 333–352.

Bergmann, M. (1963). "The Place of Paul Federn's Ego Psychology in Psychoanalytic Metapsychology," *J. Am. Psychoanal. Assoc.*, 11:97–116.

Bibring, E. (1953). "The Mechanism of Depression," in *Affective Disorders*, edited by P. Greenacre. New York: International Universities Press, pp. 13–48.

Blanck, G. and Blanck, R. (1972). "Toward a Psychoanalytic Developmental Psychology," *J. Am. Psychoanal. Assoc.*, 20:668–710.

———. (1974). *Frontiers of Psychotherapy*, New York: Columbia University Press.

Bonnard, A. (1958). "Pre-Body-Ego Types of (Pathological) Mental Functioning," *J. Am. Psychoanal. Assoc.*, 6:581–611.

Bornstein, B. (1945). "Clinical Notes on Child Analysis," in *The Psychoanalytic Study of the Child*, Vol. 1. New York: International Universities Press, pp. 151–166.

Bouvet, M. (1958). "Technical Variations and the Concept of Distance," *Int. J. Psycho-Anal.*, 39:211–221.

Bowlby, J. (1958). "The Nature of the Child's Tie to the Mother," *Int. J. Psycho-Anal.*, 39:350–373.

Bowlby, J., Robertson, J., and Rosenbluth, D. (1952). "A Two-Year-Old Goes to Hospital," in *The Psychoanalytic Study of the Child*, Vol. 7. New York: International Universities Press, pp. 82–94.

Brody, S. and Axelrad, S. (1966). "Anxiety, Socialization, and Ego-Formation in Infancy," *Int. J. Psycho-Anal.*, 47:218–229.

———. (1970). *Anxiety and Ego Formation in Infancy*. New York: International University Press.

Coleman, R. W., Kris, E., and Provence, S. (1953). "The Study of Variations of Early Parental Attitudes: A Preliminary Report," in *The Psychoanalytic Study of the Child*, Vol. 8. New York: International University Press, pp. 20–47.

Eissler, K. (1962). "On the Metapsychology of the Preconscious," in *The Psychoanalytic Study of the Child*, Vol. 17. New York: International Universities Press, pp. 9–41.

References

Elkisch, P. (1953). "Simultaneous Treatment of a Child and His Mother," *Am. J. Psychother.*, 7:105–130.

———. (1971). "Initiating Separation-Individuation in the Simultaneous Treatment of a Child and his Mother," in *Separation-Individuation: Essays in Honor of Margaret S. Mahler*, edited by J. B. McDevitt and C. F. Settlage. New York: International Universities Press, pp. 356–376.

Erickson, E. H. (1959). *Identity and the Life Cycle. Psychological Issues*, Monograph No. 1. New York: International Universities Press.

Escalona, S. (1968). *The Roots of Individuality: Normal Patterns of Development in Infancy*. Chicago: Aldine Publishing.

Fantz, R. L. (1961). "The Origin of Form Perception," *Scientific American*, May 1961, pp. 66–72.

Fenichel, O. (1945). *Psychoanalytic Theory of Neurosis*. New York: Norton.

Ferenczi, S. (1913). "Stages in the Development of the Sense of Reality," in *Sex in Psychoanalysis: The Selected Papers of Sandor Ferenczi*, Vol. 1. New York: Basic Books, 1950, pp. 213–239.

Fliess, R. (1957). *Erogeneity and Libido: Addenda to the Theory of the Psychosexual Development of the Human*. New York: International Universities Press.

———. (1961). *Ego and Body Ego*. New York: International Universities Press, 1972.

Fraiberg, S. (1969). "Libidinal Object Constancy and Mental Representation," in *The Psychoanalytic Study of the Child*, Vol. 14. New York: International Universities Press, pp. 9–47.

Frank, A. (1969). "The Unrememberable and the Unforgettable: Passive Primal Repression," in *The Psychoanalytic Study of the Child*, Vol. 24. New York: International Universities Press, pp. 48–77.

Frankl, L. (1963). "Self-Preservation and the Development of Accident Proneness in Children and Adolescents," in *The Psychoanalytic Study of the Child*, Vol. 18. New York: International Universities Press, pp. 464–483.

Freud, A. (1936). *The Ego and Its Mechanisms of Defense*. London: Hogarth Press, 1937.

———. (1945). "Indications for Child Analysis," in *The Psychoanalytic Study of the Child*, Vol. 1. New York: International Universities Press, pp. 127–149.

———. (1949). "Aggression in Relation to Emotional Development: Normal and Pathological," in *The Psychoanalytic Study of the Child*, Vols. 3/4. New York: International Universities Press, pp. 37–42.

———. (1951*a*). "Negativism and Emotional Surrender," *Int. J. Psycho-Anal.*, 33 (1952): 265.

———. (1951*b*). "Observations on Child Development," in *The Psychoanalytic Study of the Child*, Vol. 6. New York: International Universities Press, pp. 18–30. Reprinted in *The Writings of Anna Freud*, Vol. 5. New York: International Universities Press, 1969, pp. 143–162.

———. (1952). "Studies in Passivity." Part 2, "Notes on a Connection Between the States of Negativism and of Emotional Surrender," in *The Writings of Anna Freud*, Vol. 4. New York: International Universities Press, 1968, pp. 256–259.

———. (1952). "The Mutual Influences in the Development of the Ego and Id," in *The Psychoanalytic Study of the Child*, Vol. 7. New York: International Universities Press, pp. 42–50.

———. (1953). "Some Remarks on Infant Observation," in *The Psychoanalytic Study of the Child*, Vol. 8. New York: International Universities Press, pp. 9–19. Reprinted in *The Writings of Anna Freud*, Vol. 4. New York: International Universities Press, 1968, pp. 569–585.

———. (1954). "Psychoanalysis and Education," in *The Psychoanalytic Study of the Child*, Vol. 9. New York: International Universities Press, pp. 9–15.

———. (1957). "The Contribution of Direct Child Observation to Psychoanalysis," in *The Writings of Anna Freud*, Vol. 5. New York: International Universities Press, 1969, pp. 95–101.

———. (1958). "Child Observation and Prediction of Development: A Memorial Lecture in Honor of Ernst Kris," in *The Psychoanalytic Study of the Child*, Vol. 13. New York: International Universities Press, pp. 92–116. Reprinted in *The Writings of Anna Freud*, Vol. 5. New York: International Universities Press, 1969, pp. 102–135.

———. (1963). "The Concept of Developmental Lines," in *The Psychoanalytic Study of the Child*, Vol. 18. New York: International Universities Press, pp. 245–266.

———. (1965*a*). "Direct Child Observation in the Service of Psychoanalytic Child Psychology," in *The Writings of Anna Freud*, Vol. 6. New York: International Universities Press, pp.10–24.

———. (1965*b*). *Normality and Pathology in Childhood: Assessments of Development*. New York: International Universities Press.

———. (1967). "About Losing and Being Lost," in *The Psychoanalytic Study of the Child*, Vol. 22. New York: International Universities Press, pp. 9–19.

———. (1971). "The Infantile Neurosis: Genetic and Dynamic Considerations," in *The Writings of Anna Freud*, Vol. 7. New York: International Universities Press, pp. 189–203.

Freud, S. (1887–1904). *The Origins of Psychoanalysis: Letters to Wilhelm Fleiss*, edited by M. Bonaparte, A. Freud, and E. Kris. New York: Basic Books, 1954.

———. (1895). "Project for a Scientific Psychology," in *Standard Edition*, Vol. 1, edited by J. Strachey. London: Hogarth Press, 1950, pp. 281–397.

———. (1900). "The Interpretation of Dreams," in *Standard Edition*, Vol. 4/5, edited by J. Strachey. London: Hogarth Press, 1953.

———. (1905). "Three Essays on the Theory of Sexuality," in *Standard Edition*, Vol. 7, edited by J. Strachey. London: Hogarth Press, 1953, pp. 135–243.

———. (1909). "Analysis of a Phobia in a Five-Year-Old Boy," in *Standard Edition*, Vol. 10, edited by J. Strachey. London: Hogarth Press, 1955, pp. 3–149.

———. (1911). "Formulations on the Two Principles of Mental Functioning," in *Standard Edition*, Vol. 12, edited by J. Strachey, London: Hogarth Press, 1958, pp. 213–226.

———. (1914*a*). "Remembering, Repeating and Working Through," in *Standard Edition*, Vol. 12, edited by J. Strachey. London: Hogarth Press, 1958, pp. 145–156.

———. (1914*b*). "On Narcissism: An Introduction," in *Standard Edition*, Vol. 14, edited by J. Strachey. London: Hogarth Press, 1967, pp. 67–102.

———. (1915*a*). "Instincts and Their Vicissitudes," in *Standard Edition*, Vol. 14, edited by J. Strachey. London: Hogarth Press, 1957, pp. 117–140.

———. (1915*b*). "Mourning and Melancholia," in *Standard Edition*, Vol. 14, edited by J. Strachey. London: Hogarth Press, 1957, pp. 237–260.

———. (1920). "Beyond the Pleasure Principle," in *Standard Edition*, Vol. 18, edited by J. Strachey. London: Hogarth Press, 1955, pp. 3–64.

———. (1923). "The Ego and the Id," in *Standard Edition*, Vol. 19, edited by J. Strachey. London: Hogarth Press, 1961, pp. 3–66.

———. (1925). "Negation," in *Standard Edition*, Vol. 19, edited by J. Strachey. London: Hogarth Press, 1961, pp. 235–239.

———. (1927). "The Future of an Illusion," in *Standard Edition*, Vol. 21, edited by J. Strachey. London: Hogarth Press, 1961, pp. 5–56.

———. (1930). "Civilization and Its Discontents," in *Standard Edition*, Vol. 21, edited by J. Strachey. London: Hogarth Press, 1961, pp. 59–145.

———. (1937). "Construction in Analysis," in *Standard Edition*, Vol. 23, edited by J. Strachey. London: Hogarth Press, 1964, pp. 255–269.

———. (1940). "An Outline of Psycho-Analysis," in *Standard Edition*, Vol. 23, edited by J. Strachey. London: Hogarth Press, 1964, pp. 141–207.

Fries, M. E. and Woolf, P. J. (1953). "Some Hypotheses on the Role of Congenital Activity Type in Personality Development," in *The Psychoanalytic Study of the Child*, Vol. 8. New York: International Universities Press, pp. 48–62.

———. (1971). "The Influence of Constitutional Complex on Developmental Phases," in *Separation-Individuation: Essays in Honor of Margaret S. Mahler*, edited by J. B. McDevitt and C. F. Settlage. New York: International Universities Press, pp. 274–296.

Frijling-Schreuder, E. C. M. (1969). "Borderline States in Children," in *The Psychoanalytic Study of the Child*, Vol. 24. New York: International Universities Press, pp. 307–327.

Furer, M. (1964). "The Development of a Preschool Symbiotic Psychotic Box," in *The Psychoanalytic Study of the Child*, Vol. 19. New York: International Universities Press, pp. 448–469.

———. (1967). "Some Developmental Aspects of the Superego," *Int. J. Psycho-Anal.*, 48:277–280.

———. (1971). "Observations on the Treatment of the Symbiotic Syndrome of Infantile Psychosis—Reality, Reconstruction, and Drive Maturation," in *Separation-Individuation: Essays in Honor of Margaret S. Mahler*, edited by J. B. McDevitt and C. F. Settlage. New York: International Universities Press, pp. 473–485.

Galenson, E. (1971). "A Consideration of the Nature of Thought in Childhood Play," in *Separation-Individuation: Essays in Honor of Margaret S. Mahler*, edited by J. B. McDevitt and C. F. Settlage. New York: International Universities Press, pp. 41–60.

Galenson, E., and Roiphe, H. (1971). "The Impact of Early Sexual Discovery on Mood, Defensive Organization and Symbolization," in *The Psychoanalytic Study of the Child*, Vol. 26. New York: Quadrangle, pp. 195–216.

Geleerd, E. R. (1956). "Clinical Contribution to the Problems of the Early Mother-Child Relationship: Some Discussion of Its Influence on Self-Destructive Tendencies and Fugue States," in *The Psychoanalytic Study of the Child*, Vol. 11. New York: International Universities Press, pp. 336–351.

Gero, G. (1936). "The Construction of Depression," *Int. J. Psycho-Anal.*, 17: 423–461.

Glenn, J., reporter. (1966). "Panel on Melanie Klein." Meeting of the New York Psychoanalytic Society, May 25, 1965. *Psychoanal. Q.*, 35:320–325.

Glover, E. (1956). *On the Early Development of Mind*. New York: International Universities Press.

Gouin-Decarie, T. (1965). *Intelligence and Affectivity in Early Childhood*. New York: International Universities Press.

Greenacre, P. (1945). "The Biologic Economy of Birth," in *The Psychoanalytic Study of the Child*, Vol. 1. New York: International Universities Press, pp. 31–51.

———. (1947). "Vision, Headache and the Halo: Reactions to Stress in the Course of Superego Formation," *Psychoanal. Q.*, 16:177–194.

———. (1948). "Anatomical Structure and Super-Ego Development," *Am. J. Orthopsychiatry*, 18:636–648.

———. (1953). "Penis Awe and Its Relation to Penis Envy," in *Emotional Growth*, Vol. 1. New York: International Universities Press, pp. 31–49.

———. (1957). "The Childhood of the Artist: Libidinal Phase Development and Giftedness," in *The Psychoanalytic Study of the Child*, Vol. 12. New York: International Universities Press, pp. 27–72.

———. (1958). "Early Physical Determinants in the Development of the Sense of Identity," *J. Am. Psychoanal. Assoc.*, 6:612–627.

———. (1959). "On Focal Symbiosis," in *Dynamic Psychology in Childhood*, edited by L. Jessner and E. Pavenstedt. New York: Grune & Stratton, pp. 243–256.

———. (1960). "Considerations Regarding the Parent-Infant Relationship," in *Emotional Growth*, Vol. 1. New York: International Universities Press, pp. 199–224.

———. (1966). "Problems of Overidealization of the Analyst and of Analysis: Their Manifestations in the Transference and Counter-Transference Relationships," in *The Psychoanalytic Study of the Child*, Vol. 21. New York: International Universities Press, pp. 193–212.

———. (1968). "Perversion: General Considerations Regarding Their Genetic and Dynamic Background," in *The Psychoanalytic Study of the Child*, Vol. 23. New York: International Universities Press, 47–62.

———. (1973). "The Primal Scene and the Sense of Reality," *Psychoanal. Q.*, 42:10–40.

Greenson, R. R. (1968). "Dis-Identification," *Int. J. Psycho-Anal.*, 49:370–374.

———. (1971). "A Dream While Drowning," in *Separation-Individuation: Essays in Honor of Margaret S. Mahler*, edited by J. B. McDevitt and C. F. Settlage. New York: International Universities Press, pp. 377–384.

Harley, M. (1971). "Some Reflections on Identity Problems in Prepuberty," in *Separation-Individuation: Essays in Honor of Margaret S. Mahler*, edited by J. B. McDevitt and C. F. Settlage. New York: International Universities Press. pp. 385–403.

Harrison, I. (1973). "On the Maternal Origins of Awe," in *The Psychoanalytic Study of the Child*, Vol. 30, in press.

Harrison, S. (1971). "Symbiotic Infantile Psychosis: Observation of an Acute Episode," in *Separation-Individuation: Essays in Honor of Margaret S. Mahler*, edited by J. B. McDevitt and C. F. Settlage. New York: International Universities Press, pp. 404–415.

Hartmann, H. (1939). *Ego Psychology and the Problem of Adaptation*. New York: International Universities Press, 1958.

———. (1950). "Psychoanalysis and Developmental Psychology," in *The Psychoanalytic Study of the Child*, Vol. 5. New York: International Universities Press, pp. 7–17.

———. (1952). "The Mutual Influences in the Development of the Ego and Id," in *The Psychoanalytic Study of the Child*, Vol. 7. New York: International Universities Press, pp. 9–30.

———. (1955). "Notes on the Theory of Sublimation," in *The Psychoanalytic Study of the Child*, Vol. 10. New York: International Universities Press, pp. 9–29.

———. (1956). "Notes on the Reality Principle," in *Essays on Ego Psychology*. New York: International Universities Press, pp. 241–267.

Hartmann, H., Kris, E., and Loewenstein, R. M. (1946). "Comments on the Formation of Psychic Structure," in *The Psychoanalytic Study of the Child*, Vol. 2. New York: International Universities Press, pp. 11–38.

———. (1949). "Notes on the Theory of Aggression," in *The Psychoanalytic*

Study of the Child, Vol. 3/4. New York: International Universities Press, pp. 9–36.

Heimann, P. (1966). "Comment on Dr. Kernberg's Paper (Structural Derivatives of Object Relationships)," *Int. J. Psycho-Anal.*, 47:254–260.

Hendrick, I. (1951). "Early Development of the Ego: Identification in Infancy," *Psychoanal. Q.*, 20:44–61.

Hermann, I. (1926). "Das System Bw," *Imago*, 12:203–210.

———. (1936). "Sich-Anklammern, Auf-Suche-Gehen," *Int. Z. Psychoanal.*, 22: 349–370.

Hoffer, W. (1949). "Mouth, Hand and Ego-Integration," in *The Psychoanalytic Study of the Child,* Vol. 3/4. New York: International Universities Press, pp. 49–56.

———. (1950*a*). "Development of the Body Ego," in *The Psychoanalytic Study of the Child,* Vol. 5. New York: International Universities Press, pp. 18–23.

———. (1950*b*). "Oral Aggressiveness and Ego Development," *Int. J. Psycho-Anal.*, 31:156–160.

———. (1952). "The Mutual Influences in the Development of Ego and Id: Earliest Stages," in *The Psychoanalytic Study of the Child,* Vol. 7. New York: International Universities Press, pp. 31–41.

———. (1955). *Psychoanalysis: Practical and Research Aspects.* Baltimore: Williams & Wilkins, p. 10.

Hollander, M. (1970). "The Need or Wish to Be Held," *Arch. Gen. Psychiatry,* 22:445–453.

Homburger, A. (1923). "Zur Gestalung der normalen menschlichen Motorik und ihre Beurteilung," *Z. Gesamte Psychiatr.*, 75. 274.

Isakower, O. (1938). "A Contribution to the Pathopsychology of Phenomena Associated with Falling Asleep," *Int. J. Psycho-Anal.*, 19:331–345.

———. (1939). "On the Exceptional Position of the Auditory Sphere," *Int. J. Psycho-Anal.*, 20:340–348.

Jackson, E., Klatskin, E., and Ethelyn, H. (1950). "Rooming-in Research Project: Development of Methodology of Parent-Child Relationship Study in a Clinical Setting," in *The Psychoanalytic Study of the Child,* Vol. 5. New York: International Universities Press, pp. 236–240.

Jacobson, E. (1953). "The Affects and Their Pleasure-Unpleasure Qualities in Relation to the Psychic Discharge Processes," in *Drives, Affects, Behavior,* edited by R. M. Loewenstein, Vol. 1. New York: International Universities Press, pp. 38–66.

———. (1954). "The Self and the Object World: Vicissitudes of Their Infantile Cathexes and Their Influence on Ideational and Affective Development," in *The Psychoanalytic Study of the Child,* Vol. 9. New York: International Universities Press, pp. 75–127.

———. (1964). *The Self and the Object World.* New York: International Universities Press.

James, M. (1960). "Premature Ego Development: Some Observations on Disturbances in the First Three Months of Life," *Int. J. Psycho-Anal.*, 41:288–294.

Joffe, W. G. and Sandler, J. (1965). "Notes on Pain, Depression, and Individuation," in *The Psychoanalytic Study of the Child,* Vol. 20. New York: International Universities Press, pp. 394–424.

Kafka, E. (1971). "On the Development of the Experience of Mental Self, Bodily Self, and Self-Consciousness," in *The Psychoanalytic Study of the Child,* Vol. 26. New York: Quadrangle, pp. 217–240.

Kanner, L. (1949). "Problems of Nosology and Psychodynamics of Early Infantile Autism," *Am. J. Orthopsychiatry,* 19:416–426.

Kaplan, L. J. (1972). "Object Constancy in Piaget's Vertical Décalage," *Bull. Menninger Clinic*, 36:322–334.

Katan, A. (1961). "Some Thoughts about the Role of Verbalization in Early Childhood," in *The Psychoanalytic Study of the Child*, Vol. 16. New York: International Universities Press, pp. 184–188.

Kaufman, I. C. and Rosenblum, L. A. (1967). "Depression in Infant Monkeys Separated from Their Mothers," *Science*, 155:1030–1031.

———. (1968). "The Reaction to Separation in Infant Monkeys: Anaclitic Depression and Conservation-Withdrawal," *Psychosom. Med.*, 29:648–675.

Kernberg, O. (1967). "Borderline Personality Organization," *J. Am. Psychoanal. Assoc.*, 15:641–685.

———. (1974). "Contrasting Viewpoints Regarding the Nature and Psychoanalytic Treatment of Narcissistic Personalities: A Preliminary Communication," *J. Am. Psychoanal. Assoc.*, 22:255–267.

Kestenberg, J. S. (1956). "On the Development of Maternal Feelings in Early Childhood: Observations and Reflections," in *The Psychoanalytic Study of the Child*, Vol. 11. New York: International Universities Press, pp. 257–291.

———. (1965*a*). "The Role of Movement Patterns in Development. I. Rhythms of Movement," *Psychoanal. Q.*, 24:1–26.

———. (1965*b*). "The Role of Movement Patterns in Development. II. Flow and Tension and Effort," *Psychoanal. Q.*, 24:517–563.

———. (1967). The Role of Movement Patterns in Development. III. The Control of Shape. *Psychoanal. Q.*, 36:356–409.

———. (1968). "Outside and Inside, Male and Female," *J. Am. Psychological Assoc.*, 16:457–520.

———. (1971). "From Organ-Object Imagery to Self and Object Representations," in *Separation-Individuation: Essays in Honor of Margaret S. Mahler*, edited by J. B. McDevitt and C. F. Settlage. New York: International Universities Press, pp. 75–99.

Khan, M. M. R. (1963). "The Concept of Cumulative Trauma," in *The Psychoanalytic Study of the Child*, Vol. 18. New York: International Universities Press, pp. 286–306.

———. (1964). "Ego Distortion, Cumulative Trauma, and the Role of Reconstruction in the Analytic Situation," *Int. J. Psycho-Anal.*, 45:272–279.

Kierkegaard, S. (1846). *Purity of Heart*. New York: Harper and Row, 1938.

Kleeman, J. A. (1967). "The Peek-a-Boo Game: Part I: Its Origins, Meanings, and Related Phenomena in the First Year," in *The Psychoanalytic Study of the Child*, Vol. 22. New York: International Universities Press, pp. 239–273.

Kohut, H. (1972). "Thoughts on Narcissism and Narcissistic Rage," in *The Psychoanalytic Study of the Child*, Vol. 27. New York: Quadrangle, pp. 360–401.

Kris, E. (1950). "Notes on the Development and on Some Current Problems of Psychoanalytic Child Psychology," in *The Psychoanalytic Study of the Child*, Vol. 5. New York: International Universities Press, pp. 24–46.

———. (1955). "Neutralization and Sublimation: Observations on Young Children," in *The Psychoanalytic Study of the Child*, Vol. 10. New York: International Universities Press, pp. 30–46.

———. (1956). "The Recovery of Childhood Memories," in *The Psychoanalytic Study of the Child*, Vol. 11. New York: International Universities Press, pp. 54–88.

———. (1962). "Decline and Recovery in the Life of a Three-Year-Old; or: Data in Psychoanalytic Perspective on the Mother-Child Relationship," in *The Psychoanalytic Study of the Child*, Vol. 17. New York: International Universities Press, pp. 175–215.

Kris, E. et al. (1954). "Problems of Infantile Neurosis: A Discussion," in *The Psychoanalytic Study of the Child*, Vol. 9. New York: International Universities Press, pp. 16–71.

Kris, M. (1957). "The Use of Prediction in a Longitudinal Study," in *The Psychoanalytic Study of the Child*, Vol. 12. New York: International Universities Press, pp. 175–189.

———. (1972). "Some Aspects of Family Interaction: A Psychoanalytic Study," *Freud Anniversary Lecture*. March 28, 1972. Unpublished.

Kupfermann, K. (1971). "The Development and Treatment of a Psychotic Child," in *Separation-Individuation: Essays in Honor of Margaret S. Mahler*, edited by J. B. McDevitt and C. F. Settlage. New York: International Universities Press, pp. 441–470.

Lampl de Groot, J. (1973). "Vicissitudes of Narcissism and Problems of Civilization," *Freud Anniversary Lecture*. March 28, 1973. Unpublished.

Levita, D. (1966). "On the Psychoanalytic Concept of Identity," *Int. J. Psycho-Anal.*, 47:299–305.

Levy, D. M. (1937). "Primary Affect Hunger," *Am. J. Psychol.*, 94:643–652.

Lewin, B. D. (1946). "Sleep, the Mouth and the Dream Screen," *Psychoanal. Q.*, 15:419–434.

———. (1948). "Inferences from the Dream Screen," *Int. J. Psycho-Anal.*, 29: 224–231.

———. (1950). *The Psychoanalysis of Elation*. New York: Norton.

———. (1953). "Reconsideration of the Dream Screen," *Psychoanal. Q.*, 22: 174–199.

Lichtenstein, H. (1964). "The Role of Narcissism in the Emergence and Maintenance of a Primary Identity," *Int. J. Psycho-Anal.*, 45:49–56.

Lley, A. W. (1972). "The Foetus as a Personalty," *Aust. N. Z. J. Psychatry*, 6: 99–105.

Loewald, H. W. (1951). "Ego and Reality," *Int. J. Psycho-Anal.*, 32:10–18.

———. (1962). "Internalization, Separation, Mourning and the Superego," *Psychoanal. Q.*, 31:483–504.

Loewenstein, R. M. (1950). "Conflict and Autonomous Ego Development During the Phallic Phase," in *The Psychoanalytic Study of the Child*, Vol. 5. New York: International Universities Press, pp. 47–52.

Löfgren, J. B. (1968). "Castration Anxiety and the Body Ego," *Int. J. Psycho-Anal.*, 49:408–410.

Lustman, S. L. (1956). "Rudiments of the Ego," in *The Psychoanalytic Study of the Child*, Vol. 11. New York: International Universities Press, pp. 89–98.

———. (1957). "Psychic Energy and the Mechanisms of Defense," in *The Psychoanalytic Study of the Child*, Vol. 12. New York: International Universities Press, pp. 151–165.

———. (1962). "Defense, Symptom, and Character," in *The Psychoanalytic Study of the Child*, Vol. 17. New York: International Universities Press, pp. 216–244.

Mahler, M. S. (1944). "Tics and Impulsions in Children: A Study of Motility," *Psychoanal. Q.*, 13:430–444.

———. (1945). "Introductory Remarks To: Symposium on Tics in Children," *Nerv. Child*, 4:307.

———. (1949*a*). "A Psychoanalytic Evaluation of Tic in Psychopathology of Children: Symptomatic Tic and Tic Syndrome," in *The Psychoanalytic Study of the Child*, Vol. 3/4. New York: International Universities Press, pp. 279–310.

———. (1949*b*). "Remarks on Psychoanalysis with Psychotic Children," *Q. J. Child Behavior*, 1:18–21. (Quoted in R. Fliess, *Ego and Body Ego*, p. 24.)

———. (1950). Discussion of Papers by Anna Freud and Ernst Kris: Symposium on "Problems of Child Development." Stockbridge, Mass., April 1950. Unpublished. (Quoted in R. Fleiss, *Ego and Body Ego*, p. 30.)

———. (1952). "On Child Psychosis and Schizophrenia: Autistic and Symbiotic Infantile Psychoses," in *The Psychoanalytic Study of the Child*, Vol. 7. New York: International Universities Press, pp. 286–305.

———. (1955). "Discussion [of papers by Kanner and Eisenberg, Despert, Lourie]," in *Psychopathology of Childhood*, edited by P. H. Hoch and J. Zubin. New York: Grune & Stratton, pp. 285–289.

———. (1958*a*). "Autism and Symbiosis: Two Extreme Disturbances of Identity," *Int. J. Psycho-Anal.*, 39:77–83.

———. (1958*b*). "On Two Crucial Phases of Integration of the Sense of Identity: Separation-Individuation and Bisexual Identity," *J. Am. Psychoanal. Assoc.*, 6:136–139.

———. (1960). "Symposium on Psychotic Object-Relationships: III. Perceptual De-Differentiation and Psychotic 'Object Relationship,'" *Int. J. Psycho-Anal.*, 41:548–553.

———. (1961). "On Sadness and Grief in Infancy and Childhood: Loss and Restoration of the Symbiotic Love Object," in *The Psychoanalytic Study of the Child*, Vol. 16. New York: International Universities Press, pp. 332–351.

———. (1963). "Thoughts about Development and Individuation," in *The Psychoanalytic Study of the Child*, Vol. 18. New York: International Universities Press, pp. 307–324.

———. (1965*a*). "On Early Infantile Psychosis: The Symbiotic and Autistic Syndromes," *J. Am. Acad. Child Psychiatry*, 4:554–568.

———. (1965*b*). "On the Significance of the Normal Separation-Individuation Phase: With Reference to Research in Symbiotic Child Psychosis," in *Drives, Affects, Behavior*, Vol. 2, edited by M. Schur. New York: International Universities Press, pp. 161–169.

———. (1966*a*). "Discussion of P. Greenacre's 'Problems of Overidealization of the Analyst and Analysis.'" Abstracted in *Psychoanal. Q.*, 36(1967):637.

———. (1966*b*). "Notes on the Development of Basic Moods: The Depressive Affect," in *Psychoanalysis—A General Psychology: Essays in Honor of Heinz Hartmann*, edited by R. M. Loewenstein, L. M. Newman, M. Schur, and A. J. Solnit. New York: International Universities Press, pp. 152–168.

———. (1967*a*). "On Human Symbiosis and the Vicissitudes of Individuation," *J. Am. Psychoanal. Assoc.*, 15:740–763.

———. (1967*b*). "Child Development and the Curriculum," *J. Am. Psychoanal. Assoc.*, 15:876–886.

———. (1968*a*). "Discussion of Börje Löfgren's paper 'Castration Anxiety and the Body Ego,'" *Int. J. Psychoanal.*, 49:410–412.

———. (1968*b*). *On Human Symbiosis and the Vicissitudes of Individuation*, Vol. 1, *Infantile Psychosis*. New York: International Universities Press.

———. (1969). "Perturbances of Symbiosis and Individuation in the Development of the Psychotic Ego," in *Problems of Psychosis*, edited by P. Doucet and C. Laurin. *Excerpt. Med. Int. Cong. Series*, Part 1, pp. 188–196 and Part 2, pp. 375–378.

———. (1971). "A Study of the Separation-Individuation Process and Its Possible Application to Borderline Phenomena in the Psychoanalytic Situation," in *The Psychoanalytic Study of the Child*, Vol. 26. New York: Quadrangle, pp. 403–424.

———. (1972*a*). "On the First Three Subphases of the Separation-Individuation Process," *Int. J. Psycho-Anal.*, 53:333–338.

———. (1972*b*). "Rapprochement Subphase of the Separation-Individuation Process," *Psychoanal. Q.*, 41:487–506.

———. (1974). "Discussion of R. Stoller's 'Healthy Parental Influences on the Earliest Development of Masculinity in Baby Boys,'" *Psychoanalytic Forum*, Vol. 5, in press.

Mahler, M. S., and Elkisch, P. (1953). "Some Observations on Disturbances of the Ego in a Case of Infantile Psychosis," in *The Psychoanalytic Study of the Child*, Vol. 8. New York: International Universities Press, pp. 252–261.

Mahler, M. S., and Furer, M. (1960). "Observations on Research Regarding the 'Symbiotic Syndrome' of Infantile Psychosis," *Psychoanal. Q.*, 29:317–327.

———. (1963*a*). "Certain Aspects of the Separation-Individuation Phase," *Psychoanal. Q.*, 32:1–14.

———. (1963*b*). "Description of the Subphases. History of the Separation-Individuation Study." Presented at Workshop IV: Research in Progress. American Psychoanalytic Association, annual meeting. St. Louis, Mo., May 4, 1963. Unpublished.

———. (1966). "Development of Symbiosis, Symbiotic Psychosis, and the Nature of Separation Anxiety: Remarks on J. Weiland's Paper," *Int. J. Psycho-Anal.*, 47:559–560.

———. (1972). "Child Psychosis: A Theoretical Statement and Its Implications," *J. Autism Child Schizo.*, 2/3:213–218.

Mahler, M. S., Furer, M., and Settlage, C. F. (1959). "Severe Emotional Disturbances in Childhood Psychosis," in *American Handbook of Psychiatry*, Vol. 1, edited by S. Arieti. New York: Basic Books, pp. 816–839.

Mahler, M. S., and Gosliner, B. J. (1955). "On Symbiotic Child Psychosis: Genetic, Dynamic and Restitutive Aspects," in *The Psychoanalytic Study of the Child*, Vol. 10. New York: International Universities Press, pp. 195–212.

Mahler, M. S., and Gross, I. H. (1945). "Psychotherapeutic Study of a Typical Case with Tic Syndrome," *Nerv. Child*, 4:359–373.

Mahler, M. S., and La Perriere, K. (1965). "Mother-Child Interaction during Separation-Individuation," *Psychoanal. Q.*, 34:483–498.

Mahler, M. S., and Luke, J. A. (1946). "Outcome of the Tic Syndrome," *J. Nerv. Ment. Dis.*, 103:433–445. Abstracted in *Digest Neurol. Psychiatry*, 14 (1946): 398.

Mahler, M. S., Luke, J. A., and Daltroff, W. (1945). "Clinical and Follow-up Study of the Tic Syndrome in Children," *Am. J. Orthopsychiatry*, 15:631–647.

Mahler, M. S., and McDevitt, J. B. (1968). "Observations on Adaptation and Defense *in Statu Nascendi*: Developmental Precursors in the First Two Years of Life," *Psychoanal. Q.*, 37:1–21.

Mahler, M. S., Pine, F., and Bergman, A. (1970). "The Mother's Reaction to her Toddler's Drive for Individuation," in *Parenthood: Its Psychology and Psychopathology*, edited by E. J. Anthony and T. Benedek. Boston: Little, Brown, pp. 257–274.

Mahler, M. S., Ross, J. R., Jr., and De Fries, Z. (1949). "Clinical Studies in Benign and Malignant Cases of Childhood Psychosis (Schizophrenia-like)," *Am. J. Orthopsychiatry*, 19:295–305.

Mahler, M. S., and Settlage, C. F. (1956). "The Classification and Treatment of Childhood Psychoses." American Psychiatric Association, Chicago, Ill., 1956. Unpublished. (Quoted in R. Fliess, *Ego and Body Ego*, p. 25.)

Masterson, J. F. (1973). "The Mother's Contribution to the Psychic Structure of the Borderline Personality." Paper read at the Margaret S. Mahler Symposium on Child Development. Philadelphia, May 1973. Unpublished.

McDevitt, J. B. (1971). "Preoedipal Determinants of an Infantile Neurosis," in

Separation-Individuation: Essays in Honor of Margaret S. Mahler, edited by J. B. McDevitt and C. F. Settlage. New York: International Universities Press, pp. 201–228.

———. (1972). "Libidinal Object Constancy: Some Developmental Considerations." Paper presented at the New York Psychoanalytic Society. New York, January 1972. Unpublished.

Modell, A. H. (1968). *Object Love and Reality*. New York: International Universities Press.

Murphy, L. B. (1962). *The Widening World of Childhood*. New York: Basic Books.

Nagera, H. (1966). *Early Childhood Disturbances: The Neurosis and the Adult Disturbances*. Monograph Series of the Psychological Study of the Child, No. 2. New York: International Universities Press.

Niederland, W. G. (1965). "The Role of the Ego in the Recovery of Early Memories." *Psychoanal. Q.*, 34:564–571.

Omwake, E. R., and Solnit, L. (1961). "It Isn't Fair," in *The Psychoanalytic Study of the Child*, Vol. 16. New York: International Universities Press, pp. 352–404.

Pacella, B. L. (1972). "Early Ego Development and the Déja Vu." Paper presented to the New York Psychoanalytic Society. New York, May 30, 1972. Unpublished.

Parens, H. (1971). "A Contribution of Separation-Individuation to the Development of Psychic Structure," in *Separation-Individuation: Essays in Honor of Margaret S. Mahler*, edited by J. B. McDevitt and C. F. Settlage. New York: International Universities Press, pp. 100–112.

———. (1973). "Aggression: A Reconsideration," *J. Am. Psychoanal. Assoc.*, 21:34–60.

———. (1974). "Aggression: Towards Its Epigenesis in Early Childhood." Unpublished.

Parens, H. and Saul, L. J. (1971). *Dependence in Man*. New York: International Universities Press.

Petö, A. (1955). "On So-Called Depersonalization," *Int. J. Psycho-Anal.*, 36: 379–386.

———. (1969). "Terrifying Eyes: A Visual Superego Forerunner," in *The Psychoanalytic Study of the Child*, Vol. 24. New York: International Universities Press, pp. 197–212.

———. (1970). "To Cast Away: An Vestibular Forerunner of the Superego," in *The Psychoanalytic Study of the Child*, Vol. 25. New York: International Universities Press, pp. 401–416.

Piaget, J. (1929*a*). *The Child's Conception of the World*. New York: Harcourt, Brace.

———. (1929*b*). *Judgment and Reasoning in the Child*. New York: Humanities Press.

———. (1930). *The Child's Conception of Physical Causality*. New York: Harcourt, Brace.

———. (1936). *The Origins of Intelligence in Children*. Paris: Delachaux & Niestle, 1936.

———. (1937). *The Construction of Reality in the Child*. New York: Basic Books, 1954.

Pine, F. (1964). "Some Patterns of Mother-Child Behavior in Toddlerhood." Paper read at the Research Career Development Award Conference. Skytop, Pa., June 1964. Unpublished.

———. (1970). "On the Structuralization of Drive-Defense Relationships," *Psychoanal. Q.*, 39:17–37.

———. (1971). "On the Separation Process: Universal Trends and Individual Differences," in *Separation-Individuation: Essays in Honor of Margaret S. Mahler*, edited by J. B. McDevitt and C. F. Settlage. New York: International Universities Press, 1971, pp. 113–130.

———. (1974). "Libidinal Object Constancy: A Theoretical Note," *Psychoanal. and Contemp. Sci.*, Vol. 3, edited by L. Goldberger and V. H. Rosen. New York: International Universities Press, pp. 307–313.

Pine, F., and Furer, M. (1963). "Studies of the Separation-Individuation Phase: A Methodological Overview," in *The Psychoanalytic Study of the Child*, Vol. 18. New York: International Universities Press, pp. 325–342.

Provence, S., and Lipton, R. C. (1962). *Infants in Institutions*. New York: International Universities Press.

Provence, S., and Ritvo, S. (1961). "Effects of Deprivation on Institutionalized Infants," in *The Psychoanalytic Study of the Child*, Vol. 16. New York: International Universities Press, pp. 189–205.

Ribble, M. A. (1943). *The Rights of Infants: Early Psychological Needs and Their Satisfaction*. New York: Columbia University Press.

Rinsley, D. B. (1965). "Intensive Psychiatric Hospital Treatment of Adolescents: An Objective Relations Review," *Psychiatr. Q.*, 39:405–429.

———. (1968). "Economic Aspects of Object-Relations," *Int. J. Psycho-Anal.*, 49:38–48.

———. (1971*a*). "The Adolescent In-Patient: Patterns of Depersonification," *Psychiatr. Q.*, 45:1–20.

———. (1971*b*). "Theory and Practice of Intensive Residential Treatment of Adolescents," in *Adolescent Psychiatry*, Vol. 1, edited by S. C. Feinstein, P. L. Giovacchini, and A. A. Miller. New York: Basic Books, pp. 479–508.

Ritvo, S., and Solnit, A. J. (1958). "Influences of Early Mother-Child Interaction on Identification Processes," in *The Psychoanalytic Study of the Child*, Vol. 13. New York: International Universities Press, pp. 64–91.

Roiphe, H., and Galenson, E. (1971). "The Impact of Early Sexual Discovery on Mood, Defensive Organization and Symbolization," in *The Psychoanalytic Study of the Child*, Vol. 26. New York: Quadrangle, pp. 195–216.

———. (1972). "Early Genital Activity and the Castration Complex," *Psychoanal. Q.*, 41:334–347.

———. (1973). "Some Observations on Transitional Object and Infantile Fetish." Paper presented to the New York Psychoanalytic Society. New York, March 27, 1973. Unpublished.

Rose, G. J. (1964). "Creative Imagination in Terms of Ego 'Core' and Boundaries," *Int. J. Psycho-Anal.*, 45:75–84.

———. (1966). "Body Ego and Reality," *Int. J. Psycho-Anal.*, 47:502–509.

Rubinfine, D. L. (1958). "Report of Panel: Problems of Identity," *J. Am. Psychoanal. Assoc.*, 6:131–142.

———. (1961). "Perception, Reality Testing, and Symbolism," in *The Psychoanalytic Study of the Child*, Vol. 16. New York: International Universities Press, pp. 73–89.

Sander, L. W. (1962*a*). "Adaptive Relationships in Early Mother-Child Interaction," *J. Am. Acad. Child Psychiatry*, 3(1964):231-264.

———. (1962*b*). "Issues in Early Mother-Child Interaction," *J. Am. Acad. Child Psychiatry*, 1(1962):141–166.

Sandler, J. (1960). "On the Concept of the Superego," in *The Psychoanalytic Study of the Child*, Vol. 15. New York: International Universities Press, pp. 128–162.

Sandler, J., Holder, A., and Meers, D. (1963). "The Ego Ideal and the Ideal Self," in *The Psychoanalytic Study of the Child*, Vol. 18. New York: International Universities Press, pp. 139–158.

Schilder, P. F. (1914). Selbstbewusstein und Persönlichkeits-bewusstsein: eine psychopathologische Studie, edited by A. Alzheimer and M. Lewandowsky. Berlin: J. Springer.

———. (1923). *The Image and Appearance of the Human Body: Studies in the Constructive Energies of the Psyche*. New York: International Universities Press, 1951.

Schur, M. (1955). "Comments on the Metapsychology of Somatization," in *The Psychoanalytic Study of the Child*, Vol. 10. New York: International Universities Press, pp. 119–164.

———. (1966). *The ID and the Regulatory Principles of Mental Functioning*. New York: International Universities Press.

Settlage, C. F. (1971). "On the Libidinal Aspect of Early Psychic Development and the Genesis of Infantile Neurosis," in *Separation-Individuation: Essays in Honor of Margaret S. Mahler*, edited by J. B. McDevitt and C. F. Settlage. New York: International Universities Press, pp. 131–156.

———. (1974). "Danger Signals in the Separation-Individuation Process: The Observations and Formulations of Margaret S. Mahler," in *The Infant at Risk*, Vol. 10, No. 2. Birth Defects: Original Article Series, edited by D. Bergsma, R. T. Gross, C. F. Settlage, A. J. Solnit, and D. Dwyer. Miami: Symposia Specialists, pp. 63–75. Distributed by Intercontinental Medical Book Corp., New York.

Solnit, A. J. (1970). "A Study of Object Loss in Infancy," in *The Psychoanalytic Study of the Child*, Vol. 25. New York: International Universities Press, pp. 257–272.

Speers, R. W. (1974). "Variations in Separation-Individuation and Implications for Play Ability and Learning," in *The Infant at Risk*, Vol. 10, No. 2. Birth Defects: Original Article Series, edited by D. Bergsma, R. T. Gross, C. F. Settlage, A. J. Solnit, and D. Dwyer. Miami: Symposia Specialists, pp. 77–100. Distributed by Intercontinental Medical Book Corp., New York.

Speers, R. W., McFarland, M. B., Arnaud, S. H., and Curry, N. E. (1971). "Recapitulation of Separation-Individuation Processes when the Normal Three-Year-Old Enters Nursery School," in *Essays in Honor of Margaret S. Mahler*, edited by J. B. McDevitt and C. F. Settlage. New York: International Universities Press, pp. 297–324.

Sperling, O. (1944). "On Appersonation," *Int. J. Psycho-Anal.*, 25:128–132.

Spiegel, L. A. (1959). "The Self, the Sense of Self, and Perception," in *The Psychoanalytic Study of the Child*, Vol. 14. New York: International Universities Press, pp. 81–109.

Spitz, R. A. (1945). "Diacritic and Coenesthetic Organizations: The Psychiatric Significance of a Functional Division of the Nervous System into a Sensory and Emotive Part," *Psychoanal. Rev.*, 32:146–162.

———. (1946). "The Smiling Response: A Contribution to the Ontogenesis of Social Relations" (with the assistance of K. M. Wolf, Ph.D.), *Genet. Psychol. Monogr.*, No. 34, pp. 57–125.

———. (1950). "Relevancy of Direct Infant Observations," in *The Psychoanalytic Study of the Child*, Vol. 10. New York: International Universities Press, pp. 215–240.

———. (1955). "The Primal Cavity: A Contribution to the Genesis of Perception and Its Role for Psychoanalytic Theory," in *The Psychoanalytic Study of the Child*, Vol. 10. New York: International Universities Press, pp. 215–240.

———. (1964). "The Derailment of Dialogue: Stimulus Overload, Action Cycles, and the Completion Gradient," *J. Am. Psychoanal. Assoc.*, 12:752–775.

———. (1965). *The First Year of Life: A Psychoanalytic Study of Normal and Deviant Development of Object Relations*. New York: International Universities Press.

———. (1972). "Bridges: On Anticipation, Duration and Meaning," *J. Am. Psychoanal. Assoc.*, 20:721–735.

Spitz, R. A., Emde, R. N., and Metcalf, D. R. (1970). "Further Prototypes of Ego Formation," in *The Psychoanalytic Study of the Child*, Vol. 25. New York: International Universities Press, pp. 417–441.

Spock, B. (1963). "The Striving for Autonomy and Regressive Objective-Relationships," *The Psychoanalytic Study of the Child*, Vol. 18. New York: International Universities Press, pp. 361–364.

———. (1965). "Innate Inhibition of Aggressiveness in Infancy," in *The Psychoanalytic Study of the Child*, Vol. 20. New York: International Universities Press, pp. 340–343.

Stoller, R. J. (1973). "Male Transsexualism: Uneasiness," *Am. J. Psychiatry*, 130:536–539.

Tolpin, M. (1972). "On the Beginnings of a Cohesive Self," in *The Psychoanalytic Study of the Child*, Vol. 26. New York: Quadrangle, pp. 316–352.

Waelder, R. (1960). *The Basic Theory of Psychoanalysis*. New York: International Universities Press, pp. 56–57.

Weil, A. P. (1956). "Some Evidences of Deviational Development in Infancy and Childhood," in *The Psychoanalytic Study of the Child*, Vol. 11. New York: International Universities Press, pp. 292–299.

———. (1970). "The Basic Core," in *The Psychoanalytic Study of the Child*, Vol. 25. New York: International Universities Press, pp. 442–460.

———. (1973). "Ego Strengthening Prior to Analysis," in *The Psychoanalytic Study of the Child*, Vol. 28. New Haven: Yale University Press, pp. 287–304.

Werner, H. (1948). *Comparative Psychology of Mental Development*. New York: International Universities Press.

Werner, H. and Kaplan, B. (1963). *Symbol Formation*. New York: John Wiley.

Winnicott, D. W. (1953). "Transitional Objects and Transitional Phenomena: A Study of the First Not-Me Possession," *Int. J. Psycho-Anal.*, 34:89–97.

———. (1956). "Primary Maternal Preoccupation," in *Collected Papers*. New York: Basic Books, 1958, pp. 300–305.

———. (1957*a*). "The Ordinary Devoted Mother and Her Baby." Nine Broadcast Talks (1949). Reprinted in *The Child and the Family*. New York, Basic Books.

———. (1957*b*). *Mother and Child: A Primer of First Relationships*. New York: Basic Books.

———. (1958). "The Capacity to Be Alone," *Int. J. Psycho-Anal.*, 39:416–420.

———. (1962). *The Maturational Processes and the Facilitating Environment*. New York: International Universities Press, 1965.

———. (1963). "Communicating and Not Communicating, Leading to a Study of Certain Opposites," in *The Maturational Processes and the Facilitating Environment*. New York: International Universities Press, 1965, pp. 179–192.

Wolf, P. and White, B. (1965). "Visual Pursuit and Attention in Young Infants," *J. Am. Acad. Child Psychiatry*, 4:473–484.

Wolff, P. H. (1959). "Observations on Newborn Infants," *Psychosom. Med.*, 21: 110–118.

Woodbury, M. A. (1966). "Altered Body-Ego Experiences: A Contribution to the Study of Regression, Perception, and Early Development," *J. Am. Psychoanal. Assoc.*, 14:273–303.

Zetzel, E. R. (1949). "Anxiety and the Capacity to Bear It," ***Int. J. Psycho-Anal.,*** **30:1–12.**

———. (1965). "Depression and the Incapacity to Bear It," in ***Drives, Affects, Behavior,*** **Vol. 2, edited by M. Schur. New York: International Universities Press, pp. 243–274.**

———. (1966). "The Predisposition to Depression," ***Can. Psychiatr. Assoc. J. Supp.,*** **11:236–249.**

PERMISSIONS

Permission to quote from the following works is gratefully acknowledged.

Ferenczi, S., "Stages in the Development of the Sense of Reality," in *Sex in Psychoanalysis: Selected Papers of Sandor Ferenczi*, translated by Ernest Jones, Vol. 1, pp. 213–239. © 1950 by Basic Books, Inc., Publishers, New York.

Freud, S., "Mourning and Melancholia," in *Collected Papers of Sigmund Freud*, edited by Ernest Jones, Vol. 4, pp. 152–170. Published by Basic Books, Inc., Publishers, by arrangement with The Hogarth Press, Ltd., and The Institute of Psycho-Analysis, London. Also in *Standard Edition*, edited by J. Strachey, Vol. 14, pp. 237–260. London: Hogarth Press, 1957. Reprinted by permission of the publisher.

Freud, S., "Negation," in *Collected Papers of Sigmund Freud*, edited by Ernest Jones, Vol. 5, pp. 181–185. Published by Basic Books, Inc., Publishers, by arrangement with The Hogarth Press, Ltd. and The Institute of Psycho-Analysis, London. Also in *Standard Edition*, edited by J. Strachey, Vol. 19, pp. 235–239. London: Hogarth Press, 1961. Reprinted by permission of the publisher.

Greenacre, P., "Considerations Regarding the Parent-Infant Relationship," *Int. J. Psycho-Anal.*, 41(1960): 571–584.

Jacobson, E., "The Self and the Object World: Vicissitudes of Their Infantile Cathexes and Their Influence on Ideational and Affective Development," in *The Psychoanalytic Study of the Child*, Vol. 9. New York: International Universities Press, 1954, pp. 75–127.

Lewin, B. D., "Reconsideration of the Dream Screen," *Psychoanal. Q.*, 22(1953): 174–199.

Mahler, M. S., "Thoughts about Development and Individuation," in *The Psychoanalytic Study of the Child*, Vol. 18. New York: International Universities Press, 1963, pp. 307–324.

Mahler, M. S. and Gosliner, B. J., "On Symbiotic Child Psychosis: Genetic, Dynamic and Restitutive Aspects," in *The Psychoanalytic Study of the Child*, Vol. 10. New York: International Universities Press, 1955, pp. 195–212.

GLOSSARY OF CONCEPTS

Ambitendency. The simultaneous presence of two contrasting, behaviorally manifest tendencies; for example, a child may cry and smile virtually at the same time, approach mother and at the last minute veer away, or kiss mother and then suddenly bite her. Ambitendency is behaviorally biphasic; it may or may not soon be replaced by ambivalence, where the biphasic tendency is integrated and no longer observable.

Approach-distancing patterns. The changing patterns with which the infant distances from mother and returns to her. Each subphase has its characteristic patterns, determined by the progressive motor and cognitive development of the child and by the changing needs for distance or closeness.

Autistic child psychosis. In the syndrome of infantile autism, there is fixation or regression to the autistic phase of earliest infancy, that is, the mother does not seem to be perceived at all by the child as representative of the outside world. There is a frozen wall between the autistic child and the human environment. Psychotic autism constitutes an attempt to achieve dedifferentiation and deanimation; it serves to counteract the multitudinous complexities of external stimuli and inner excitations which threaten the rudimentary ego of the autistic child with annihilation. The maintenance of sameness is the cardinal feature of the autistic psychosis syndrome.

Consolidation of individuality and emotional object constancy. The fourth subphase of separation-individuation, which begins toward the end of the second year and is open-ended. During this period, a degree of object constancy is achieved, and the separation of self and object representations is sufficiently established. Mother is clearly perceived as a separate person in the outside world, and at the same time has an existence in the internal representational world of the child. *See also* Differentiation; Practicing; Rapprochement.

Darting away. *See* Shadowing and darting away.

Differentiation. The first subphase of the separation-individuation process, manifested from 5 to 9 months of age. Total bodily dependence on mother begins to decrease as the maturation of locomotor partial functions brings about the first tentative moving away from her. Characteristic behaviors that make possible the demarcation of self from nonself are visual and tactile exploration of mother's face and body; pulling away from mother to scan the wider world and look at her; checking back from mother to others. Pleasure in emerging ego functions and the outside world is expressed in close proximity to mother. At the same time, differentiation of a primitive, but distinct, body image seems to occur. *See also* Practicing, Rapprochement, Consolidation of individuality.

Dual unity. The symbiotic unit of mother and child, imbued by the infant with omnipotent qualities, in which there is a vague sensing of the symbiotic half of the self (Spitz's "external ego").

Emotional or libidinal refueling. During the practicing subphase, the infant forays away from mother, but when he becomes fatigued or depleted of energy, he seeks to reestablish bodily contact with her. This "refueling" perks him up and restores his previous momentum to practice and explore.

Fear of reengulfment. Fear of regression to a symbiotic state from which the toddler has only recently individuated (emerged). The fear of reengulfment is the defense against the perpetual longing of the human being for reunion with the erstwhile symbiotic mother, a longing that threatens individual entity and identity and, therefore, has to be warded off even beyond childhood.

Hatching. The process of emerging from the symbiotic state of oneness with mother, in the intrapsychic sense. It is the "second," the psychological, birth experience—the process by which the "other-than-mother" world begins to be cathected. The hatched infant has left the vague twilight state of symbiosis and has become more permanently alert and perceptive to the stimuli of his environment, rather than to his own bodily sensations, or to sensations emanating within the symbiotic orbit only.

Mutual cueing. A circular process of interaction established very early between mother and infant by which they "empathically" read each other's signs and signals and react to each other. For example, the mother learns the meanings of the baby's different cries and movements; the baby learns to anticipate the mother's ministrations; he also learns soon which cues his mother (unconsciously) picks up and which she does not. No mother perfectly responds to a baby's cues, but serious mismatching of cues is an obstacle in the path of smooth development.

Normal autistic phase. The first weeks of extrauterine life, during which the neonate or young infant appears to be an almost purely biological organism, his instinctual responses to stimuli being on a reflex and thalamic level. During this phase we can speak only of primitive unintegrated ego apparatuses and purely somatic defense mechanisms, consisting of overflow and discharge reactions, the goal of which is the maintenance of homeostatic equilibrium. The libido position is a predominantly visceral one with no discriminaton between inside and outside, animate and inanimate. Initially, because of his very high threshold for external stimuli, the infant seems to be in a state of primitive negative hallucinatory disorientation, in which need satisfaction belongs to his own omnipotent autistic orbit.

Normal symbiotic phase. Normal symbiosis is ushered in by the lifting of the innate strong stimulus barrier that protected the young infant from internal and external stimuli up to the third or fourth week of life. Since, in the human young the instinct for self-preservation has atrophied, the ego has to take over the role of managing the human being's adaptation to reality. However, the rudimentary ego of the young infant is not adequate to the task of organizing his inner and outer stimuli in such a way as to ensure his survival; it is the psychobiological rapport between the nursing mother and the baby that complements the infant's undifferentiated ego. Empathy on the part of a mother is, under normal circumstances, the substitute among human beings for those instincts on which the altricial animal relies for its survival. Normal symbiosis develops concomitantly with the lowering of the innate stimulus barrier (Benjamin, 1961), through the predictably repetitious experience of an outside mothering agency alleviating need, hunger, and tension coming from within, that is, functioning as an auxiliary ego (Spitz).

Symbiosis refers to a stage of sociobiological interdependence between the 1- to 5-month-old infant and his mother, a stage of preobject or need satisfying relationship, in which self and maternal intrapsychic representations have not yet been differentiated. From the second month on, the infant behaves and functions as though he and his mother were an omnipotent dual unity within one common boundary (the "symbiotic membrane").

The mother's availability and the infant's innate capacity to engage in the symbiotic relationship are essential at this point. This relationship marks the inception of ego organization by the establishment of intrapsychic connections on the infant's part between memory traces of gratification and the gestalt of the human face; there is a shift of cathexis from inside the body, from the predominantly visceral position of the autistic phase to the periphery, the sensory perceptive organs (from coenesthetic to diacritic organization).

Optimal distance. As the infant grows and develops, there is for each stage a position between mother and child that best allows the infant to develop those faculties which he needs in order to grow, that is, to individuate. During the symbiotic stage the infant molds into the mother's body; during the differentiation subphase he begins to push away from mother's chest in order to be able freely to explore her tactilely and near-visually. The practicing infant distances in space in order to have a chance to explore; during rapprochement the toddler needs to go and come to find mother available, but not intruding. The optimal distance is dictated by the developing secondary narcissism as well as by the changing object relationship and the developing ego functions.

Practicing. The second subphase of separation-individuation, lasting from about 9 months to about 14 months of age. During this period the infant is able to actively move away from mother and return to her, first by crawling and later by the mastery of upright locomotion. It is a period in which the exploration of the environment, animate and inanimate, and the practicing of locomotor skills are highly invested with libidinal energy. *See also* Differentiation, Rapprochement, Consolidation of individuality.

Precursors of defense. During the separation-individuation process we find primitive behaviors that can be regarded as precursors of later defense mechanisms. For example, pushing away from mother, not looking at her, veering away, ignoring her presence or her departure are behaviors leading to mechanisms of denial or disavowal. We also find primitive identification with mother—"becoming mother"—in her absence and premature independence (false self) where there is a deficiency in mothering. These mechanisms are relatively unstable; they come and go. They serve adaptation as well as defense. Choice of these mechanisms depends on the characteristics of the child and the selective response of the parents to the child.

Primary narcissism. A state prevailing during the first week of life in which need satisfaction is not perceived as coming from the outside and in which there is no awareness of a mothering agent. It is akin to Ferenczi's "absolute infantile omnipotence." This stage is followed by one of dim awareness that need satisfaction cannot be provided by oneself.

Proprioceptive-enteroceptive cathexis. The cathexis of the inside of the body, experienced as tensions or sensations emanating from within and discharged by coughing, spitting, vomiting, squirming, crying, and so on, which prevail during the first weeks of life.

Rapprochement. The third subphase of separation-individuation, lasting from 14 or 15 months to about 24 months of age and even beyond. It is characterized by a rediscovery of mother, now a separate individual, and a returning to her after the obligatory forays of the practicing period. The toddler loves to share his experiences and possessions with mother, who is now more clearly perceived as separate and outside. The narcissistic inflation of the practicing subphase is slowly replaced by a growing realization of separateness and, with it, vulnerability. Adverse reactions to brief separations are common, and mother can no longer be easily substituted for, even by familiar adults. It often culminates in a more or less transient rapprochement crisis which is of great developmental significance. *See also* Differentiation, Practicing, Consolidation of individuality.

Rapprochement crisis. A period during the rapprochement subphase occurring in all children, but with great intensity in some, during which the realization of separateness is acute. The toddler's belief in his omnipotence is severely threatened and the environment is coerced as he tries to restore the status quo, which is impossible. Ambitendency, which develops into ambivalence, is often intense; the toddler wants to be united with, and at the same time separate from, mother. Temper tantrums, whining, sad moods, and intense separation reactions are at their height.

Sensoriperceptive cathexis. Cathexis of the sensorium and the periphery of the body, particularly the sensory perceptive organs—tactile, near-visual, auditory. Shift to sensoriperceptive cathexis is an important step in development, taking place at 3 or 4 weeks of age. (Replacing the hitherto predominantly proprioceptive-enteroceptive cathexis).

Separation-individuation phase. The phase of normal development commencing around 4 to 5 months of age, at the height of symbiosis and overlapping it. The infant shows increasing capacity to recognize mother as a special person, to cathect and inspect the nonmother world, and to move ever so slightly, and later quite deliberately, away from mother. It is a phase of development that lasts from about 5 months to 2½ years, and moves along two separate but intertwining tracks: the one of separation, leading to intrapsychic awareness of separateness, and the other of individuation, leading to the acquisition of a distinct and unique individuality. Four subphases of the separation-individuation process have been identified. Although they overlap, each subphase has its own characteristic clusters of behaviors that distinguish it from the preceding and following ones. The four subphases are: (1) Differentiation, (2) Practicing, (3) Rapprochement, and (4) Consolidation of individuality and beginning emotional object constancy.

Separation reactions. These vary in kind and intensity in the progressive course of the separation-individuation process. During differentiation, we characteristically see low-keyedness at brief separations, which sometimes, however, culminates in desperate crying; during the practicing period, there is relative obliviousness to mother's presence; during rapprochement, a host of reactions, such as searching, crying, or pointedly ignoring mother occur. During the fourth subphase, brief separations are generally better tolerated.

Shadowing and darting away. During the rapprochement subphase the child at times follows his mother's every move ("shadows" her); he cannot let her be out of sight or out of his immediate vicinity. At times we observe the opposite behavior: the child darts away, and waits for and expects mother to swoop him up in her arms and thus for brief moments undo the "separateness."

Splitting. A defense mechanism often found during the rapprochement subphase (once a certain measure of ego development has been achieved); the toddler cannot easily tolerate simultaneous love and hate feelings toward the same person. Love and hate are not amalgamated; mother is experienced alternately as all good or all bad. Another possibility is that the absent mother is felt to be all good, while others become all bad. Hence the toddler may displace aggression onto the nonmother world while exaggerating love for (overidealizing) the absent, longed-for mother. When mother returns she disrupts the ideal image, and reunions with her are often painful, since the young ego's synthetic function cannot heal the split. In most cases gradual synthesis of all "good" and all "bad" by the growing ego becomes possible.

Stranger reactions. A variety of reactions to people other than mother, particularly pronounced during the differentiation subphase, when a special relationship to mother has been well established, as evidenced by the special smile to her. Stranger reactions include curiosity and interest, as well as wariness and mild or even severe anxiety. They subside at the beginning of the practicing period, but reappear at various times throughout the separation-individuation process.

Symbiotic child psychosis. The symbiotic developmental phase, although grossly distorted, has been reached; the child treats the mother as if she were part of the self, that is, not external to the self but fused with it. He is unable to integrate an image of mother as a distinct and whole external object, but instead seems to maintain fragmented good and bad part images (introjects) of the object. He alternates between the wish to incorporate and to expel. There is, without therapy, insurmountable interference with any progress toward separation-individuation, that is to say, there is fixation at or regression to the pathological symbiosis phase. Restitution mechanisms which create the varied symptomatology are attempts to restore and perpetuate the delusional omnipotent mother-child symbiotic unity; because of continuous abysmal panic-stricken states, the patient is compelled to take recourse to a secondary retreat into a quasi-stabilizing (*secondary*) autism. "Panic tantrums," as well as autoaggressive behavior, every so often dominate the clinical picture.

Symbiotic orbit. Mother and all parts and attributes of mother—her voice, her gestures, her clothes, and the space in which she comes and goes—which form the magic circle of the symbiotic mother-infant world.

AUTHOR INDEX

SUBJECT INDEX

For Product Safety Concerns and Information please contact our EU representative GPSR@taylorandfrancis.com Taylor & Francis Verlag GmbH, Kaufingerstraße 24, 80331 München, Germany

Batch number: 10725891

Printed by Printforce, the Netherlands